Imperial steam

Manchester University Press

STUDIES IN IMPERIALISM

General editors: Andrew S. Thompson and Alan Lester
Founding editor: John M. MacKenzie

When the 'Studies in Imperialism' series was founded by Professor John M. MacKenzie more than thirty years ago, emphasis was laid upon the conviction that 'imperialism as a cultural phenomenon had as significant an effect on the dominant as on the subordinate societies'. With well over a hundred titles now published, this remains the prime concern of the series. Cross-disciplinary work has indeed appeared covering the full spectrum of cultural phenomena, as well as examining aspects of gender and sex, frontiers and law, science and the environment, language and literature, migration and patriotic societies, and much else. Moreover, the series has always wished to present comparative work on European and American imperialism, and particularly welcomes the submission of books in these areas. The fascination with imperialism, in all its aspects, shows no sign of abating, and this series will continue to lead the way in encouraging the widest possible range of studies in the field. 'Studies in Imperialism' is fully organic in its development, always seeking to be at the cutting edge, responding to the latest interests of scholars and the needs of this ever-expanding area of scholarship.

To buy or to find out more about the books currently available in this series, please go to: https://manchesteruniversitypress.co.uk/series/studies-in-imperialism/

Imperial steam

Modernity on the sea route to India, 1837–74

Jonathan Stafford

MANCHESTER UNIVERSITY PRESS

The right of Jonathan Stafford to be identified as the author of this work has been asserted in accordance with the Copyright, Designs and Patents Act 1988.

Published by Manchester University Press
Oxford Road, Manchester M13 9PL

www.manchesteruniversitypress.co.uk

British Library Cataloguing-in-Publication Data
A catalogue record for this book is available from the British Library

ISBN   978 1 5261 6448 3   hardback

First published 2023

The publisher has no responsibility for the persistence or accuracy of URLs for any external or third-party internet websites referred to in this book, and does not guarantee that any content on such websites is, or will remain, accurate or appropriate.

Typeset
by New Best-set Typesetters Ltd

Contents

Illustrations

Acknowledgements

The writing of this book has been a long journey, and has inevitably benefited from the camaraderie and intellectual generosity of many people along the way. Trevor Keeble, Charles Rice and Howard Caygill offered feedback on early drafts. Miles Ogborn has been an ungrudging source of insight and guidance over the years. Toby Bennett has been an indulgent interlocutor and friend throughout the book's writing. A reading group on the sea that met at Birkbeck College over several years provided an invaluable forum for debate and comradeship, for which I owe my thanks to Liam Campling, Alex Colas, Stephanie Jones, Stewart Motha and David Styan. The book's evolution took place in a number of institutions, and I have been fortunate to have enjoyed the company and support of many dear colleagues at both Nottingham Trent University and the University of Nottingham, particularly Ben Taylor, Steven Jones, Craig Lundy, Dean Blackburn and Kate Law. Martin O'Shaughnessy provided encouragement when it was most needed. James Mansell has been an endlessly giving and patient colleague. I owe a great deal to Maiken Umbach's wisdom and indulgence, and I am a better historian for our time together. David Laven offered advice and support at a critical time. I am also blessed by the abundant goodwill of my colleagues at the Leibniz Zentrum für Literatur- und Kulturforschung in Berlin, where this book ends its journey, particularly Henning Trüper, who has provided much welcome advice. Alexandra Heimes has been a true friend. My experience of working with Manchester University Press has been a pleasure throughout, and I am particularly grateful to Emma Brennan and Meredith Carroll for their patient and adroit stewardship of the book. I was fortunate to have academic readers whose engagement with my writing was indulgent and insightful, and the book is much improved for their feedback. This book couldn't have come to fruition without the forbearance and warmth of my family: my mum and dad, Lesley and David Stafford, offered not only their love and support, but also a home during a critical period of the book's writing. My siblings Holly and James Stafford, and their partners and children have also been unfailing sources of distraction and generosity.

Vicky Sparrow saw this book through its various stages, and was witness to its many ups and downs. This book owes more to her love and kindness than to anyone else.

Some of the material in this book has appeared previously. Earlier versions of material in Chapters 1 and 5 appeared in my article 'A Sea View: Perceptions of Maritime Space and Landscape in Accounts of Nineteenth-Century Colonial Steamship Travel', published in the *Journal of Historical Geography*, 55 (2017) (www.sciencedirect.com). Parts of Chapter 4 are based on my article 'Home on the Waves: Domesticity and Discomfort Aboard the Overland Route Steamship, 1842–1862', published in *Mobilities*, 14 (2019) (www.tandfonline.com). I am grateful to the editors of the journals and the anonymous reviewers of the articles, and to the publishers for permission to reproduce this material.

Introduction

'The Peninsular and Oriental Steam Navigation Company's magnificent vessels employed on what is called the Overland Indian Route' begins *The Anglo-Indian Passage* (1845), 'start from the Southampton Docks for Alexandria on the 3rd and 20th of every month'.[1] Written by David Lester Richardson, a retired East India Company officer, academic and journal editor, the book is an early example of the proliferation of travel narratives and guides dedicated to the then nascent steamship route connecting England and India. While Richardson's opening sentence is decidedly prosaic, it narrates a revolution in global mobilities: P&O, as the shipping line became known, had only three years previously become the first company to provide a regular, integrated steamship service between Britain and the East, as an alternative to the protracted voyage around the Cape of Good Hope by sailing vessel.[2] Travelling via Egypt on what was dubbed the 'overland route', the company's steamers had radically shortened the transit time of the journey and, in the process, had captured the public imagination, a circumstance Richardson's book capitalised upon; while it provided a range of practical information for passengers travelling on the new route connecting Britain and its increasingly important imperial possessions in the East, *The Anglo-Indian Passage* was not merely a guidebook. Like many such publications, it was also a technophilic paean to the steamship's impact on the experiences, sensations, social relations and politics of the modern world – and nowhere was this impact seen to be more keenly felt that in the imperial possessions with which the steamship provided a crucial logistical connection.

In the book's preface, Richardson presents what he terms 'a consideration of the practical good which steam has already wrought, and is about to work, in the Eastern world'.[3] The steamship was, for Richardson, responsible for a revolution in imperial society, the agent of thoroughgoing social change at a global level – a perspective informed by the pervasive and widespread belief in the transformative power of modern technology. Richardson had served as aide-de-camp to Lord William Bentinck, Governor-General of

India from 1828 to 1835, and shared his former superior's zeal for imperial social reform. India's route to modernity, it was believed, would be
driven by the power of Western science and technology.[4] Furthermore, the
steamship, through its sheer size and visual impact, was not just a practical means of effecting such far-reaching developments, but also provided
a prominent representational manifestation of this potency. Certainly for
the steamship's passengers, the colonial actors whose lives were intimately
caught up with the workings of British imperialism, the impact of this
new form of maritime mobility's introduction to the journey East was
immeasurable. 'The contemplation of a passage between England and
India', Richardson opined, 'now creates as little uneasiness in the mind of
the most nervous traveller, who is made aware of its real nature, as a trip
from England to America.'[5] If steam had been responsible for a revolution in global mobilities, it was a distinctly prosaic one – in Richardson's
account, the modernity of the steamship was one characterised by ease and
convenience.

For Richardson, steam had not only shortened the passage to India, but
normalised it, bridging the gap between West and East in both a practical
sense, and in the imagination. In the days before the steamship, the alienation
of distance had been keenly felt by the colonial servant in India, who,
Richardson claimed, 'almost forgot that he was a Briton'. Colonial steamship
mobilities helped to maintain a sense of connectedness between imperial
centre and periphery. For the British Indian, steam's ramifications were
manifested at the level of affect and identity: 'his mind and heart are benefitted;
they are kept warm and awake'.[6] The significance of this shift was felt,
however, not just in the small circle of imperial actors whose mobility it
facilitated, whose time it saved, and whose connection with a sense of shared
British identity it helped produce. For Richardson, the mobilities of imperial
steam at sea provided a compelling *symbolic* link between metropole and
periphery, foregrounding the place of Britain's imperial world in the imaginations of the Victorian public at home:

> Indian affairs are now home affairs. Oriental politics are familiarly discussed
> not only in the British Senate, but in drawing-rooms and taverns. And yet
> before the introduction of steam navigation, the majority of the British people
> only knew the East in the 'Arabian Nights Entertainments.' ... But steam has
> wrought a wondrous change in these matters.[7]

The steamship voyage to India was thus not just a faster, more predictable
and convenient form of imperial mobility. It also performed a discursive
passage, from a fantastical imagined orient to the prosaic day-to-day
administration of a British imperial possession. The steamship was framed
as being at the heart of a significant historical transition (specifically as a

departure from the age of sail), responsible for shifting conceptions of India in the metropole. Richardson's account exhibits a vivid example of the technological determinism which held powerful sway over the Victorian discourse surrounding the steamship.

Imperial Steam is the first cultural history of a steamship service that was intimately caught up with the workings of the British Empire. This book charts the first decades of this service, from P&O's 1837 beginnings until 1874, in the wake of the opening of the Suez Canal, the event which brought the history of the overland route (and the company's near-monopoly of the passage East) to a close.[8] This focus, on the steamship's introduction and its formative years, foregrounds the significance of historical change in tracing shifting attitudes toward technology, imperialism and modernity – and their intersections. Steam was seen to have effected a fundamental shift in the imaginative geographies of empire.[9] The unprecedented sensation of proximity between East and West, claimed Richardson, engendered a keener interest in the workings of British imperial India in the metropole – a familiarity characterised by both an affirmative identification with empire, and the normalisation of a formerly exotic, 'distant' East. This was a quotidian modernity, in tension with the grander, utopian claims regarding steam frequently lauded by Richardson and numerous other contemporary commentators. As Richardson's hyperbolic plaudits illustrate, the overland route (and the wealth of literature which documented it) not only provided a logistical and imaginative connection between metropole and periphery: it bound together an imaginative nexus which linked the experiences of the ship's passengers, the colonial world, and the British public. The steamship was more than a conduit for travel between Britain and its Eastern empire: it acted as an important means for foregrounding the significance of imperialism, and particularly of the British Empire in India, not just for colonial actors but in the British cultural and geographical imagination more widely. Steamship mobilities – and specifically the way they are framed in the profusion of written accounts which accompanied their rise – occupied a privileged place in the production of knowledge and conceptions of the British Empire in the metropole.

Writing imperial mobilities at sea

Since the facilities of steam-navigation have brought the Nile within the scope of everybody's possibility, and rendered Constantinople an easier undertaking than the Giants' Causeway formerly was, so much has been published upon the East, that the subject has been completely exhausted by minds of every calibre, and books of Oriental travel have become a mere drug.[10]

So begins English novelist and travel writer Isabella Frances Romer's 1846 account of the sightseeing tour of the Middle East she had undertaken the previous year. Romer's claim, that a scant few years after the introduction of a regular steamship service to the East the journey had become so convenient that accounts of Eastern travel were ubiquitous to the point of banality, exhibits a kind of literary technological determinism. Steam had, according to Romer, been responsible for a simultaneous explosion in writing on the topic, and a figurative bringing closer of a formerly exotic East, which had resulted in its normalisation. *Imperial Steam* explores the nexus hinted at by Romer: between steam's mobilities at sea, travel writing and the imaginative geographies of imperial space. In doing so, it sheds light on the role played by steamship mobilities in shaping the discursive production of the British imperial world view.[11]

For the facilitation of a transport and communication link with the East, steam proved highly attractive. It offered not just a more regular, reliable, predictable means of transport, but enabled a novel geography of global mobility. Travelling through the Mediterranean to Alexandria, transporting the cargo, mail and passengers across Egypt to Suez, and continuing on another steamship down the Red Sea and across the Indian Ocean, steam made possible the channel of mobility known as the overland route.[12] As prevailing winds in the Red Sea meant that it would have been impossible to provide a regular service by sailing vessel, this route represented a new geography of imperial transit, facilitated specifically by the technology of steam.[13] The introduction of steam power to maritime communications with the East meant that an unpredictable sailing voyage around the Cape of Good Hope of between three and six months could be supplemented by a journey of under a month and a half (decreasing over the period covered by this book to less than a month), which was able to obey a regular, predictable timetable. However, the driving force behind this revolution had little to do with the mobilities of the imperial bourgeoisie – it was rather driven by a British government mail subsidy to improve communications between Britain and the colonial East. By 1843, the year after the implementation of the Suez–India service, the company was already transporting 100,000 letters per ship.[14]

The overland route revolutionised transport and communication between the East and West. Yet little scholarly attention has been dedicated to this important imperial network. Existing research has emphasised technological innovations, prominent individuals and personal networks as the drivers of the steamship's history.[15] The subjective experience of imperial steamship mobilities remains underexplored. 'The number of books on the overland route from time to time which have been "done" by various hands would constitute a library *per se*', wrote the Irish journalist William Howard

Russell, in his own contribution to this library, his 1860 account of an overland route trip to India.[16] *Imperial Steam* draws upon this wealth of written responses to P&O's steamships, to dozens of voyage narratives published in books, journal and newspaper articles in the first thirty years of the overland route, supplemented with a number of archival accounts.[17] From these sources, a composite picture is constructed of the experiences, sensations, encounters and affective world of the steamship passenger travelling between Britain and the East.[18] While these sources include books, like David Lester Richardson's, solely dedicated to the route, in the majority of cases, like Russell, the voyage forms just a small part of a wider work concerned with Eastern life or travel. In addition, numerous guidebooks to the East include information for the traveller regarding the route.[19]

In a sense, these texts can be seen as productive of the voyage itself, framing and making legible the experience of travel for both those who wrote them, and for their readers. British colonial administrator and author William Delafield Arnold wrote an 1856 account of an overland route journey from England to the East. As his narrative was concerned with the section of the voyage between Ceylon and China, Arnold justified his omission of much of the detail of the route. In doing so, he highlights the parallels between the textual and the mobile, the reader's experiences and those of the traveller: 'I do not propose to travel over again the overland route', he writes. 'I have gone it often enough in the flesh to satisfy myself; my readers have probably travelled it often enough in spirit to satisfy them.'[20] Not only does Arnold's discursive device again highlight the ubiquity (and familiarity) of published narratives of the overland route – it invites us to consider the parallel between the overland route voyage and its textual representation, drawing attention to the vicarious nature of Victorian practices of textual consumption.

While the profusion of writing about the overland route reflected the wider explosion in publishing which was gathering steam throughout the nineteenth century, it also bears witness to a keen public interest in the quotidian circumstances of steamship travel to the East. This situates the overland route narrative within a larger corpus of imperial travel literature, which allowed those in the metropole to engage vicariously with the world of the British Empire.[21] However, much of this genre was concerned with the excitement of travel in exotic climes, with novel experiences and noteworthy encounters with the racial Other.[22] Overland route narratives often sit ill with this embrace of the exhilarating life of global adventure – accounts of shipboard life generally document a regimented, repeatable journey with little but open sea and distant shorelines to distract from the leisured monotony of the time spent in transit. However, as the nineteenth-century's imperial expansion gathered pace, the majority of global travel was just the type of banal, repetitive and functional voyaging documented by these accounts. No less than the thrilling adventures of explorers and scientists, in order to understand Britain's Victorian Empire it is necessary to also look at global mobilities which were becoming increasingly prosaic.

Despite the quotidian character of the overland route, all too often shipboard life constitutes a significant focus in narratives of Eastern travel. This ubiquity can be seen in part as a reflection of the usefulness of the processes of mobility for narrating imperial travel – rather than beginning the narrative in the East, the voyage's inclusion invited the reader to join the narrator in an imaginative journey linking metropole with periphery. It also reflects the popular appeal of first-hand accounts of the world of imperial steam shipping – with the steamship's space, its inhabitants, and with the everyday experiences of travel. Indeed, much of the time, overland route narratives merely reproduce the mundane details of the voyage, offering little material for a historical analysis which hopes to engage with the social, political and cultural life of imperial mobilities. Yet these quotidian minutiae, accounts of eating, sleeping, washing, socialising, leisure activities, gazing at the view, encounters with the ship's crew, the weather, and countless other shipboard trivialities, frequently offer distinctive perspectives on the making of the modern world. Within these prosaic passages, their authors often attempt to articulate something more specific, something novel and different about the steamship, the voyage, their experiences in transit. Taken from the first three decades of steamship travel to the East, they are often preoccupied with the shifting cultural meanings undergone by sea travel in the age of steam.[23] Simply put, they are concerned with the steamship's modernity.

Modernity at sea

This book argues that the overland route steamship voyage provided a powerful discursive vehicle for narrating a confident, affirmative, comprehensible British imperial world view. Furthermore, it highlights the extent to which this discourse operated through the diverse imaginative investments associated with the 'modernity' which was ascribed to the steamship.[24] Voyage narratives evince a number of preoccupations which will be familiar to even the passing scholar of modernity: with the notion of progress; with the rhythms and texture of experience; with historical change; with shifts in the constitution of time and space, and so on. Persistently, these accounts characterise the overland route as marking a profound historical shift – a form of mobility distinguished by its newness – as a departure from the world of sail which had dominated transnational mobility for millennia.

In his 1872 account of life in India, the colonial administrator and author Sir Edward Braddon looks back on three decades of the overland route. Characteristically, he compares the journey by steamship to the sailing voyage:

> The voyage round the Cape was a formidable undertaking, not to be thought of save when stern necessity made it inevitable. The eastward bound traveller of that time was, as compared with the modern specimen, an adventurous navigator like unto the Argonauts ... he had to abandon himself to a life on the ocean wave ... for the next three, six, or nine months.

In comparison, he wrote, the overland route was 'a different affair altogether'.[25] Braddon's claims encapsulate the discourse of the overland route as a historical departure. They emphasise that, both in terms of the duration of the passage, and in its cultural associations, the sailing ship voyage presented a marked interruption of normal life. The steamship's characterisation as a radical historical break thus has to be seen in dialogue with the wider history of seafaring. In the days before steamships, passengers who travelled by sailing vessel to India around the Cape of Good Hope underwent a protracted, unpredictable voyage whose duration ranged from around three to six months. They arrived ready to perform the work of empire weary, jaded and malnourished, after an uncomfortable, sometimes terrifying and taxing voyage – circumstances perhaps ill-suited to a colonising race's sense of its innate superiority and global mastery.[26]

The steamship voyage, on the other hand, offered a – relatively – comfortable, expeditious and orderly means for travelling to the imperial East. It provided passengers with a familiar, regimented, and above all modern vantage point from which to comprehend the British imperial world. Long sea voyages could destabilise the Western sense of self.[27] This book explores how the steamship acted as not just a mode of transport, but a means for imperial actors to retain (and even shape) a stable, coherent sense of their identity in transit and many miles from home. While the overland route voyage in its first decades fell short in many ways of the hubristic claims with which it was invested, it gave passengers a discursive hook from which to hang their sense of themselves: as Western, European, superior, clean, intelligent – and most of all as modern. The steamship was a symbol around which they could construct a coherent narrative of their place in the world. It is no surprise, then, that accounts of the overland route exhibit a persistent concern with the steamship as a radical historical break, a departure from the past.

Imperial Steam explores the particularity of the various claims for the steamship's modernity, its newness. The 'other' in this narrative was of course the sailing ship. But this technological story obscures the wider sense in which the overland route steamship's modernity was a distinctly imperial concept, in which the past was not just 'back then' but also 'out there'.[28] The steamship's history thus provides a means for coming to terms with the historical production of imperial identities. By being attentive to the complexity (and contradictions) of Victorian attitudes toward new technologies, *Imperial Steam* contributes to debates concerning the convoluted intersections of technology, modernity and imperialism. Modernity can be understood in this context less as a claim to any innate property of the nineteenth-century world, but rather as a discursive model which people used to constitute their identity and their sense of their place in that world. It provided those whose lives were enmeshed with empire – and the technological developments and social change which were associated with it – with an imaginative resource which they employed to come to terms with the diverse experiences which they encountered in their mobile lives.[29] The claims to modernity found in the archive of the overland route provide a distinctive historical perspective on the British Empire. Just as they invited the Victorian reader to engage with the shifting relationship between metropole and periphery, so they offer the historian an opportunity to understand the discursive production of the nineteenth-century imperial world view.

Global subjectivities

Charting this modernity means being attentive to the subjective experiences of those who narrate the accounts this book draws upon – to the embodied, affective, imaginative claims they make about their encounters. This book documents the thoughts, feelings, sensations, perceptions and imaginaries found in the texts produced by the peripatetic subjects who peopled the overland route steamship. In doing so, it builds on a growing body of literature which engages with imperialism's history from the perspective of first-hand accounts – the lived experiences of empire found in ego documents which have been frequently overlooked in favour of less ambiguous, less subjective source materials.[30] This is an approach indebted to the methodologies and preoccupations of the 'new' imperial history, a diverse field which has drawn attention to the intersections of identity, culture and power in the archive of imperialism.[31] Such a focus engenders new perspectives on the history of imperialism – the feelings, fantasies and encounters of those involved in the day-to-day life of empire shed light on the production of global subjectivities and the British imperial world view.

Conceptions of the global and the modern were deeply interconnected in the Victorian imagination, tied up with bourgeois identity and subjectivity.[32] This book's first chapter particularly contributes to an understanding of this interplay, employing the overland route as a case study to engage with some of the core discourses of modernity in a global context. As I will explore, the overland route steamship was an engine of the processes of globalisation – its mobility brought Britain and its Eastern empire closer together, intensifying the entanglements of their political, economic, social and cultural worlds.[33] Yet the steamship provided more than a functional link between metropole and periphery; it constituted a significant imaginative nexus which was used to tell the story of this interconnectedness, to engage with the global.

It is thus necessary to consider ships as not just producers of mobility, but, as Tamson Pietsch has argued, significant mobile spheres of imperial social relations in themselves. For Pietsch, 'the moving space of the steamship functioned as a particularly important and largely overlooked site in which travellers' political and racial ideas were gradually and actively reworked as they moved along the routes of global and imperial trade'.[34] Paying attention to this 'moving space' highlights that the steamship was in fact a significant sphere for shaping the passenger's imperial world view, and in turn, that of those who read the narratives produced by travellers. It is thus necessary to dwell upon the 'space between' of the ship as a political space – one which has its own social codes and hierarchies, temporal rhythms and cultural meanings. The details of shipboard life, both material and imaginative, render visible what Tim Cresswell has called the 'politics of mobility' – the particular way in which mobilities intersect with the production of power through social relations. Insisting upon the imperative to develop this political engagement with mobility, Cresswell poses a set of questions which serve as a point of departure: 'How is mobility discursively constituted? What narratives have been constructed around mobility? How are mobilities represented?'[35]

Engaging with these questions in relation to the lived world of the steamship sheds light on the historical interrelation of imperialism and globalisation, deepening our understanding of the latter's past.[36] As Martin Thomas and Andrew Thompson have insisted, globalisation can be understood as pertaining 'not only to the physical compression of the world, but also to the realm of perception and the imagination'.[37] The profound shifts in the production of global space which characterised the nineteenth-century world were first encountered in the lived experiences of those whose lives were enmeshed with these processes, as a shifting consciousness of their place in the world. Passengers on the overland route were the consumers of a new type of global mobility. As such they can be seen as pioneers of globalisation – they were among the first to experience first-hand the spatial compression and interconnectedness the steamship facilitated. How did these imperial actors understand the global character of their lives? How was it reflected in their lived experiences of travel and their conception of the world? In its focus on emotion, attitudes and experience, and on the production of identity and difference, a cultural history is best placed to explore these questions.[38] Such an approach allows for an attentiveness to landscape, to place, space, temporality, and to the cultural meanings invested in the steamship and its mobilities.

An 1846 book by the pre-eminent nineteenth-century author William Makepeace Thackeray offers one of the earliest comprehensive accounts of travel aboard the P&O steamship. *Notes of a Journey from Cornhill to Grand Cairo* documents the complimentary leisure voyage around the Mediterranean which Thackeray enjoyed aboard several of the company's steamers in 1844. This highly sardonic account was published under the moniker of Michael Angelo Titmarsh, a literary persona which Thackeray had employed extensively in his journalistic writing for the satirical periodical *Punch*. Yet it was Thackeray who signed the book's dedication. We thus must see the factual experiences of steamship travel documented by Thackeray as filtered through the fictional figure of Titmarsh. Although other sources are less emphatically suspended between fact and fiction, the case of Thackeray's book is instructive: accounts of overland route travel are not merely records of the experiences of the journey, but offer distinctive commentary and perspectives on the new world of imperial steamship mobility.

Imperial Steam is thus concerned with the discursive production of its source materials: with the words used, the patterns which emerge within and between texts, with the contradictions, the textures, the structures of feeling, the associations and cultural meanings invested in them. It pays close attention to the similes, metaphors, images, descriptive and imaginative techniques employed by their authors. Narratives give sometimes contradictory accounts of travel on the overland route, ranging from fawning praise to hostile criticism. However, whether sources describe the voyage as stultifyingly boring or a stimulating excursion; whether they are preoccupied with the ship's discomforts or its luxurious interiors, these contradictions have much to tell us. They illuminate the shared preoccupations of these diverse passenger experiences: with concerns of the spatial, the mobile, the temporal, with the quality of experience, and so on. Around these tensions are narrated the fraught relationships between Britain and its empire, white and black, modernity and its 'other'.

Cultures of imperial logistics

The impact of technological shifts on human experience is at the heart of accounts of the modern world, rooted in claims of novel visual, temporal, spatial and embodied sensations.[39] Yet in many such accounts of modern experience, insights have been limited to the Western world.[40] Scholars such as Douglas Burgess have attempted to address this oversight, foregrounding the steamship's relevance to these concerns, including in the context of imperial mobility. At the centre of this thesis is what he terms the 'phantasmagoria of steam': the steamship was an object of wood and iron, but also of spectacle and the imagination. 'Just as steam travel transformed the landscape of the modern world,' he writes, 'it remapped the landscape of the modern mind.'[41]

Histories of technology have drawn attention to the role played by the steamship as an innovative means for Western imperial powers to secure superior control over global space and resources, lending them a tactical, geopolitical advantage over other nations.[42] A focus, however, on the colonial domination of Western technologies risks overlooking the ways in which the drawbacks and limitations of these technologies could be drowned out by the imperialist hubris of their association with modernity.[43] Jürgen Osterhammel has written of the steamship's place in the nineteenth century's increasingly integrated world system: 'in the history of transportation, there is often no way around a mild form of technological determinism'. As Osterhammel suggests, it would be foolish to argue that the technology of steam was not responsible for forms of global mobility which revolutionised colonial social relations and imperial geopolitics.[44] 'It is another story', Osterhammel continues, 'whether they then … are endowed with special meanings and functions.'[45] As this book will show, this 'other story' is in many ways no less significant in the steamship's making of the modern world than the material functionality of mobility.

Frances Steel, in her exploration of imperial steam shipping's history in the context of Oceania, has insisted on the need to avoid 'conceiving of imperialism as an abstract system in order to talk in general terms about the "impacts" and "outcomes" of steam'. Instead, she insists, it is imperative for the historian to 'locate transport technologies and systems in the contexts of their everyday use'.[46] Paying close attention to the lived world of the imperial steamship, Steel argues, allows us to 'open up an historical analysis of steamships and empire to the more complex and layered histories of transnational and transcolonial activities, lives and identities'. There is thus much to be gained from studying textual representations of steam at sea, the subjective, affective investments found in ego documents of imperial travel. Close analysis of such source materials reveals the plurality and difference found in the cultural associations of steamship mobilities. 'Technologies did not have stable meanings that were neatly defined by the elite', Steel insists. 'They were transformed and found meaning in specific colonial settings.'[47]

However, I argue that much of the novel experiences and imaginaries which accompanied the nineteenth-century revolution in mobilities were not necessarily the causal outcome of technological innovation. Rather, they have to be seen as part of wider social and cultural imaginaries which were projected onto technologies often in themselves less than adequate to such utopian visions. Jeffrey Auerbach has suggested that a more comprehensive understanding of imperialism's histories can be reached through 'focusing on the divergence between the fantasy and reality of empire'.[48] Analogously, the shortfall between the frequently utopian, hubristic, sometimes problematic stories which have been told about imperial mobilities at sea, and the disappointments, monotony and discomforts of shipboard life is itself revealing. It conveys the extent to which the technophilic exuberance at the heart of much of the discourse concerning steamships was invested in an imaginative modernity which often exceeded the realities of technological innovation. The degree to which these visions and narratives were tied up in wider ideological narratives of capitalism, progress and empire needs to be further interrogated.

Imperial networks, spaces in between

Studying the history of shipboard lives on the overland route engages with imperial history's long-standing concern with the convoluted relationship between metropole and periphery.[49] 'New' imperial historians have insisted on the need to go beyond the fixity and localisation of this conceptualisation of empire. Rather, they have privileged approaches which transcend the bounds of individual states and regions, embracing webs, networks, connections, flows, circulation, linkages.[50] Yet, despite this emphasis, imperial lives lived in transit remain something of a lacuna in this historiography. As Alan Lester has suggested, imperial networks were conduits through which 'British colonial discourses were made and remade rather than simply transferred or imposed.'[51] While such work increasingly highlights the role of global networks as the *medium* of such discourses, less has been said about networks as significant historical sites for the production of imperial discourse.

Recent scholarship has increasingly drawn attention to the sea, particularly to the ship at sea, as a distinctive yet neglected object of scholarly inquiry.[52] Mobilities research has particularly insisted on the need to engage with the interstitial conditions of shipboard spaces and their inhabitants.[53] Such an approach foregrounds the ship as an overlooked mobile space which should not merely be seen as a vehicle for effecting the transfer of people, goods, information and money between two points, but as a site no less important than the land-based locations it connects. *Imperial Steam* argues that ships were significant imperial sites where conceptions of identity, empire and the global were produced in transit, through the social, cultural, material and imaginative practices of shipboard life; and that its very betweenness, its being in transit, makes the ship a significant site for coming to terms with the British Empire's history.[54] P&O's steamships are particularly significant in this regard, given the extent to which the company's history is intertwined with nineteenth-century British imperialism.

Simon Potter and Jonathan Saha have drawn attention to what they term 'the long-standing but often misleading tendency to examine the British Empire as a singular, hermetically-sealed world-system'.[55] Being attentive to the links and networks which connected imperial sites, they claim, can help historians move beyond such limited perspectives, highlighting the difference and specificity of imperial experiences. Engaging with imperial mobilities rather than the binary of metropole and periphery can also help us to understand how such perspectives arose in the first place – the overland route provided both passengers and those in the metropole with a powerful discursive vehicle for comprehending the British Empire as a coherent, homogeneous whole. This book thus doesn't set out to write a history which reflects the need – identified by Antoinette Burton – for 'displacing the West as the originary site of knowledge, power, resources, history'.[56] Rather, it seeks to contribute to our understanding of the origins of such beliefs; their construction socially, culturally, discursively, textually, imaginatively, representationally. How were the cultural meanings attached to the imperial steamship employed to construct narratives of the West's place in the world?

Spatially, this book's engagement is with both a constrained space (the ship itself) and with a vast 'imperial network' (the geographical space of the overland route). Focusing on the moving space of the ship at sea offers a distinctive set of perspectives and preoccupations.[57] In the most obvious sense, as a moving space which goes beyond the geographical fixity of much imperial history, it emphasises transnational imperial perspectives. While imperial India inevitably loomed large in passengers' imaginative investments in the voyage, the overland route steamship intersected with more than just one nation's imperial history – in its very mobility, it was also caught up to varying degrees with that of Egypt, Arabia, Sri Lanka, Australia, China, Japan and numerous other locations. Travel writer Eliot Warburton opened his hugely successful 1844 account of Middle Eastern travel, *The Crescent and the Cross*, by detailing his voyage from Southampton to Alexandria aboard the *Oriental*. This was one of the two large wooden paddle steamers which the company had acquired from the failing Transatlantic Steamship Company in 1840, to commence the Southampton–Alexandria route. The new means of mobility, which had made the Eastern world more accessible, provided Warburton with a powerful discursive vehicle to draw his readers into this world. A description he furnishes of the passengers he encountered on board the steamer emphasises the extent to which their itinerant lives were tied up with the European colonial project:

> You will hear places, that sound most strange and distant, spoken of with the familiarity of citizens: if you enquire upon any locality in the wide East, up starts a native of the spot; and a gazetteer of voices is ready to enlighten you on any subject of geography, from Cairo to Hong-Kong.[58]

Not only does Warburton's account highlight the trans-imperial nature of the overland steamship's passengers, it also emphasises that the ship was a space in which these figures could come together and perceive themselves as part of a shared project – a common grouping of imperial subjects in transit. Irrespective of where their journey took them, and the heterogeneous nature of the imperial experiences they would encounter there, the overland route provided imperial actors with a common discourse, a unified sense of their place in the imperial world. The 'modern' global mobility provided by the steamship, then, allowed passengers to imagine themselves part of a global empire, both contained within and propagated by the ship. It contributed to what Gareth Curless et al. have described as 'the perception among historical actors that they themselves were part of a system of interconnected global empires'.[59] Exploring such sentiments means asking how steamship mobilities contributed to passengers' sense of connectedness to empire as a network and their comprehension of the imperial world as a totality. What did the overland route mean to them? How did they experience it? How did they articulate their experiences? Above all, it requires us to consider how imperial actors' sense of self spanned the discursive gulf between metropole and periphery. As I will explore, an important aspect of the overland route's mythology lay in passengers' affective investments in the processes of mobility itself.

The sea, and mobilities at sea, have long been at the centre of discourses about Britain's place in the world, often featuring in highly politicised, partial narratives.[60] The potent symbolism of the steamship – as modernity, as progress, as the hubristic overcoming of nature – provided an effective discursive means for those in the metropole to encounter imperial lives lived through the imaginative apparatus of a real logistical system. This book does not, however, attempt to make any direct claims regarding the specific impacts of these texts on the reader in the metropole. My assertions regarding the place of the steamship in the British imperial imaginary are rooted rather in the sheer profusion of voyage narratives. These sources give us an idea of how the general reader of books, journals and newspapers in the metropole – white, bourgeois, urbane, predominantly male – would encounter the world of imperial mobility, and the locations in the British Empire to which the steamship travelled. They provide an overview of the core discursive concerns which would animate such a reader's encounter with the imperial world.[61] The steamship provided a powerful narrative device which allowed readers in the metropole to imaginatively travel to the imperial East – above all, it allowed them to perform this imaginative journey using a distinctly modern form of mobility.

Summary of chapter themes

Imperial Steam is structured according to thematic configurations which emerge out of the primary source material – significant cultural associations of the overland route which occur repeatedly in historical accounts of overland route steamship travel. Chapter 1 explores what exactly was modern about the colonial steamship experience, utilising as an organising principle four key aspects of modernity defined by an 1857 publication eulogising the overland route steamship's revolutionary impact on the voyage to India. Exploring these themes of 'bustle, motion, progress and change', the chapter tests their veracity against the archive of the P&O steamer. Bustle emphasises the texture of modern experience, particularly the sensory overstimulation associated with urban modernity. The steamship voyage was, however, seen as an oasis of calm, only described as overwhelming in the transitions of the external world, the different sights and experiences outside of the ship and the various stops along the way, described as increasingly exotic and 'oriental' in character. Motion foregrounds the significance of mobility in the making of the modern world, with accounts repeatedly attesting to shifting conceptions of imperial geographies as a result of the overland route, describing a familiar sensation of the compression of global space. Progress engages with the Victorian preoccupation with technology's developmental role in promulgating enlightenment values and societal improvement. Accounts of the steamship's progressive symbolism are revealing of the racial hierarchies at the heart of the imperial project. Change assesses just what was new about steamship travel to the East. Passengers described a spectacular overcoming of nature which, I argue, was rooted in the steamship's liberation from the influence of wind and wave. However, this characterisation relied on an ignoring of both the nascent steamship's continued reliance upon sail and modern forms of subaltern shipboard labour whose impact reached beyond the steamer's engine rooms.

Passengers stepping on board the overland route steamship reported their amazement at what they described as a radically new kind of shipboard space, a vast, complex one which at first proved difficult to navigate. The early steamer was certainly larger than most of the sailing vessels that passengers had until that time travelled on to the East, but what exactly was so novel about this space that it provoked such reactions? Chapter 2 documents the emergence of dedicated passenger spaces which accompanied the introduction of steam propulsion. While sailing ships travelling to India did offer passenger accommodation, it was provided in an improvised, indiscriminate manner, with passenger cabins built using temporary partitions and furnished by their occupants. The steamship formalised passenger accommodation on the journey to the East, with permanent cabins and a range of other luxurious dedicated passenger spaces: dining saloons, bathrooms, toilets, ladies' dressing rooms, smoking rooms. The ship's deck particularly underwent a transformation, from a space of labour aboard the sailing vessel into a bourgeois social sphere of leisured display and spectatorship, due in part to the decline of the traditional maritime labour practices in this space effected by steam propulsion.

Steamship space was distinguished not only by practical changes, but was invested by passengers with the practices and associations of other – specifically modern – spaces from beyond the ship. Whether sources compare the steamer to the factory, the city, the coffee house or the private club, they unequivocally converge on claims that its space was distinctly un-shiplike. Steam propulsion also introduced new labour spaces such as the engine room and stokehole to the ship, and the new labour roles of the engineer and stoker. A clear tension emerges in voyage narratives between the two sets of shipboard spaces and occupants, with rules, structures and spatial practices designed to ensure that the increasingly subaltern crew members were spatially segregated from privileged white passengers. While the sailing ship had for centuries been characterised by rigid forms of discipline, the steamer was more clearly demarcated spatially, in terms of who could access certain spaces, and how they could behave in this space. Even passengers deemed problematic (due to reasons of class, race or gender) were denied access to the leisured, bourgeois passenger spaces of the ship – or from the ship altogether. The chapter culminates in an examination of how the various aspects of steamship space designate it as an idiosyncratically imperial environment.

Chapter 3 focuses on a striking concern in source materials with the steamship's temporality: on passengers' preoccupations with the passage of time, with temporal precision, and with the rhythms of shipboard life. The steamship had injected a new temporal urgency into the sea voyage to the East: no longer reliant on the whims of nature, steamships were not just faster than sailing vessels, but could travel to precise, repeatable timetables, unprecedented in global travel. This bureaucratic precision, temporal discipline and repetition which governed the steamer's mobility was echoed in the passenger experience. From the steamer's mealtimes to the popular pastime of gambling on the steamer's insignificant deviations from its schedule, passengers appeared to be obsessed with the temporality of shipboard life. Yet while the steamship was lauded by contemporary commentators for the radical temporal abbreviation of the journey to the East, overland route narratives are marked by repeated references to the monotony of the voyage. This boredom, at odds with the ubiquitous emphasis upon acceleration and flux as the defining modes of modern experience, differs little from accounts of sailing ship voyages from the previous century, despite the overland's route brevity, and the steamer's numerous calling points. These claims emphasise an acute sense of the passengers' separation from the flow of time associated with their everyday lives on land. Suspended between the temporalities (both real and perceived) of the British and imperial worlds, this dislocation contributed to a sense of being 'outside' the passage of time in the modern world. The chapter engages with this shipboard phenomenon in the context of the wider rationalisation of the temporality of everyday life which characterised Western modernity. In doing so, it clarifies the extent to which the passengers' sense of themselves as passive consumers of mobility was seen as problematic, due to its identification of the time spent in transit as the inversion of the productive, busy time of modern life. These preoccupations with temporality, whether positive or negative, helped mediate the passenger's sense of their place between metropole and periphery, warding off the threat of difference.

The framing of the steamship as simultaneously a radical departure from sail and almost routinely quotidian was a persistent feature of accounts of travel aboard P&O steamers. The revolution in global mobility facilitated by steam is repeatedly characterised by passengers as ordinary, everyday, articulated specifically through a distinctive homeliness ascribed to the steamer. Chapter 4 explores this domesticity as a set of social, material and representational practices which helped passengers to identify the steamship as a distinctly modern (Western) environment, acting as a corrective to the dislocation of imperial mobilities identified in Chapter 3. The steamship's domesticity can be seen as a kind of cushioning of the passenger from both the industrial production of mobility (and the associated labour practices), the tribulations of travel at sea, and the unfamiliarity of the imperial world. Passenger accounts of the steamship's domesticity exist in a state of tension between descriptions of interior decoration and concerns regarding the level of comfort on board. P&O's steamships featured an opulent if conservative décor whose familiarity appealed to an increasingly discerning bourgeois consumer. Florid papier mâché ornamentation, oil lamps, walls hung with paintings and gilded mirrors produced luxurious shipboard interior spaces which helped to mask the trials of life at sea. Yet this décor was often seen by passengers as superfluous, inappropriate to the gravity and potential dangers of maritime travel, and to an imperial climate which tested the very limits of comfort. Descriptions of the inevitable discomforts of life on board foreground the embodied experience of steamship travel, for both the bourgeois consumers of mobility and the subaltern workers who made their experience of mobility possible.

Chapter 5 moves away from the space of the ship itself, to focus on passenger descriptions of the maritime landscape viewed from the steamship. With striking frequency, passenger accounts of the view from the ship employ the popular Victorian entertainment form of the panorama as a means of framing and articulating their perception of the Eastern landscape. In fact, P&O's steamship service to the East was represented in one of the nineteenth century's most successful spectacles of this type, 1851's *Overland Mail Panorama*. The popularity of this panorama was testament to the overland route's place in the Victorian popular imagination, particularly situating the steamship line in relation to Britain's global empire. While the *Overland Mail Panorama* presented an aesthetic mode of engaging with the geographies of global space that had been made possible by P&O's introduction of steam to colonial shipping scarcely a decade before, it also fed back into passengers' experiences of the overland route itself. The mechanical form of vision facilitated by the panorama not only offered passengers a means of representing their experience of steamship travel, but also, I argue, presented a Western mode of viewing the Eastern landscape in which representation came to precede reality – travellers reported that the Eastern landscape viewed from the steamer resembled the panorama, rather than the other way round. Furthermore, passenger descriptions of these landscapes compare favourably with their accounts of disembarking and experiencing the imperial world at first hand, an experience often met with disappointment. This phenomenon supports the notion that the steamship offered Western travellers a means for viewing the Eastern landscape in a way that they found comprehensible. I conclude by arguing that this was in fact indicative of a broader sense in which the steamship could be said to have acted as a significant device for framing and forming the passenger's – and the British public's – imperial world view.

Notes

1 David Lester Richardson, *The Anglo-Indian Passage, Homeward and Outward; or, a Card for the Overland Traveller from Southampton to Bombay, Madras, and Calcutta: With Letters Descriptive of the Homeward Passage and Notices of Gibraltar [etc.]* (London: Madden and Malcolm, 1845), p. 1.
2 Incorporated by Royal Charter in 1840 to provide steamship communication with the colonial East, P&O's ships facilitated a vitally important logistical system

which connected and sustained the fluid functioning of British imperialism. For an account of the company's early years, see Gordon Boyce, *Information, Mediation, and Institutional Development: The Rise of Large-Scale Enterprise in British Shipping, 1870–1919* (Manchester: Manchester University Press, 1995), pp. 66–7. The company relied on a number of British government contracts to carry mail, their first major contract, to the Iberian Peninsula, being awarded in 1837. P&O's main steamship routes ran from Southampton to Alexandria (from 1840); from Suez to Ceylon, Madras and Calcutta (from 1842); from Ceylon to Penang, Singapore and Hong Kong (from 1845), extending to Shanghai in 1849. The company ran a Malta–Constantinople branch line from 1845 to 1854. Their steam service to Australia began in 1852. Until 1854, when P&O took the line over completely, the Suez–Bombay branch route was maintained in part by East India Company steamers. Freda Harcourt, *Flagships of Imperialism: The P&O Company and the Politics of Empire from its Origins to 1867* (Manchester: Manchester University Press, 2006), pp. 72–7, 105.

3 Richardson, *The Anglo-Indian Passage*, p. vii.

4 David Arnold, *Science, Technology and Medicine in Colonial India* (Cambridge: Cambridge University Press, 2000), p. 63.

5 Richardson, *The Anglo-Indian Passage*, p. ix. Steamships were at this time regularly crossing the Atlantic in around two weeks.

6 *Ibid.*, p. viii.

7 *Ibid.*, pp. viii–ix

8 The company continued to employ the Egyptian railway for some years after the canal's opening, owing partly to their government contract stipulating that the mail had to be carried by this method. P&O would not finally cease utilising the Egyptian railway to transport mail, and begin to exclusively employ the Suez Canal, until 1888, after the canal had been considerably improved. See Yrjö Kaukiainen, 'Shrinking the World: Improvements in the Speed of Information Transmission, *c.*1820–1870', *European Review of Economic History*, 5 (2001), 1–28, p. 16. Although severely prejudicial to P&O's near-monopolistic hold on Eastern steam navigation, the Canal meant that the steamship's place as the dominant means of global maritime mobility was realised. The year 1870 also marked the completion of the telegraph connecting Britain and India, a development which meant that the steamship's primacy as the means of communication with the colonial East also came to an end at this time.

9 A concept indebted to the work of Edward Said, imaginative geographies have been described by Derek Gregory as 'figurations of place, space and landscape that dramatize distance and difference in such a way that "our" space is divided and demarcated from "their" space'. Derek Gregory, 'Between the Book and the Lamp: Imaginative Geographies of Egypt, 1849–50', *Transactions of the Institute of British Geographers*, 20 (1995), 29–57, p. 29. See also Derek Gregory, 'Imaginative Geographies', *Progress in Human Geography*, 19 (1995), 447–85, and Edward W. Said, *Orientalism* (London: Penguin, 2003), pp. 49–73.

10 Isabella Frances Romer, *A Pilgrimage to the Temples and Tombs of Egypt, Nubia, and Palestine, in 1845–6, Volume 1* (London: R. Bentley, 1846), p. v.

Romer's reference to a 'drug' is probably to the now obsolete meaning of a commodity which is no longer in demand.

11   Much has been said of the 'British imperial world view'. See, for example, John Mackenzie, *Propaganda and Empire: The Manipulation of British Public Opinion 1880–1960* (Manchester: Manchester University Press, 1984), pp. 253–8. I do not attempt to suggest that there was a single, monolithic 'British imperial world view'. Rather, I hope to show that the history this book explores constitutes a powerful and distinctive contribution to the discursive production of a world view which privileged England (and the West more generally) as the centre of the world, from which modernity spread out over the globe.

12   The transit across Egypt, from Alexandria to Suez, was initially performed in a fairly primitive manner: small steamboats carried the passengers along the Mahmoudiyah Canal and up the Nile to Cairo. Travellers would often take advantage of the opportunity for sightseeing before the arduous journey across the desert to Suez by horse-drawn carriage. The company exerted pressure upon the Egyptian government to construct a railway network, the Alexandria–Cairo section of which was inaugurated in 1856, with the Cairo–Suez section following in 1858. While this part of the voyage, of course, constituted a significant aspect of the narrative of the overland route, it is not engaged with in detail here. Nor are the various touristic excursions passengers engaged in at the various stops along the route. This is due to the book's emphasis on the space of the ship itself as a significant and overlooked vantage point from which to explore the history of the British imperial world. For a compelling cultural history of the overland section of the route, see On Barak, *On Time: Technology and Temporality in Modern Egypt* (Berkeley: University of California Press, 2013), pp. 26–39.

13   See Valeska Huber, *Channelling Mobilities: Migration and Globalisation in the Suez Canal Region and Beyond, 1869–1914* (Cambridge: Cambridge University Press, 2013), p. 22, and Robert Blyth, 'Aden, British India and the Development of Steam Power in the Red Sea, 1825–1839', in *Maritime Empires: British Imperial Maritime Trade in the Nineteenth Century*, ed. by David Killingray, Margarette Lincoln and Nigel Rigby (Woodbridge: Boydell Press, 2004), pp. 68–83, p. 69. For a pre-history of the overland route, documenting earlier attempts to run steamships to the East via Egypt, see On Barak, *On Time*, pp. 21–9. See also Huber, *Channelling Mobilities*, pp. 22–3, and Alan Lester, Kate Boehme and Peter Mitchell, 'Steam and Opium', in *Ruling the World: Freedom, Civilisation and Liberalism in the Nineteenth-Century British Empire* (Cambridge: Cambridge University Press, 2020), pp. 168–82.

14   'Communication with the East', *Asiatic Journal and Monthly Register for British and Foreign India China and Australasia, Volume 1*, May–October 1843, p. 573.

15   Freda Harcourt's business history of P&O focuses on the company's management, its financial infrastructure, the activities of its owners and other significant figures in its history, and the impact of the policies of the British government upon the business. Crosbie Smith's history of nineteenth-century steam shipping also engages with the company, focusing on the technological developments of

the steamship, the biographies of entrepreneurs, engineers and naval officers, inventors and investors behind the major steamship lines. Harcourt, *Flagships of Imperialism*; Crosbie Smith, *Coal, Steam and Ships: Engineering, Enterprise and Empire on the Nineteenth-Century Seas* (Cambridge: Cambridge University Press, 2018), pp. 225–82.

16 William Howard Russell, *My Diary in India, in the Year 1858–9* (London: Routledge, 1860), p. 3. There was a marked burgeoning of accounts of the voyage East which accompanied the advent of steamship travel, compared to a relative dearth in the age of sail.

17 This book draws upon overland route narratives from nearly fifty books published in the first three decades of P&O's steamship service to India, representing an average of one and a half accounts every year for thirty years. It also employs numerous articles published in journals and newspapers during the same period. The overland route was rarely out of the public eye. Of course, not all of the accounts which engage with the overland route are travel narratives – much of the writing about P&O's steamships was produced by those who remained in Britain. A significant genre within this corpus consists of the elaborate journalistic descriptions of new vessels which accompanied their launch.

18 This approach has perhaps more in common with the methodology of German cultural critic Walter Benjamin, in his unfinished *Arcades Project*, than it does with much imperial history. Benjamin's accumulation of a wealth of quotations documenting life in nineteenth-century Paris was intended as a means to come to terms with the quality of modern experience. Walter Benjamin, *The Arcades Project*, trans. by Howard Eiland and Kevin McLaughlin (Cambridge, MA: Harvard University Press, 1999), p. 461. See also Irving Wohlfarth, 'Et Cetera? The Historian as Chiffonnier', in *Walter Benjamin and the Arcades Project*, ed. by Beatrice Hanssen (London: Continuum, 2006), pp. 12–32.

19 For example, John Murray, one of the most prominent nineteenth-century British publishers of guidebooks, produced the *Handbook for India*, which provides extensive information on the route. Edward B. Eastwick, *A Handbook for India: Being an Account of the Three Presidencies, and of the Overland Route; Intended as A Guide for Travellers, Officers, and Civilians, Part I. – Madras* (London: John Murray, 1859).

20 William Delafield Arnold, 'An Overland Mail Adventure', *Fraser's Magazine for Town and Country*, July 1856, p. 113.

21 Travel writing scholarship has emphasised the role of mobility in the production of imperial knowledge. See Paul Smethurst, 'Introduction', in *Travel Writing, Form and Empire: The Poetic and Politics of Mobility*, ed. by Julia Kuehn and Paul Smethurst (New York: Routledge, 2009), pp. 1–18, pp. 1–7.

22 See Mary Louise Pratt, *Imperial Eyes: Travel Writing and Transculturation* (London: Routledge, 1992); Felix Driver and Luciana Martins (eds), *Tropical Visions in an Age of Empire* (Chicago: University of Chicago Press, 2005).

23 Such narratives also had a life on board the ship itself: no less than the social and material conditions of shipboard life, passenger conceptions of steamship mobility were managed and mediated by guidebooks and literary and journalistic

accounts which employed familiar textual tropes to discursively mitigate against the uncertainty and disorientation of mobility at sea. As James Duncan and Derek Gregory have suggested, travel and texts were produced in a process of co-constitution, with narratives informing the experiences of subsequent travellers, and the texts they themselves produced. James Duncan and Derek Gregory, 'Introduction', in *Writes of Passage: Reading Travel Writing*, ed. by James Duncan and Derek Gregory (London and New York: Routledge, 1999), pp. 1–13, p. 7.

24 'Some of the foundational narratives of modernity', Tim Cresswell has written, 'have been constructed around the brute fact of moving. Mobility as liberty, mobility as progress.' Tim Cresswell, 'Towards a Politics of Mobility', *Environment and Planning D: Society and Space*, 2 (2010), 17–31, p. 21. As John Armstrong and David Williams have argued, the modernity of the early steamship has been largely ignored, particularly in the important formative decades which preceded the opening of the Suez Canal. John Armstrong and David Williams, 'The Steamship as an Agent of Modernisation, 1812–1840', *International Journal of Maritime History*, 19 (2007), 145–60.

25 Edward Braddon, *Life in India: A Series of Sketches Showing Something of the Anglo-Indian, the Land He Lives In, and the People Among Whom He Lives* (London: Longmans, Green & Co., 1872), pp. 303, 307.

26 For a detailed account of the various tribulations of the sailing ship voyage to India, see Jeffrey Auerbach, 'Voyages', *Imperial Boredom: Monotony and the British Empire* (Oxford: Oxford University Press, 2018), pp. 12–43.

27 Tamson Pietsch, 'Bodies at Sea: Travelling to Australia in the Age of Sail', *Journal of Global History*, 11 (2016), 209–28, p. 224.

28 This claim resonates with what Bruno Latour has termed the 'Great Divide' he identifies at the heart of modernity's constitution, the gulf which he argues 'moderns' believe separates them from 'primitives'. This divide is both temporal and spatial, in that modernity is conceived as a historical departure from the past, but also that the very idea of modernity is constituted through moderns' sense of themselves as set apart geographically. Bruno Latour, *We Have Never Been Modern*, trans. by Catherine Porter (Cambridge: Harvard University Press, 1993), p. 12. See also Timothy Mitchell, 'Introduction', in *Questions of Modernity*, ed. by Timothy Mitchell (Minneapolis, MN: University of Minnesota Press, 2000), pp. xi–xxvii, p. xiii. As David Arnold has argued, such technologies were instrumental in producing Western subjects' conceptions of their own innate superiority. They helped to emphasise racial, national difference and to justify the ideological claims which underpinned imperialism: 'By the early nineteenth century ... the British saw science, technology, and medicine as exemplary attributes of their "civilizing mission," clear evidence of their own superiority over, and imperial responsibility for, a land they identified as superstitious and backward. Science thus conceived served to heighten a growing sense of difference between Britain and India. In the wake of Britain's industrial revolution, technology (especially that of the steam age, heralded by steamships and railways) critically informed this perspective.' Arnold, *Science, Technology*

and Medicine in Colonial India, p. 15. See also Michael Adas, *Machines as the Measure of Men: Science, Technology, and Ideologies of Western Dominance* (Ithaca, NY: Cornell University Press, 1990). In her cultural history of the Indian railway, Marian Aguiar has explored the interweaving narratives of mobility, technology, colonialism and modernity at stake in that history. 'Modernity and mobility are closely connected in a relation charged by the power of rhetoric and representation', she writes. As Aguiar suggests, viewing developments in mobility in their colonial contexts emphasises the extent to which claims regarding the modern and its relationship with technologies of mobility were fraught with the politics of empire and their attendant geographical imaginaries. Marian Aguiar, *Tracking Modernity: India's Railway and the Culture of Mobility* (Minneapolis: University of Minnesota Press, 2011), p. 2.

29 Dipesh Chakrabarty has insisted that we be aware of the plural meanings and social uses of a modernity constituted through the history of colonialism. 'Claims to modernity,' he writes, 'are artifacts of both ideology and imagination. To be "modern" is to judge one's experience of time and space and thus create new possibilities for oneself.' Dipesh Chakrabarty, 'The Muddle of Modernity', *American Historical Review*, 116 (2011), 663–75, p. 674.

30 See, for example, Andrew Rotter, *Empires of the Senses: Bodily Encounters in Imperial India and the Philippines* (Oxford: Oxford University Press, 2019); Auerbach, *Imperial Boredom*; Pietsch, 'Bodies at Sea'; Tony Ballantyne and Antoinette Burton (eds), *Moving Subjects: Gender, Mobility, and Intimacy in an Age of Global Empire* (Urbana: University of Illinois Press, 2009). The use of biographical texts to write imperial history has been explored in some detail in David Lambert and Alan Lester (eds), *Colonial Lives across the British Empire: Imperial Careering in the Long Nineteenth Century* (Cambridge: Cambridge University Press, 2006), pp. 16–21, and David Lambert, 'Reflections on the Concept of Imperial Biographies: The British Case', *Geschichte und Gesellschaft*, 40 (2014), 22–41.

31 See Kathleen Wilson, 'Introduction: Histories, Empires, Modernities', in *A New Imperial History: Culture, Identity and Modernity in Britain and the Empire, 1660–1840*, ed. by Kathleen Wilson (Cambridge: Cambridge University Press, 2004), pp. 1–26. I am particularly mindful of Tony Ballantyne and Antoinette Burton's suggestion that imperial history benefit from situating colonial encounters in space, drawing attention to the embodied experiences of mobility at stake in the production of identity and affect. Tony Ballantyne and Antoinette Burton, 'Introduction: The Politics of Intimacy in an Age of Empire', in *Moving Subjects*, 1–28.

32 As Adam McKeown has explored, modernity and globalisation are closely related, sharing a sense of newness and perpetual change. Adam McKeown, 'Periodizing Globalization', *History Workshop Journal*, 63 (2007), 218–30. See also Mike Featherstone, Scott Lash and Roland Robertson (eds), *Global Modernities* (London: Sage, 1995); Arjun Appadurai, *Modernity at Large: Cultural Dimensions of Globalization* (Minneapolis, MN: University of Minnesota Press, 1996); Timothy Mitchell (ed.), *Questions of Modernity*.

33 'Globalisation', write Gary Magee and Andrew Thompson, 'is about the interconnectedness of different parts of the world. It is best understood as a process, or a set of processes, that compress time and space, and accelerate the "interdependence" of societies and states'. Gary Magee and Andrew Thompson, *Empire and Globalisation: Networks of People, Goods and Capital in the British World, c.1850–1914* (Cambridge: Cambridge University Press, 2010), p. 2. For John Darwin, the transition from sail to steam in global shipping is at the heart of the long history of globalisation. John Darwin, *Unlocking the World: Port Cities and Globalisation in the Age of Steam 1830–1930* (London: Penguin, 2020).

34 Tamson Pietsch, 'A British Sea: Making Sense of Global Space in the Late Nineteenth Century', *Journal of Global History*, 5 (2010), 423–46, pp. 423–4. See also Auerbach, *Imperial Boredom*. Drawing on narratives of sailing ship voyages to India, Jeffrey Auerbach has identified the significance of the ship as an imperial social sphere, emphasising that for many of those whose lives were lived in the British imperial world, their experience of this world began with their departure from Britain, rather than at the moment of their arrival at their destination.

35 Cresswell, 'Towards a Politics of Mobility', p. 21.

36 For a detailed discussion of the relationship between imperialism and globalisation, see Martin Thomas and Andrew Thompson, 'Empire and Globalisation: From "High Imperialism" to Decolonisation', *The International History Review*, 36 (2014), 142–70.

37 Thomas and Thompson, 'Empire and Globalisation', p. 143. This imaginative aspect of globalisation, they note, comprises the perception of the world as a totality.

38 In making this claim, we might usefully draw upon the definition of culture provided by Magee and Thompson. Writing in the context of imperial history, they refer to 'the idea of "culture" as the embodiment of a group's experiences, which refers to patterns of thinking, feeling and acting that are shared by groups of people (large or small) who live in the same social environment'. Magee and Thompson, *Empire and Globalisation*, p. 13.

39 An approach to the mobilities of steam which privileges the interplay of technology and the imagination, paying attention to the subtle textures of modern life, owes a debt to the work of Wolfgang Schivelbusch, particularly his influential study of the steam train, *The Railway Journey*. Schivelbusch, in a work which could itself be accused of a form of technological determinism, insists on the significance of steam propulsion's influence in understanding shifts in modern subjectivity and experience, particularly in the perception of time and space. Wolfgang Schivelbusch, *The Railway Journey: The Industrialization of Time and Space in the 19th Century* (Berkeley: University of California Press, 1986). For other prominent accounts of the modern world which privilege the quality of experience, see also Benjamin, *The Arcades Project*; Marshall Berman, *All That Is Solid Melts into Air: The Experience of Modernity* (London: Verso, 1993).

40 As Douglas Burgess has argued, this is in part because accounts of steam transportation's place in the historiography of modernity have overwhelmingly privileged

the train over the ship, employing the former to explore 'the transformative impact of mechanized speed on the landscape, social relations, tourism, perception of distance, even the concept of time itself'. Douglas Burgess, *Engines of Empire: Steamships and the Victorian Imagination* (Stanford, CA: Stanford University Press, 2016), pp. 10–11.

41 *Ibid.*, p. 5. As Magee and Thompson have explored, developments in the technologies of transport and communication, 'affected how migrants ... imagined their social and political spaces, thereby making their migrations a defining aspect of their identity'. Magee and Thompson, *Empire and Globalisation*, p. 112.

42 Daniel Headrick, *The Tentacles of Progress: Technology Transfer in the Age of Imperialism, 1850–1940* (Oxford: Oxford University Press, 1988); Ben Marsden and Crosbie Smith, *Engineering Empires: A Cultural History of Technology in Nineteenth-Century Britain* (Basingstoke: Palgrave Macmillan, 2007), pp. 88–128.

43 Walter Johnson has cautioned against narratives which emphasise the role of technologicy. Such stories, he writes, can 'invisibly shape the history they seem to relate. They re-frame economic history as a story of self-made men, of inventors and entrepreneurs. [They] elided deeper structures of history. They overwrote the history of conquest with the history of technology. They transformed the history of capitalism into the history of technology.' Walter Johnson, *River of Dark Dreams: Slavery and Empire in the Cotton Kingdom* (Cambridge, MA: Harvard University Press, 2013), p. 74.

44 Lester, Boehme and Mitchell have referred to the 'disruptive' technology of the steamship in the context of the British Empire in India. Lester, Boehme and Mitchell, *Ruling the World*, p. 173.

45 Jürgen Osterhammel, *The Transformation of the World: A Global History of the Nineteenth Century* (Princeton: Princeton University Press, 2014), p. 712.

46 Frances Steel, *Oceania under Steam: Sea Transport and the Cultures of Colonialism, c.1870–1914* (Manchester: Manchester University Press, 2011), p. 5.

47 *Ibid.* John Law's seminal essay on the topic of sixteenth-century Portuguese colonial sailing ships demonstrated that changes in the technologies of maritime mobility had not merely functional corollaries, but were often tied up with and productive of new forms of global imaginaries and subjectivities. In order to understand the role of mobilities in the making of empire, Law insists upon the need to recognise the role of not just human and non-human actors in this process, but also that 'the technological, the economic, the political, the social, and the natural are all seen as being interrelated'. John Law, 'On the Methods of Long-Distance Control: Vessels, Navigation and the Portuguese Route to India', *The Sociological Review*, 32 (1984), 234–63, p. 235. As Gary Magee and Andrew Thompson have explored, developments in the technologies of transport and communication, 'affected how migrants – and the families they left behind – imagined their social and political spaces, thereby making their migrations a defining aspect of their identity'. Magee and Thompson, *Empire and Globalisation*, p. 112.

48 Auerbach, *Imperial Boredom*, p. 11.

49 For an overview of this relationship and its role in the production of imperial discourses, see Alan Lester, 'Imperial Circuits and Networks: Geographies of the British Empire', *History Compass*, 4 (2006), 124–41.

50 *Ibid.* See also Tony Ballantyne, *Orientalism and Race: Aryanism in the British Empire* (Basingstoke: Palgrave, 2002); Gareth Curless, Stacey Hynd, Temilola Alanamu and Katherine Roscoe, 'Editors' Introduction: Networks in Imperial History', *Journal of World History*, 26 (2015), 705–32.

51 Alan Lester, *Imperial Networks: Creating Identities in Nineteenth-century South Africa and Britain* (London: Routledge, 2001), p. 4.

52 This turn has been especially well documented in David Lambert, Lucianna Martins and Miles Ogborn, 'Currents, Visions and Voyages: Historical Geographies of the Sea', *Journal of Historical Geography*, 32 (2006), 479–93. See also Steve Mentz, *At the Bottom of Shakespeare's Ocean* (London: Continuum, 2009); *Sea Narratives: Cultural Responses to the Sea, 1600-Present*, ed. by Charlotte Mathieson (Basingstoke: Palgrave Macmillan, 2016); Martin Dusinberre and Roland Wenzlhuemer, 'Being in Transit: Ships and Global Incompatibilities', *Journal of Global History*, 11 (2016), 155–62 (the editors' introduction to a special issue of the same name). This turn has seen increased attention paid to steamships in their colonial context. Examples of such work include Anyaa Anim-Addo, '"A Wretched and Slave-like Mode of Labor": Slavery, Emancipation, and the Royal Mail Steam Packet Company's Coaling Stations', *Historical Geography*, 39 (2011), 65–84; Anyaa Anim-Addo, '"The Great Event of the Fortnight": Steamship Rhythms and Colonial Communication', *Mobilities*, 9 (2014), 369–83; Anyaa Anim-Addo, '"Thence to the River Plate": Steamship Mobilities in the South Atlantic, 1842–1869', *Atlantic Studies*, 13 (2016), 6–24; Gopalan Balachandran, 'Cultures of Protest in Transnational Contexts: Indian Seamen Abroad, 1886–1945', *Transforming Cultures eJournal*, 3 (2008), 45–75; Gopalan Balachandran, 'Indefinite Transits: Mobility and Confinement in the Age of Steam', *Journal of Global History*, 11 (2016), 187–208; Janet J. Ewald, 'Crossers of the Sea: Slaves, Freedmen, and Other Migrants in the Northwestern Indian Ocean, *c.*1750–1914', *American Historical Review*, 105 (2005), 69–91; Ravi Ahuja, 'Capital at Sea, Shaitan Below Decks? A Note on Global Narratives, Narrow Spaces, and the Limits of Experience', *History of the Present*, 2 (2012), 78–85.

53 This position has been persuasively articulated by Anyaa Anim-Addo, William Hasty and Kimberley Peters: 'At sea, there are an abundance of "gaps" between A's and B's – journeys, moments in transit, lives lived on the move – which have been hitherto overlooked in favour of the apparent fixity and thus importance of points of departure and arrival at either side, on land'. Anyaa Anim-Addo, William Hasty and Kimberley Peters, 'The Mobilities of Ships and Shipped Mobilities', *Mobilities*, 9 (2014), 337–49, p. 342. Such a perspective is indebted to the insights of the new mobilities paradigm. See Mimi Sheller and John Urry, 'The New Mobilities Paradigm', *Environment and Planning A*, 38 (2006), 207–26, pp. 213–4. The mobilities paradigm has been characterised by an insistence on the centrality of processes of movement in the formation of subjectivity and

the production of meaning. See also Tim Cresswell, *On the Move: Mobility in the Modern Western World* (London: Routledge, 2006), pp. 2–3. Gopalan Balachandran, writing in the context of the history of imperial steamship mobilities, echoes this call for greater attention to this 'space between'. 'Global histories of mobility', he argues, 'cannot simply be about departures, arrivals, admittance, and eventual inclusion. They are also about conditions in between.' Balachandran, 'Indefinite Transits', p. 207.

54 David Lambert and Peter Merriman have insisted on the need to foreground the question of mobility in engaging with histories of imperialism: 'A thorough engagement with questions of mobility – and immobility – has much to offer to the study of empire more broadly, and not merely in terms of transport technologies and infrastructures, but also the cultures, discourses, practices and subjectivities with which they are associated.' David Lambert and Peter Merriman, 'Empire and Mobility: An Introduction', in *Empire and Mobility in the Long Nineteenth Century*, ed. by David Lambert and Peter Merriman (Manchester: Manchester University Press, 2020), pp. 1–28, p. 3.

55 Simon Potter and Jonathan Saha, 'Global History, Imperial History and Connected Histories of Empire', *Journal of Colonialism and Colonial History*, 16 (2015), https://muse.jhu.edu/article/577738.

56 Antoinette Burton, 'When Was Britain? Nostalgia for the Nation at the End of the "American Century"', *Journal of Modern History*, 75 (2003), 359–74, p. 371.

57 Alison Bashford, in arguing for the maritime's significance to global history, suggests overcoming the binary of land and sea, in order to think more productively about the histories which were animated by the connections and intersections between and across both spaces. Alison Bashford, 'Terraqueous Histories', *The Historical Journal*, 60 (2017), 253–72. Paul Gilroy has suggested that paying attention to the cultural history of the ship affords the opportunity to develop a deeper understanding of the constitution of Western identity and the production of modernity in relation to imperialism. Paul Gilroy, *The Black Atlantic: Modernity and Double Consciousness* (London: Verso, 1993), pp. 16–17.

58 Eliot Warburton, *The Crescent and the Cross; Or, Romance and Realities of Eastern Travel, Volumes 1–2* (London: Henry Colburn. 1844), p. 6.

59 Curless et al., 'Editors' Introduction: Networks in Imperial History', p. 708.

60 Miles Taylor, 'Introduction', *The Victorian Empire and Britain's Maritime Worlds, 1837–1901: The Sea and Global History*, ed. by Miles Taylor (New York: Palgrave Macmillan, 2013), pp. 1–18.

61 David Lambert and Alan Lester have explored the impact of imperial travel narratives in the metropole. 'Such narratives', they write, 'were influential in constructing the geographical imaginations of those who had stayed "at home" in Britain itself.' David Lambert and Alan Lester, 'Introduction: Imperial Spaces, Imperial Subjects', in *Colonial Lives across the British Empire: Imperial Careering in the Long Nineteenth Century*, ed. by David Lambert and Alan Lester (Cambridge: Cambridge University Press, 2006), pp. 1–31, p. 1.

1

'Bustle, motion, progress, change': Steamship modernity

A series of articles published under the title 'The Overland Route to India' appeared in the periodical *Leisure Hour* in late 1857, narrating the journey from England to India by P&O's steamship service. Written in the aftermath of the Indian Rebellion's outbreak that year – an event which raised the profile of the rapid steam route in the public imagination – the first in this series of articles employs a vocabulary more often reserved to describe the revolutionary changes associated with a firmly terrestrial modernity than the vicissitudes of travel at sea.[1] 'We live in stirring times,' its author enthuses, 'all is now bustle, motion, progress, change.'[2] In attempting to convey the revolutionary changes brought about by P&O's introduction of a regular steam service to the voyage East less than two decades before, the article mobilises the vocabulary of a modernity subject to constant transformation and instability: a present in constant flux. This was a modernity characterised as both chronological ('stirring times') and qualitative ('bustle, motion, progress, change').[3]

Locating the steamship at the centre of this process of relentless flux and renewal, the article comprehends technological innovation in imperial mobilities specifically within the framework of a historical break, invoking the preindustrial past in order to emphasise the revolutionary nature of this maritime, global transition:

> In days of yore our worthy sires, in this sea-girt isle, seldom travelled far from home. ... Not so now. Steam has changed all that. These are the days of rapid, easy, economical transit. Oceans are now bridged, and distance is well nigh destroyed, by the wonder-working achievements of human intellect and skill.[4]

The *Leisure Hour* article's energetic, excessive tribute to P&O's steam service invokes the familiar trope of a modernity characterised by novelty and innovation. It describes a transformative, visceral mode of being distinguished by cataclysmic shifts in experience associated with technological, social and cultural change. The speed of the steamship's mobility, identified as a pivotal concern of the era, is articulated in association with its apparent effortlessness.

The technology of steam is characterised as the vehicle of historical change, with the overcoming of the natural space of the sea emphasising steam's role in a radical reappraisal of global geographies. Such references, to what can best be described as the steamship's modernity, were widespread. As has been suggested, this discursive trope provided writers with an effective shorthand for articulating the place of imperial mobilities in a wider narrative of British global supremacy and the role of technology in the making of the modern world. This chapter explores the core characteristics of the steamship's modernity as they are manifested in the archive of the overland route. As an organising principle, it utilises the four modern qualities identified by the *Leisure Hour* article: 'bustle, motion, progress [and] change'.

Bustle: The texture of shipboard life

The Dutch-German naturalist Franz Junghuhn travelled from Singapore to Southampton by the overland route in 1848. In his account of the journey, Junghuhn recounted his experience of transferring at Point de Galle from the smaller P&O steamship *Braganza* to the *Bentinck*, one of the two large, luxurious vessels the company had ordered to serve the Eastern section of the overland route just five years before.[5] For Junghuhn, this was a transition which rendered him 'weary like someone coming from a small provincial town into a capital city, like Paris or London'.[6] Junghuhn's description of the marked experiential change he encountered on boarding the *Bentinck* plays into nineteenth-century discourses regarding the city as an overwhelming environment characterised by an excess of sensory stimulation. The description of this experience that he goes on to furnish is certainly reminiscent of the sensation of the shocks and strain of modern urban life:

> When I had withdrawn from the crowd, from within the tangled mass of the intersecting multitude and settled down at the aft of the *Bentinck*, it was difficult to become accustomed to the conviction that I was on the deck of a ship, so far did the plateau of planks stretch before me; a wealth of objects of the most diverse kind afforded incessant variety and diversion for the crowd, who walked on the deck, which was partly covered with canopies and filled with chairs and benches.[7]

In Junghuhn's description, the steamship is depicted as an exhilarating new sphere of social relations, specifically expressed through its departure from the recognisable characteristics of the traditional environment of the ship. Instead, he compares the steamer to the big city, a characterisation distinguished by sensory change and distraction, centring on the figure of the crowd. Accounts of shipboard bustle are often association with an urbanity that is explored in more detail Chapter 2. Like urban space, the bustling environment of the steamer presented the simultaneous experience of anonymity and of being flung into close proximity with large numbers of strangers.[8]

Junghuhn's was one of the first of a number of overland route narratives published in Dutch. No less than for British imperialists, the steamship had had a profound impact on those whose lives were tied up with the Dutch colonial project, offering a far more expedient means of transport and communication between the Dutch East Indies and Europe. While Dutch imperialism was in the shade of the greater British imperial project, this was a period of expansion and consolidation of the Dutch empire in the Indonesian archipelago. The majority of the seven Dutch accounts which appear in this book record overland route journeys from Java to Europe, providing highly detailed and penetrating descriptions of the various new experiences encountered in transit, to a Dutch public hungry for the novelty of modern imperial mobilities. These accounts tend to exhibit an emphatic, if at times grudging, admiration for the pioneering infrastructure of British imperialism. Their vivid, energetic descriptions of steamship mobility might be accounted for in part by their authors' relative lack of exposure to the experiences of industrial modernity which their British counterparts were already thoroughly inured to, due to the Netherlands' relatively late industrialisation. Junghuhn had departed Europe for the Dutch East Indies in 1835, working in the Dutch colonial service on Java, where he also pursued his enthusiasm for geological and botanical exploration on the island. Returning to Europe over a decade later, it could be said that boarding the steamship offered him his first encounter with British industrial modernity. His stupefied response to this experience is thus perhaps unsurprising.

Of the four categories of modern experience which structure this chapter, bustle is the most evocative of the experiential character of modern life, a modernity explicated at the level of sensory experience. To be characterised by bustle is to be alive with activity – the word is evocative of the modern city, the flux and commotion of urban life famously characterised by Charles Baudelaire as 'the ephemeral, the fugitive, [and] the contingent'.[9] Georg Simmel's 'The Metropolis and Mental Life' provides the classic account of the sensorial impact of the modern city upon its residents. Simmel identifies a defining quality of modern experience whereby sense perceptions were increasingly subjected to the intensification and kaleidoscopic fragmentation of external stimuli. He describes this idiosyncratically urban phenomenon as one characterised by the 'rapidly shifting stimulations of the nerves which are thrown together in all their contrasts'.[10] This description diagnoses the impact upon human perceptions of the varied colliding and intermingling sensory phenomena which constitute the experience of modern life. For Simmel, this was manifested in such explicitly modern symptoms as nervous overstimulation, fatigue and a blasé outlook on the world.[11] Far from the commotion, diversions and shocks of city life, the ship would perhaps seem an unlikely setting for engaging with such a category of experience. Nevertheless, like the city, in the nineteenth century the experience of mobility took on new facets and imaginaries, which were particularly associated with its industrialisation.[12] The categories of experience described by Simmel and other scholars of modernity do in fact find significant resonances in accounts of steamship voyages.

Like Junghuhn, many passengers' accounts were acutely sensitive to articulating the qualities of shipboard experience, coming to terms with what they considered to be the novel, distinctive, modern characteristics of life on the steamship. They record the sights, sounds and sensations of shipboard life, its spatial and temporal idiosyncrasies, their emotional responses to, and cultural associations of, the voyage. This attentiveness to describing the distinctive experiences of steamship mobility reinforces the sense that this was a historical departure, a new category of experience which demanded to be articulated. An anonymous 1868 account from the *Manchester Weekly Times* provides another such example, even some decades after the line's establishment. Again, its author mobilises bustle as the defining quality of steamship mobility, specifically in terms which distinguishes it from the tradition of travel by sailing ship:

> The overland trip to India scarcely deserves to be dignified with the title of a voyage; it is too bustling and too feverish for such an appellation. My notion of a voyage is where you take some pains to fit up your cabin comfortably, knowing that you are going to inhabit it for three or four months at least.[13]

The temporal protraction of the sailing voyage is employed to emphasise the steamship's speed as a break with the past, characterising the latter by its frenetic activity and ephemerality. Again, this activity is seen to find its origin in the numerous passengers who made up the steamer's transitory population: 'On board the Peninsular and Oriental steamer', the account continues, 'people are always coming and going – it is a sort of an ocean omnibus.'[14] The omnibus, a distinctly modern, urban form of transport, was characterised by its frequent stops and by the continually renewed crowd of people who consequently comprised its occupants. For the article's author, the bustle of the steamship voyage was rooted in its calling, like the omnibus, at regular points on its route: Gibraltar, Malta, Aden, Ceylon. This was consequent of the steamer's need for a regular supply of coal, and the conditions of the company's mail contract. At each of these stops, the ship would take on and drop off mail, passengers, cargo, fuel and supplies.

Passengers were encouraged to visit the shore at these points, partly owing to the lengthy and dirty process of coaling. These interruptions provided opportunities for sightseeing at the nodal points of the British Empire's global logistical network. The short overland section of the journey, across Egypt from Alexandria to Suez via Cairo also became an increasingly touristic interlude in the journey East.[15] It is clear from these sources that the bustle attributed to overland steamship mobilities was rooted in this new tempo of mobility, and in the concomitantly fleeting and shifting character of social relations during the voyage.

In 1843 the East India Company army officer Albert Hervey boarded the steamship *Hindostan* at Madras to begin his homeward voyage on the newly inaugurated overland route.[16] The *Hindostan* had been launched only the previous year, built by the company especially for the Eastern section of the overland route, and was considered to be at the cutting edge of shipbuilding: large, powerful and commodious. Hervey's account of the journey, *The Ocean and the Desert*, provides one of the earliest and most comprehensive accounts of the route. Styling himself as 'A Madras Officer', Hervey was keen to capitalise on the increasing public interest in the British Empire in India, and specifically in the details of the new geography of transit which connected Britain with the colonial East. Running to several hundred pages, Hervey's account provides detailed descriptions of the sights and sensations of the overland voyage, including the various ports of call. It is also at pains to articulate a vivid sense of the experience of the new form of mobility, providing extensive details of what he terms the ship's 'interior economy'.

Hervey is unambiguous regarding his book's intentions, emphatically advocating for the new steam route over sail. However, in the book's concluding remarks, which he uses to persuade the reader of the overland route's unequivocal superiority to the voyage by sail, Hervey makes a passing concession to the latter. This remark seemingly ascribes to steamship mobilities a category of experience which is markedly evocative of the overstimulation contingent upon the shocks and acceleration of modern life. 'Parties having large families of children,' he cautions the reader, 'a good respectable sailing ship … is better than going the overland route; for the rapidity of motion, and the consequent fatigue would be inconvenient to young children; the same reason holds good to the generality of invalids.'[17] In Hervey's reckoning, the very speed with which the overland route journey was undertaken risked taxing a developing or impaired constitution. In this formulation, the sailing ship was deemed to offer a more subdued mode of travel. The antidote to the overstimulation caused by a modern technological form of mobility at sea could, Hervey suggests, be found in a reversion to the earlier, pre-industrial means of transportation.

It is, however, unclear what exactly Hervey considered fatiguing about the overland route. An observation he makes earlier in his narrative appears to contradict such a characterisation. In this passage, he defines the sensory experience of steamship travel as one typified not by the fatiguing sensation of motion, but, compared to the sailing ship, by its relative serenity. On board the *Hindostan*, Hervey writes, he experienced

> no noise of sailors ... no words of command; no bawling through speaking-trumpets; nor any coarse swearing or cursing, so general on board of sailing-craft. Our ears were not saluted with any vulgarisms, nor our nerves tested by any disagreeable noises; all that was heard, and that most indistinctly, was the clanking of the engines; and all that was felt, a sort of vibratory, trembling motion.[18]

The experience of steamship travel presented for Hervey a distinct departure from the still-prevalent maritime environment of the sailing ship. In this description, the steamship betrays little of the dynamic activity which was frequently associated with industrial technologies of mobility. In contrast to the sailing vessel, characterised by the noisy activity and commotion of shipboard labour, the industrialised ship presented for Hervey the absence of such maritime practices. This description is again couched in terms of the impact of sea travel on the nervous system, playing into Victorian discourses about sensory overstimulation as a source of nervous disorder.[19] Yet for Hervey, the steamship was not in itself a bustling environment, specifically due to the passenger's remoteness from the sphere of maritime labour. Indeed, while boarding the *Hindostan* at Madras he described the scene as 'one of bustle and confusion', but soon after the vessel was underway, he writes, 'the bustle and noise of departure subsided into silence'.[20]

Ruth Coopland, the widow of an East India Company chaplain who had been killed in the Indian Rebellion, returned to Britain by the overland route in 1857. In her account of the voyage to Suez on board the *Oriental*, she describes the experience of commotion and chaos upon boarding the steamer at Bombay:

> On the 18th of March the 'Oriental' was to leave, so we bade good-bye to our hospitable friends, and drove down to the Apollo Bunder; when finding the steamer had not yet come round, we put off in a boat, and were soon on board. Only those who have been on board a large vessel can know the bustle and confusion that goes on at first, and how soon people settle quietly down.[21]

For Coopland, like Hervey and Junghuhn, the experience of the steamship as an environment characterised by bustle was associated with the vessel's contact with the land. As passengers boarded, cargo and belongings were loaded, and the crew prepared the vessel for departure, the steamship was a space of noise and confusion. While in transit on the open sea, however,

the steamer was a space of calm and quiet. Such a characterisation of the
steamship is again expressed by Richard Lepsius, a Prussian Egyptologist
who travelled from Southampton to Alexandria on board the *Oriental* in
1842. Lepsius recounts the experience of departure after his hectic preparations
for the trip in London, which he refers to as 'the whirl of the last days and
weeks'. In contrast, the steamer was an environment of marked serenity:

> From the immeasurable world-city, I entered on the uniform desert of the
> ocean, in the narrow-bounded, soon-traversed house of planks. And now there
> was nothing more to be provided, nothing to be hurried ... The want of
> anxiety caused for some time a new and indefinite uneasiness, a solicitude
> without any object of solicitude.[22]

In an inversion of Junghuhn's claims, Lepsius's lyrical account explicitly
contrasts the steamship with the space of the modern city. While the latter
was capacious and frenetic, the delimited, discrete space of the steamer in
transit presented an absence of activity, framed by Lepsius as a spontaneous
departure from the urban as a mode of experience.

For William Makepeace Thackeray, recounting his 1844 leisure voyage
around the Mediterranean, the forced interruption of his return journey
provided a welcome respite from the overstimulation he had encountered
during the trip. This respite was found, he writes, 'in the Quarantine Harbour
at Malta, where seventeen days of prison and quiet were almost agreeable,
after the incessant sight-seeing of the last two months'.[23] Thackeray appears
to suggest that the lazaretto offered him relief from the sensory overload
of a modern, rapid mobility. However, again it was not the shipboard
environment itself which appears to have given rise to this sensation of
overstimulation, but the number and diversity of locations which Thackeray
had visited.[24] Of course, Thackeray's account is different in tone from the
majority of overland route narratives – while most of the latter relate the
journey between England and India or the Far East, mainly taken for
functional purposes, Thackeray embarked on his proto-cruise for purely
touristic reasons, which didn't take him further than Egypt.

The characterisation of the steamship as a source of sensory overstimulation
can be understood as rooted in steam's geographies of mobility. The Dutch
politician Gevers Deynoot travelled to the Dutch East Indies by the overland
route in 1862. Deynoot's account articulates a kind of jouissance associated
with the steamship's mobility, which is explored in the next section. 'This
mode of transport brings great pleasures which cannot be ignored', he
remarks. Again, this is rooted in a distinctly touristic pleasure in the thrill
of geographical encounter: 'I have already talked about the speed with
which the passage is completed, but this is especially significant for such a
journey through the various nations which are seen, and the countries and

places that one calls at.'[25] The velocity of steamship mobility was articulated for Deynoot in the brevity with which a large number of diverse and distinctive geographical locations could be encountered:

> If you start your mail journey in Marseille ... then you first visit the quaint Island of Malta, soon afterwards Egypt, which is so important in many respects, further still arid Aden with its black population, before long setting foot in the Indian world, so completely foreign to Europeans, at Bombay or Ceylon, and at last to become acquainted with the Chinese race on the islands of Penang and Singapore.

The steamship's mobility was experienced through the interruptions of the voyage provided by the overland route's stopping points, 'rapid transitions', Deynoot concludes, which 'make the journey all the more remarkable'.[26] As the steamship traversed vast distances in an unprecedentedly short period of time, the passenger was subject to a sometimes-disorienting exposure to a variety of new and heterogeneous places and landscapes.

The experience of modernity might have been marked by overwhelming stimulation, but it was also characterised by the escape from such experiences: from industrial technologies; from labour; from the overwhelming social experience of the busy crowd. As well as imperialism, modernity, mobility, technology and so on, the overland route's history is concerned in many ways with bourgeois sociality, and particularly with the refined leisure practices of the passenger: with their material and representative manifestations; cultural and textual production; and how these performative, embodied practices themselves defined a certain kind of imperial modernity. In accounts of the overland route, imperial steamship mobilities are persistently associated with distinctive forms of bourgeois leisure, enjoyed specifically at a remove from the bustle of shipboard labour and mobility's production. This was a period which saw the democratisation of forms of leisure previously only available to the very wealthy, but increasingly enjoyed by an ascendant bourgeoisie. As Shelley Baranowski and Ellen Furlough have argued, Victorian bourgeois leisure practices 'articulated middle-class values of self-improvement, time discipline, privacy, and predictability, modifying the hedonistic pleasure-seeking that the bourgeoisie attributed to the aristocracy'.[27] Bourgeois leisure thus had an important role to play in identity formation – the refined, relaxed pursuits of the steamship passenger were not merely defined in opposition to the bustle of shipboard labour. They had a distinctly imperial dimension, helping those who traversed the boundaries between metropole and periphery to maintain a sense of self rooted in class, race and gender in a world of flux and difference. Passengers emphasised the edifying, useful, values of such pursuits, associating them with the distinctive frisson of being privileged consumers of the global mobility at sea provided by the steamship.

As this section has explored, it is clear that passenger preoccupations with the new sensations and experiences of overland route travel were rooted more than anything in their engagement with the new mobilities of steam.

Motion: The imperial mobilities of steam at sea

Bound for Suez on board the *Hindostan* in 1843, Albert Hervey went on deck shortly after the vessel's departure from Madras. Hervey was eager to articulate for his readers the new experiences of the recently inaugurated overland route. His characterisation of the peaceful serenity of steamship travel contrasts with his effusive veneration of the ship's mobility: 'I never witnessed any thing to equal her speed. The power of five hundred horses brought into action propelling such a vast body at so rapid a rate, is indeed matter for admiration and wonder!'[28]

Narratives of overland route travel emphasised the vessel's mobility as a radical technological achievement, emphasising the steamship's status as a wonder of the modern age. The steamship's means of propulsion was particularly seen as a radical departure from sail, which had revolutionised global mobility, constituting the industrialisation of travel at sea. Indeed, with the use of steam, seagoing vessels were no longer constrained by the contingency of the elements which dictated the mobility of the sailing ship. This allowed them to leave port without having to wait for favourable conditions, to travel against the prevailing wind and to steam through storms which could render sailing ships incapacitated, sometimes dangerously so. However, the speed of the early steamship was in fact often little more than that of a sailing vessel in favourable conditions. Nevertheless, steam's ability to overcome the constraints of natural forces, and to travel in a straight line rather than obeying the back-and-forth tacking of the sailing vessel travelling against the wind, meant that it could cover greater distances in shorter periods of time, and travel at times of the year impractical or impossible for many sailing vessels. Coming to terms with the cultural meanings of steamship mobilities is at the heart of this book's engagement with the overland route's history. Being attentive to the cultural investments in steam allows these significant material developments to be embedded in the social relations and cultural imaginary of imperialism and the expansion of global markets.

Accounts of the overland route persistently have recourse to emphatic claims regarding steam's impact on shifting conceptions of imperial geography, particularly mobilising a compelling narrative of the compression of global space. David Lester Richardson, in *The Anglo-Indian Passage* (1845), provides an emphatically laudatory celebration of the new steam route's impact on the imperial world. This is expressed in his veneration of what he terms

> that great magician – STEAM. By that wondrous power the lover's wish is realised – 'time and space' are 'annihilated,' and gigantic India and her proud Ruler, small sized but mighty-hearted England, are brought into closer contact, and made to afford a noble exemplification of the power of science in the nineteenth century.[29]

Richardson's technophilic exuberance characterises the steamship's emergent mobility as a seismic break with tradition. His mobilisation of the 'annihilation of space and time' plays into a familiar discourse about Victorian technologies of mobility. He refers to the steamship's apparent bringing-closer of distant locations, which he also terms (in somewhat less emphatic language) the 'approximation of distant lands – the abbreviation of time and space'.[30] This trope was one more often employed to eulogise the steam train's revolutionary impact than that of steam at sea.[31] More so than the train, however, the overland route steamship's impact emphasises the role of mobilities in the British imperial project as a specifically global concern. An 1843 *Illustrated London News* article announcing the launch of the *Bentinck* refers to P&O's 'patriotic efforts to shorten the distance between Europe and the East'.[32] Moreover, this impact was felt not just in a functional sense, but in terms of the imaginative geographies which contributed to the legitimising and naturalising of the British Empire.

This was the concept that Karl Marx famously nuanced as the annihilation of space *by* time: in Marx's formulation, the space and time of travel were not simply both 'annihilated' by technologies of mobility, but the impact of geographical distance was lessened through the reduction in the time taken to traverse it. This shift, rooted in the globalising tendency of imperial capitalism, resulted in a perceived reduction of distance.[33] Much has been said of this concept, particularly in the context of the Victorian railway. Less attention has been devoted to its imperial iterations – yet the specifics of how this shift was actually experienced, both on and off the steamer, and how it was textually articulated, have much to tell us about the relationship between the mobilities of steam and the British imperial world view. For those imperial actors whose lives were caught up in the expanding global market, the world began to appear smaller – and this had important corollaries for thinking about empire in Britain, and the relationship between metropole and periphery. A new consciousness of global space was thus fostered through the experience of steamship travel, one which was deeply tied up with the imaginative geographies of the British imperial world. This sensation, of the apparent shrinking of the space of the earth, the perceptual diminishing of distance which David Harvey has referred to as 'time–space compression', was implicated in an imperial conception of global space.[34] It helped facilitate the conceptualisation of empire as a coherent, unified global system. In this phenomenon the economic, political and technological intersected with the cultural, the imaginary, the subjective.

The extent to which this development was reflected in contemporary discourses of steamship mobility is articulated by Richardson's comparison of the new steam service with the conditions which had prevailed under sail: 'An Englishman in India, but a few years ago, regarded himself as in a condition of hopeless exile – it almost amounted to banishment for life. All home ties were severed.' The sailing voyage's duration emphasised the separation of metropole and periphery, not merely as geographical distance, but for imperial actors living in the East in the sense of emotional and imaginative distance. Imperial lives were lived, according to Richardson, in an acute state of affective isolation from the metropole, with all of its connotations of British identity and belonging. In a radical departure from these conditions, Richardson asserted, 'a twice-a-month regular Mail will make the majority of Englishmen in India almost fancy themselves in their own land. They will feel that they are rather in a remote *county* than in a foreign *country*.'[35] For Richardson, the time–space compression facilitated by steamship mobilities allowed British colonial actors in the East to conceive of themselves as part of a greater Britain. This was the conception of global space as British imperial space which was famously expressed by Benjamin Disraeli in 1866: 'England has outgrown the continent of Europe. Her position is no longer that of a mere European Power; England is the metropolis of a great maritime empire extending to the boundaries of the farthest oceans.'[36] Colonial territory was subsumed under the conceptual limits of the British imperial state, expressed as maritime space, a conception which owed much to the imaginative geographies of the overland route.

The significance of the overland route in the production of new imperial imaginative geographies is illustrated by a pamphlet published by Captain James Barber in 1839, promoting the steam route to India. Barber was a former servant of the East India Company who was employed by P&O in the 1840s. At the time of writing, three years before P&O sent its first steamers east of Suez, he considered the impact made upon Anglo-Indians by the proposed steamship service: 'Imagination presented to them a grand high-road, connecting the two empires, by which the geographical distance would be shortened one half, and the time occupied be two-thirds less than had hitherto been required to perform an uncomfortable and expensive sea-voyage round the "Cape of Storms".'[37] Barber's observations exhibit an unconventional yet instructive form of technological determinism. The imaginative geographies of British imperialism in this case preceded the impact of technological change – steamship mobilities had not merely functional corollaries, but were invested with the weight of cultural expectations.

The imaginative geographies of steam are again encountered in an 1855 overland route narrative by an anonymous passenger who returned by steamship to Britain from China. This exuberant piece of writing is infused with a global perspective on the radical changes which the steamship had effected in little more than a decade:

> What a revolution steam has created in the world! In the East as well as in the West! When I went out to Hong-Kong at first, letters took four or five, sometimes six, months to come from England by sailing ships. When I left that place a few years ago, letters and newspapers reached us, per overland and by steamers, in seven weeks.[38]

Colonial subjects operating at the periphery of empire in the days before the overland route are characterised by their disconnection from the social relations of the metropole. 'After the establishment of steam communication', the article continues, 'the distance between Great Britain and China seemed actually abridged, and we felt as if we were brought a great deal nearer home than before.'[39] The impact of the voyage's temporal brevity again finds expression in its relation to the comprehension of spatial distance. In Anthony Giddens's reckoning, the modern world is characterised by the intensification of what he terms 'time–space distanciation', the extension of formerly localised social relations across increasing temporal and spatial distances.[40] In reducing the temporal interval of communications between Britain and the East, steam effaced the experience of distance, resulting in an altered conception of global space. The radical reduction of the protracted time lapse in communication which had existed before the advent of steam gave rise to the feeling of a shared present, of coexisting with those in distant lands. This is a transnational iteration of what Benedict Anderson has referred to as an 'imagined community', the production (by modern communication technologies) of a shared sense of unity and simultaneity created in social groupings, whose members have no direct physical contact.[41] The geographical imaginaries associated with imperial steamship mobilities contributed to a shared global consciousness which allowed empire to be thought of as a coherent totality.

The shipboard imaginative geographies of steam

> Our progress today was 219 miles. As the stock of coal taken at Aden diminishes, our speed increases to the same extent. The Oriental burns 40 tons of coal every day. Now, if one considers that the coal at Aden costs 2 pounds per ton, one can understand how great the expenses are which the P&O Company has to meet every day. But the yield of the mail subsidy must also be fabulous.[42]

So writes Steven Adriaan Buddingh, a Dutch pastor who travelled from Europe to Java by the overland route in 1852. Aboard the *Oriental*, travelling from Suez to Ceylon, his speculations regarding the economic, technological and logistical elements of the steamship's mobility exhibits a keen sensitivity to the infrastructural, which is distinctly absent from most accounts. As this section explores, overland route narratives more frequently articulate their engagement with the logistics of steamship mobilities through imaginative and performative shipboard practices.

The Scottish clergyman and editor of the popular Victorian periodical *Good Words*, Norman Macleod, undertaking a tour of the Holy Land, travelled on the *Valetta* from Southampton to Alexandria in 1864. Macleod's account of the voyage reveals the extent to which the steamship's mobility constituted a significant preoccupation for overland route travellers. 'At sea,' he writes, 'our position is known every day at twelve o'clock; and the spot upon the globe's surface which we at that moment occupy becomes a matter of serious speculation until dinner-time.'[43] As Macleod's anecdote suggests, passengers engaged with the vessel's mobility, and their comprehension of their place in global and imperial space, through a range of shipboard social and cultural practices. He provides a striking example of such practices in his account of another overland route journey he undertook just three years later, in 1867, on a missionary trip to India. Underpinned by Christian sentiment, Macleod's accounts are concerned with providing his readers with a sober, edifying encounter with the world which steam was making more accessible. He peppers his narratives with historical detail and amateur scientific engagement with the novel experiences he encountered.

Recounting his 1867 voyage from Suez to Bombay aboard the *Rangoon*, Macleod relates an anecdote which presents a distinctive example of shipboard engagements with the imaginative geographies of colonial mobility. 'Being very anxious to see that great sign of the tropics, the Southern Cross,' he writes, 'and having been told that it was visible about three in the morning from the forecastle, I managed to awake about that time.'[44] A view of the Southern Cross – a constellation visible in the southern hemisphere, which can also be viewed in tropical regions of the northern hemisphere for short periods of the night in winter and spring – could provide the passenger with a visual testament to their global mobility. However, Macleod's intention to gaze at the stars was met instead by the spectacle of the ship's subaltern labourers at rest:

> I clambered on deck. It is strange to contemplate a native crew lying asleep. They are all covered up, including their heads, in the sacks used for loading the ship, and they lie side by side in rows, as if dead. Their dreams, if they have any, must have some ethnographical, and, in the case of the Africans especially, geographical interest.[45]

The body of the subaltern worker provided Macleod with what he had sought in the night sky – projected onto their sleeping forms, he encountered an imaginative geography of empire, a dream-space which invoked the global character of the steamship's social relations. The steamship's apparent compression of global space had an impact not only at the two poles of metropole and periphery, but was encountered in the midst of mobility, inflecting social life on board. In turn, the reader of such accounts was exposed to a global subjectivity which afforded novel perspectives on imperial space.

For the subaltern workers in Macleod's account, the steam revolution provided an almost carceral experience of the vessel's global mobility. Their imaginative geographies would likely offer perspectives on the compression, distanciation, or annihilation of space and time distinctly heterogeneous to those of the Western passenger. Although such perspectives are lost to history, and in their place we have the kind of bourgeois imperial fantasies mobilised by Macleod, the few accounts by Eastern passengers which exist furnish distinctive modes of engagement with the experience of global mobility aboard the steamship. The Indian Muslim Lutfullah travelled from Ceylon to England by the overland route in 1844. In his account of the journey, Lutfullah recalls a conversation with his companions on board the *Bentinck*, steaming up the Red Sea bound for Suez. As Indian Muslims, they had always faced west to direct their prayers toward Mecca, and were unaccustomed to the idea that they would need to adjust these religious practices in accordance with their global mobility. Lutfullah describes his companions' scepticism regarding this change:

> This day, in the afternoon, I found, by the mariner's compass, that the Kaba, the criterion point of our prayers, began to incline to the East. I mentioned the fact to my Muslim companions, who, instead of believing me, laughed at me heartily, and said that too much reading in English books most certainly had made my religious feelings too weak. 'How could it be possible', said they, 'that the Kaba, the most sacred house of God, which is the centre of the universe, should change its position!'[46]

Lutfullah's account presents an embodied, cultural orientation to the global geographies of steamship mobility. Shifting perceptions of global travel were engaged with through performative, social, shipboard practices.

The Dutch colonial politician Jacob van Heerdt travelled on board the *Hindostan* from Point de Galle to Suez in 1846. Like most of the Dutch overland route narratives, van Heerdt's 1851 account of the journey is characterised by an exuberant curiosity, a marked preoccupation with steamship mobilities as a startlingly novel experience, with the social and spatial world of the ship. The overland route had fundamentally transformed the geographies of the Dutch imperial world. Van Heerdt's account of the voyage emphasises the extent to which the preoccupation with global space was manifested in the passengers' recreational activities. He relates his enjoyment of the popular shipboard pastime of perusing maps and charts, mentioning noted geographer and map-seller James Wyld's 1840 *Map of the Countries Between England & India, Designed to Shew the Over-land and Sea-routes to the East*.[47] Van Heerdt describes how the passengers communicated their own various journeys to each other by tracing their routes on the maps with their fingers, 'with a swiftness as if the journey had been made as quickly as indicated'. These cartographic recreational practices helped to facilitate the passengers' identification with the global scale of their mobility. They normalised the imaginative geographies of the imperial world, pictorially rendering the routes of steamship travel as permanent lines on a map. Maps represented imperial logistics as linear, repeatable, simplified. Such a perspective on the imaginative geographies of imperial mobilities is dramatically expressed in van Heerdt's subsequent observations:

> It is difficult to create an impression of the low level of concern that a traveller on the overland route – having arrived in Egypt and still many thousands of miles away from his destination – has for the distance still to be covered. The world is for him too small, and seems now no larger than as it appears inscribed upon the map. Only the expense prevents him, otherwise an expedition to Bougainville would in his eyes be but child's play, and he, drifting from one country to another, would be able to forget that he possesses a 'sweet home and dear relations' who yearn for his return, and perhaps calculate the hour at which he will clasp them in his arms.[48]

Van Heerdt's fantastical musings provide a striking instance of the geographical imaginary of the globally mobile steamship passenger. His outlook emphasises the compression of geographical space which the steamship was implicated in, experienced subjectively through a blasé disregard for the vastness of global space. This was a traveller for whom the sheer jouissance of steamship mobility, the ease, fluidity and pleasure of global travel, was presented as an end in itself, rather than the voyage's destination. Through such shipboard social and imaginative practices, passengers could identify with an imperial world system whose expanding limits also established the parameters of their geographical imagination.

This expansive characterisation of steamship mobilities is again evoked in an article from the *Hobart Town Daily Courier* of 30 March 1853. Playing into notions of a modernity characterised by the veneration of technological advancement, the article emphasises the numerical scale of P&O's fleet of steamships. 'The P. and O.S.N.C.', it reports, 'have a fleet of forty steamers, 52,000 tons and 16,000 horse power; they run annually a distance amongst them of a million of miles.'[49] An image of progress signified by quantity, mass and power is augmented by a mobility which threatens to exceed the limits of global space. The article continues, tracing this concept's trajectory through the vastness of spatial categories which are no longer grasped within the confines of the globe:

> The length of time a cannon-ball would take to travel from the earth to the sun used to be given as an illustration of the enormous distance between the two – ninety-six millions of miles: stationed at proper intervals and with a navigable medium, the fleet referred to would traverse the space within a century.[50]

That the steamship's mobility was expressed in these fantastical, interplanetary terms reflects its perceived role in a process of expansion which continually strove to overcome spatial barriers, the limits of global space. This fantastical image emphasises the extent to which global space was perceived as a merely contingent barrier to steamship mobility, subsumed under the time taken to traverse it. All that was needed for the steamer to overcome even the vast distance between the earth and sun was enough time.

The steamship was at the heart of the discursive production of a world which wasn't simply perceived as smaller, but which could be thought increasingly as a coherent imperial world system. The bombastic, energetic claims regarding the overland route which are found in contemporary texts contributed to a cultural conceptualisation of global space (and imperial territory) as a finite, comprehensible totality. For passengers, for imperial actors in the East, and for those in the metropole who read these accounts, steamship mobilities had a profound impact on the geographical imaginary of British imperialism, and in turn on their imperial world view. And for many of them, this vision of the world's integration in a fundamentally Western, capitalist global economy was deeply implicated with the concept of progress.

Progress: Steam as imperial utopia

> We are like passengers ... upon one of the P. and O. steamers. We meet each other day by day on deck and see very little difference in our position or in the sea or the sky. But every day we are nearer our destined port. So it is with human society. We may not appear to be making much progress, but depend upon it we are ceaselessly forging ahead.[51]
>
> William T. Stead, Gladstone: *A Character Sketch*, 1898

The Crystal Palace's Naval Gallery was one of the numerous exhibitions which occupied the gigantic glass structure, both before and after its 1854 relocation to Sydenham. P&O chairman and co-founder Arthur Anderson was also chairman of the Crystal Palace Company, and was instrumental in the Naval Gallery's ongoing prioritisation as a presence there. Its contents are described in an 1864 guide to the Palace: 'Here is the history and progress of naval architecture,' it reads, 'represented by evidences of that skill and ingenuity for which Englishmen are so pre-eminent, and on which is based the supremacy and glory of our country.'[52] The progress of Western civilisation was narrated by the material culture of maritime transportation. Technologies of mobility provided a powerful signifier of British national identity, reflecting an imperialistic hierarchy of racial superiority.[53] The nineteenth-century ideology of progress was deeply tied up with the development of modern technology, which provided a convincing material manifestation of Western advances in science and industry.

English author Charles Henry Newmarch travelled widely in the East, returning from India to England by the overland route in 1847. In the account of his voyage aboard the *Hindostan* from Aden to Suez, which closes his two-volume narrative of Eastern travel, he furnishes a particularly hubristic commentary on steamship mobilities:

> How wonderful is the power of steam, and how varied the application of it. What innumerable benefits have resulted to man from the discovery of an agent which can be alike applied to the fabrication of the finest thread, or the moving of a mass of upwards of two thousand tons.[54]

Newmarch provides a particularly emphatic example of the widespread technophilia seen in the early years of transnational steamship travel, in which steam was seen to have had not merely material corollaries, but moral, social outcomes. As Susan Buck-Morss has written, in the nineteenth century 'spatial movement became ... wedded to the concept of historical movement'.[55] P&O's steamships provided a powerful – global – vision of the concept of progress, associated with the role of technological development in promulgating enlightenment values and societal improvement.

The progressive symbolism of the steamship

'Power of the P. and O. Company', an article from an 1845 edition of the *Malta Times* presents a typically technophilic panegyric to the nascent company's fleet of steamships. 'The P. and O. Company have now in service and progress of construction 30 steamers', the article states. In possessing vessels in such numbers, the company's fleet was subject to comparisons with the naval force of a nation state:

> No single power in Europe, France not excepted, can boast of such a steam squadron as this single branch of British private enterprize [*sic*] has produced

in the short period of four years ... With a few more years of peace, and of the reign of railroads and steam boats, Britain will so far outstrip all her rivals in resources, as to bid defiance to the world.[56]

The P&O steamship is presented as a symbolic technology of British imperial might, occupying a position alongside the steam train as a signifier of progress and power. As has been explored, the nineteenth-century concept of the annihilation of space and time was seen as a progressive force: in their overcoming of spatial distance, as huge concentrations of capital, vast spectacles of industrial technology, steamships came to stand as signifiers of the potency and advancement of Western society.

The steamship's capacity as a representational manifestation of progress was in part indebted to its sheer physical presence. Jacob van Heerdt described his first impression at Point de Galle in 1846 of the *Hindostan*, which he was to travel to Suez aboard:

> With a force equivalent to that of 220 horses, she had the previous day arrived at Point de Galle from Calcutta occupied by more than 100 passengers. Seen from the ramparts this vessel certainly yielded a proud and impressive spectacle, due to its immense size and peculiar construction. In the midst of the numerous vessels which were anchored around this steamship, she was as it were a mother amongst her children, so prominently did she stand out from the others.[57]

For van Heerdt, the vessel's visual impact was contingent upon its novelty and size, which were unprecedented in the seas where it had commenced operations four years earlier. As physically imposing manifestations of modern engineering, early steamships provided a distinctive visual spectacle. Their presence in Eastern waters only served to emphasise racial and geographical difference for many onlookers. Travellers like van Heerdt mobilised notions of the advancement of national identity on the world stage, with the steamship embodying the technological modernity of British industrial capitalism. Upon boarding the *Hindostan*, van Heerdt found that in addition to the steamer's commanding physical presence when viewed from the shore, its internal arrangements also acted as a signifier of national and ethnic superiority:

> The whole provides the fastidious observer with a really noteworthy object to satisfy his curiosity upon. He admires there the good taste of the English, the soundness of their labours, their ingenuity, and their financial capacity, with which virtually every object strikes him in the eyes.[58]

The steamship's interior was characterised by van Heerdt as a representational manifestation of British national values. As will be explored in Chapter 4, its interior design played an important role in establishing the steamship as a powerful symbol of ethnic and national identity.

Accounts of the steamship's progressive symbolism are revealing of the racial hierarchies at the heart of the imperial project. The steamship's representational capacity as a signifier of British identity finds a particularly imperious, chauvinistic voice in an overland route narrative by Sir Syed Ahmed Khan, one of the few such accounts narrated by a non-white author. Khan was an Indian Muslim who had worked for the East India Company and was a prominent Islamic reformer. He was a complex figure who, during the 1857 rebellion, had remained loyal to the British, although he blamed the aggressive expansionism of company rule for the rebellion, as well as British ignorance of Indian culture.[59] Nonetheless, he was broadly positive about what he saw as the advances of Western civilisation. He was also a significant figure in the British Indian Association, an organisation representing Indian landlords and the upper class, intended to promote the interests of Indians within the parameters of British rule. His ambivalent perspective on the British Empire, and his conviction of the need for the Muslim world to adapt to Western modernity, means that he provides a particularly insightful perspective on the shipboard manifestations of technology, race and modernity, and their intersections.

Khan's account of his 1869 overland route journey from India to England was published in Urdu in the *Aligarh Institute Gazette*, the journal of the Scientific Society of Aligarh. Khan had founded the society, intended to make Western works on arts and science available to Indians, and to promote Western education among the masses. In his account, Khan relates a conversation he had with a colonial army officer while travelling on board the *Baroda* from Bombay to Suez. The officer, keen to extol the superiority of the Christian faith – and Western civilisation – mobilised the vessel, an iron screw steamer launched in 1864, as evidence of this claim: 'See this steamer, the skill and acumen that have gone into it and the scientific wisdom that helps it sail ... If there was any other true religion, God would have showered the same favours on the followers of that as well.'[60] The steamship is portrayed as a divinely ordained, technological substantiation of Western superiority. While progress was associated in the nineteenth century with an enlightenment conception of the advance of a universal human spirit, this 'universalism' was often inflected with racially charged rhetoric. The technological assemblage of the steamship provided British passengers with a convincing sense of their superiority over other races. Although Khan registered some disquietude concerning what he felt was a divisive conversation, his own opinions seem to have differed little from those of his fellow passenger. He was deeply impressed by the Western civilisation which his trip exposed him to: 'The moment one steps into the boundary of England, one comes across such a world that one feels convinced that the Englishmen are not wrong in regarding us, the people of Hindustan, as beasts.'[61] Above all, Khan seems to have been concerned to maintain the ethnic, national and religious character of Indian Muslims in the face of a Western modernity which he viewed as both inevitable and desirable.

While Khan's account illustrates the extent to which the steamship's status as a symbol of progress was employed in a narrative of racial superiority, it is useful to consider the rare examples of accounts which offer Eastern perspectives on this symbolism. Lutfullah, who had encountered the *Bentinck*'s mobility through distinctively Indian Muslim cultural practices during his 1844 voyage from Point de Galle to Suez, relates his experience of the vessel's arrival at the former port. It describes, in very different terms, almost exactly the same view as van Heerdt's account, from just two years later:

> We discerned the large steamer *Bentinck* forcing its way through the sea, with its four [*sic*] tremendous wheels at work, making a dreadful noise, and sending up its smoke to the sky. Upon the whole, the sight of this exceedingly big sea monster will give you an idea of a roaring Satan making its appearance to devour up all that may come in its way.[62]

While it would be tempting to attribute this arresting description of the steamship to an Eastern subjectivity horrified by Western technological progress, clearly Lutfullah's diabolical, monstrous description of the steamship was intended as a fanciful exaggeration. His other references to the vessel are distinctly prosaic, and he reported himself 'delighted' by this spectacle. As David Nye has explored, early encounters with industrial technology were often textually articulated using such language, as part of what he refers to as the 'technological sublime'.[63] The hellish agency attributed to the steamship by Lutfullah has more to do with its novelty than a racialised perspective.

Other than what is found in the autobiography from which this account is taken, little is known of Lutfullah, but he had certainly had little exposure to modern Western technology. It is unclear – but unlikely – that he would have been aware of similar discursive responses to such technologies. Published in the aftermath of the Indian Rebellion, Lutfullah's book offered an Indian perspective on the West to a British public eager to gain insight into the traumatic events which had unfolded there. Lutfullah's perspective was a sympathetic, educated one: like Syed Khan, he was overwhelmingly positive regarding his visit to the West, impressed by the technology and culture he encountered, both in transit and upon his arrival. The trip forms a significant section in the book, and his encounter with the overland route steamship can be seen as part of a continuum of encounters with Western culture which begins in British India and extends into the metropole.

The theme of the stunned Eastern encounter with the steamship's novelty is again found in an 1843 account of an overland route voyage by journalist and lecturer Joachim Stocqueler from the *Asiatic Journal and Monthly Register* (the organ of the East India Company). The article relates the allegedly widespread belief among Indians that the steamship was propelled by supernatural forces: 'The magic by which [the steamship] was impelled earned for her the unenviable appellation of the *Shitan ke jaj*, or devil's ship. It was in vain to shew the inquiring native that she was furnished with wheels and engines, boilers, pumps, &c.' Stocqueler attributes the eventual dispelling of such notions to the 1842 arrival of the *Hindostan* in the East, the first steamship to make regular, scheduled voyages between Calcutta and Suez: 'The scepticism of the Hindoo then vanished, and what was once confidently believed to originate in an understanding with a demoniacal power, is now justly ascribed to the effort of the human intellect, and the prudent direction of abundant capital.'[64] Stocqueler suggests that the normalisation of the steamship's presence in Indian waters helped convince the local population that the steamer was in fact driven not by a demonic force, but rather by another form of non-human agency – that of capital. If belief in the steamship's diabolical power attributed to Indians appears absurdly naive, it was certainly no less so than the identification (of the British passenger in Syed Khan's account) of this potency's source in the agency of a Christian God. Of course, Stocqueler was in the business of travel writing and entertainment – his claims should be seen in the context of the satire and hyperbole which characterised much of the published material on this topic. Nevertheless, identifying the Indian population as a sort of pre-modern, primitive other, bewildered by modern Western technology, provided an unambiguous articulation of racial difference, and helped to emphasise the steamship's innovative modernity.

Progress as imperial control

The discourse of imperialism was narrated as the progressive overcoming of ignorance and barbarism through the dissemination of knowledge and civilisation. The steamship was seen as a vehicle for the promotion of this process. In the body of literature which endorsed steam propulsion's application to the voyage East, the justification for this development was couched in terms whereby steam was conceived of as a civilising force. This was wed to the notion of modernity as the dissemination of the ideas of the enlightenment, borne forth in the steamship as a mobile embodiment and bearer of these values. The essence of this ideology is succinctly expressed in the words of Louis Moser, an employee of P&O who used the dedication of his 1856 book to praise his employer, 'the great company which has taken so prominent a part in ... bringing European energy to bear on Asiatic torpor'.[65] The thermodynamic principle of the steam engine inflects the language employed by Moser to articulate the steamship's geopolitical impact, expressed as an energy exchange between West and East.

Lord William Bentinck, Governor-General of India from 1828 to 1835, had campaigned extensively for the introduction of steam communication between East and West as a vehicle for facilitating his modernising project in British India. In 1842 P&O would name the second ship on their Suez to Calcutta line *Bentinck* in recognition of this patronage. In an 1834 letter, the colonial administrator clearly aligns himself with an imperial ideology of progress which positioned the East as having fallen behind in the global advancement of the human species. It was an area where, he wrote, 'the human mind has been buried for ages in universal darkness'. For Bentinck, the mission of the Western coloniser was the emancipation of this primitive, unenlightened East. Technology would be the means. 'Steam navigation', he wrote, was 'the great engine of working this moral improvement. In proportion as the communication between the two countries shall be facilitated and shortened, so will civilized Europe be approximated, as it were, to these benighted regions.'[66] Bentinck's utopian conception of the steamship's impact on the East mobilises time–space compression as the means for 'civilising' this benighted land.

The overland route was envisaged as a conduit not merely for the mobility of people, information, capital and commodities, but for the diffusion of progress, as the universalisation of Western modernity. Such notions play into what Marian Aguiar has referred to as 'the colonial discourse that promoted mobility as a means for social evolution'.[67] Even the overland route's passage through Egypt was considered to have had a 'civilising' impact on the country's capital, according to an 1847 account from the *Illustrated London News*:

> The immense importance of the overland passage through Cairo ... is sufficiently obvious in the rapid communication with our eastern possessions. The effects of this intercourse are also very visible in the city, in the changes that have taken place during the last few years in the manners and customs of the inhabitants, especially in their treatment of foreigners. Order and security of property has been established, the laws have been more equitably administered, manufactories of all kinds have risen, and more useful institutions have been called into existence by the Pasha, than by any other sovereign of Egypt.[68]

This account describes a progress which is conceptualised as the movement toward a Western capitalist modernity, characterised by developments in social discipline, private property, legal bureaucratic structures and the industrial means of production. The overland route is construed as the agent of this civilising force.

The enlightenment ideal of universal human advancement was seen to have been manifested in material form with the industrial revolution. Technology provided a means for disseminating the fruits of progress between an apparently enlightened metropole and a periphery in primitive darkness. David Lester Richardson, who had been aide-de-camp to Lord Bentinck in Bengal in 1835, echoed his former superior's characterisation of the steamship, as a progressive force whose bringing closer of the metropole and periphery would act as a conduit for promulgating Western knowledge in a benighted East. Writing in 1845, shortly after the inception of the overland route, Richardson considered the impact of the recently increased regularity of the monthly steamship service P&O provided on the route:

> The establishment at the beginning of the present year of a twice-a-month steam communication with the East Indies … will not only increase to an indefinite extent the value of our Eastern territories, but it will diffuse with magic rapidity the living radiance of knowledge over regions buried for ages in the night of ignorance.[69]

These words feed into the discourse regarding technological progress as a vehicle for the distribution of the perceived superiority of Western civilisation (fittingly, Richardson positions this benefit as a *supplement* to the route's economic advantages). Steam is identified as not merely implicated in this process, but as the instrument of transformation. 'The vast agency of steam', continues Richardson, 'of all physical powers the one calculated to effect the mightiest moral revolutions – must lead to the mental manumission of millions of our fellow creatures. The East and the West will meet.'[70] Again mobilising the notion of time–space compression, the apparent geographical joining of metropole and periphery is presented as the unification of the ideologically divided occident and orient in which the values of the enlightenment are universalised at a global level. While the technological determinism manifested here is of a distinctly utopian character, the civilising mission which Richardson assigns to steam is redolent with the universalisation of the conditions of Western capitalism.[71]

This rhetoric was one which P&O's senior representatives themselves purported to subscribe to. Arthur Anderson, one of the company's chairmen, who served in this role from his co-founding of the company until his death in 1868, wrote a short pamphlet advocating for the construction of the Suez Canal in 1843. For Anderson, the logistical developments he endorsed were not merely functional, but underpinned by enlightenment utopianism: 'That facility of intercourse creates commerce,' he wrote, 'and commerce carries with it civilisation, is an axiom founded on universal experience'. The project would, he claimed, 'approximate by many thousand miles the knowledge and industry of the west to the ignorance and barbarism of the east'.[72] The notion of progress which animates the discourse of the overland route was thus a racially charged one, at its heart tied to capitalist global expansion and the imperial project. It is indicative of a British imperial world view, a world in which progress was a movement toward Western norms and values. William Makepeace Thackeray, writing of his 1844 steamship tour, describes the normalising impact of the steamship's increasingly regular presence in the East. For Thackeray, the steamship was the bearer of Western values and civilisation, dispelling all the romance of the Muslim world. Reflecting on the failure of the Crusades to 'civilise' the East, Thackeray suggests that the steam engine, as the agent of Western capitalism, had achieved that which the Crusades had failed to do. 'An allegory might be made showing how much stronger commerce is than chivalry,' he writes, 'finishing with a grand image of Mahomet's crescent being extinguished in Fulton's boiler.'[73] Imperial control could be more easily effected with efficient, fast and reliable transport and communications linking the metropole and periphery.

Behind the ideology of technological progress as a force for liberating those outside of the ambit of Western modernity lay the reality of technologies of mobility as a means of controlling geographical space. This is illustrated in an 1854 article from *The Times*, announcing the building of P&O's huge steamship the *Himalaya*. At the date of its 1854 launch, the *Himalaya* was the largest vessel in existence and was widely lauded for its great size and speed. The article suggests that such a ship's capacity for the spontaneous mobility of large cargoes had the potential to effect a radical geopolitical shift. Written during the period shortly before the Crimean War, it recognises the new technology's potential for application to warfare:

> The possession of such a stupendous steamship as the *Himalaya* must be a matter not merely of local, but national interest. If, unhappily, the threatened war should break out, there is no telling the uses to which [this vessel] might be applied. 3,000 men could be embarked at Southampton, and conveyed by the Himalaya in 11 days to Constantinople or the Black Sea ... A small army might in fact be rapidly thrown upon any particular point of the European or Asiatic coast ... For rapidly transporting immense supplies of provisions, ammunition, artillery, of men to the fleets in the Black Sea in the Mediterranean, or in the Baltic, it is difficult to say what enormous services might not, on emergency, be rendered by a few steamers such as these.[74]

Geopolitical power, this passage suggests, is contingent upon the capacity for the rapid distribution in geographical space of the raw materials of warfare. The strategic advantage of access to superior forms of mobility emphasises that the steamship afforded a means of controlling territory: transportation as the logistics of imperial power. Indeed, in the context of

India, overland route steamships were employed to dramatically reduce the passage time for troop reinforcements to reach the country during the rebellion of 1857.[75] The *Himalaya* was in fact used extensively in the Crimean War as a troop transport ship, in an arrangement which formed part of P&O's government mail contract whereby the company's ships were made available to the navy in times of war. It would also be used to transport troops to Calcutta in 1857 to help suppress the rebellion. P&O's story is inextricably linked with the British imperialist state. No less for commerce than for the nation state, steamship mobility facilitated the superior command of global space.

The *Himalaya*'s vast size inevitably meant that it was also lauded as a symbol of Western superiority and progress. J. Willett Spalding, in his account of the US expeditions to open up Japan to global trade, comments on this symbolism. 'There are no more characteristic things of a people than their water vehicles', he writes. For Spalding, the East Asian sailing vessel, which he termed 'the stupid, cumbersome, unsightly junk' thus presented a rendering in material form of 'the inertia of the opinionated Mongolian'. Conversely, he claimed, 'the enormous "Himalaya" steamship is the card that Great Britain sends out upon the ocean'.[76] The company's gigantic steamer was conceived by Spalding as the material manifestation of the national superiority of the British state on the global stage. As the largest steamship then in existence, utilising the relatively innovative means of propulsion of the screw propeller rather than the more commonly utilised side paddles, the *Himalaya* provided an apparently unambiguous symbol of the imperial British state's technological, social and racial superiority.

This racially charged account is useful in clarifying the homogenising tendency inherent in the process of uneven technological development at the global level; progress is always posited for the 'primitive' other as a teleology whose end point is the contemporaneous ideal of Western development: 'A scale of development which defines "progress" in terms of the projection of certain people's presents as other people's futures', as Peter Osborne has expressed it.[77] However, while technological change was employed as an apparently unambiguous signifier of ethnically charged notions of progress, this progress was not always straightforward. Two historical instances give the lie to Spalding's claims: first, such assertions ignore the influence of traditional non-Western shipbuilding practices on the design of modern Western vessels;[78] second, the progressive symbolism attributed to the *Himalaya* by Spalding was contingent upon the notion of the ever-increasing size of the ship as a signifier of progress. However, the *Himalaya* was in fact a much larger ship than the colonial market at the time required, and the fuel consumption for propelling such a large vessel would have been unsustainable for P&O. When the British government purchased the ship from the company at cost price only months after its launch, it saved them from the prematurity of this level of technological 'progress'.[79]

Change: Steam as historical rupture

Where the rude hamlet rested on its banks in rural solitude, the never weary din of commerce rolls through the city of the world. The locomotive rushes like a thunder-roll upon the rail; the steamer ploughs against the adverse wind; and, rapid as lightning, the telegraph cripples time.[80]

Samuel W. Baker, *Eight Years' Wanderings in Ceylon*, 1855

'There is no limit to the effects of steam-power, which will work more changes on society than either the needle, gunpowder, or the art of printing', claims an 1843 article from the *Asiatic Journal and Monthly Register*, exploring P&O's recent introduction of steam to the voyage East.[81] The article exhibits a conspicuous technological determinism, characterising technological innovations as the agents of historical, social change – and none more so than steam. Such a perspective was widespread in the nineteenth century, and was particularly prominent in the discourse of the colonial steamship's impact upon global mobilities. Of course, it would be foolish to argue that steam did not facilitate profound transitions.[82] A sea which had for millennia been traversed only by vessels propelled by human muscle and the wind and currents saw the arrival of an ever-increasing volume of ships which travelled under their own steam. However, as already suggested, it is essential to understand the broader historical shifts which accompanied this development as not merely the straightforward outcome of technological developments. Such a perspective risks ignoring the social and cultural construction of technology, attributing agency to technology itself. Coming to terms with the steamship's modernity requires close attention to the stories that were told about new technological forms, to the cultural meanings invested in the steamship.

What precisely was considered historically new about overland route steamship mobilities? The themes already explored in this chapter have frequently touched upon aspects of the changes associated with the introduction of steam to global shipping: new forms of social experience in the rhythms and textures of shipboard life; a technological revolution in imperial mobilities, implicated in new imaginative geographies of global space; a hubristic – and thoroughly Eurocentric – ideology of progress which conflated technological development with societal advancement and racial superiority. All of these aspects contributed to the imaginative reserves of the British imperial world view. Indeed, accounts of the overland route exhibit a distinctive concern with the 'newness' of the steamship. They persistently characterise its mobility as a historical break, a manifest departure from the conditions of the sailing ship voyage. John Tillotson, in his 1859 popular illustrated guide to the route, provides a particularly chauvinistic example of this trend:

> British pluck, Anglo Saxon energy – what is there these cannot accomplish? How much they have done, not only to found and to consolidate the Indian Empire, but to annihilate both space and time; and by steam and electricity to hurry us near to our possessions. Of old we sailed to India and had a five months' voyage, full of discomfort and disaster; but we have changed all this for a rapid transit by steam.[83]

An imperially infused notion of progress and technophilic utopianism inform this account of historical change, emphasising national difference and ethnic superiority. The trope of space–time compression is mobilised to illustrate the revolutionary impact of steam on the relationship between imperial metropole and periphery. Only two decades after steam's introduction to the voyage East, the (still existent) sailing voyage is portrayed as a relic of times past, replaced by the fast, comfortable, safe and reliable mobility of steam.

As James Vernon has suggested, modernity is characterised as a departure from the past. 'Becoming modern', he writes, 'is a process that entails the demolition of "traditional" forms of life and the construction of new, "modern" alternatives to them.'[84] Modernity takes leave of the past in a sometimes violent, volatile manner, brushing aside and destroying traditional ways of life with great rapidity. Yet the steamship's ostensible modernity was not the clean break with the past that sources frequently portrayed it as: any claims to radical historical change in the context of colonial mobilities at sea have to be tempered by the fact that the steamship was anything but a stable, complete technology. In reality the technological modernity presented by the steamship was at best only partial. In the mid-nineteenth century, the technology of maritime steam propulsion was still quite rudimentary: engines were inefficient and prone to mechanical failure, and until near to the end of the century steamships still possessed sails as an auxiliary means of propulsion. Steam power was at this early stage not yet a practical choice for the majority of ocean-going traffic: it was expensive, relatively unreliable, and significantly limited a ship's cargo-carrying capacity. Thus steam in its maritime context did not present the same break with tradition as its land-based counterparts: with steam-driven ships at the nascent stage in their development and thus relatively uncommon, sail was itself not a thing of the past, but continued to dominate British shipping for some years. It would not in fact be until 1883 that the total tonnage of all British steam vessels surpassed that of sail.[85]

Despite the effusive claims regarding the steamship's modernity, steam thus marked only a partial departure from the past, characterised by the intermingling of the old and the new. In the transition from sail to steam in global shipping, the former continued to play a significant role long into the latter's history. The coexistence of the two technologies of propulsion made the early steamship an ambiguous symbol of modernity, one which retained elements of maritime tradition. Nevertheless, if steam presented a distinctly partial historical departure in the maritime means of propulsion, the imaginative investments and cultural meanings projected onto the steamship often conveyed a more emphatic, at times utopian modernity than these conditions might have suggested. Coming to terms with this history thus means interrogating how the trope of the steamship as historical departure was constituted in part through the repression of tradition, and how images of the maritime past continued to surface and circulate in the experience of passengers, taking on new meanings in the era of steam.

One significant transition which the emergence of the steamship did see was the seismic shifts undergone in shipboard labour. With steam, new modes of labour emerged which were the reflection of a specifically industrial means of production. This included mechanisation, shifts in spatial discipline, the division of labour (particularly along racial lines), repetitive labour practices, and de-skilling.[86] A (decidedly high-ranking) example of the new labour practices and roles which accompanied steam power at sea can be seen in P&O's pamphlet *Instructions for Chief Engineers* from 1867. This was an internal document printed by the company to be kept on board vessels, mainly intended to ensure that the ship's steam apparatus was maintained and cared for appropriately. It also registers tensions regarding the uneasy hierarchy of shipboard labour roles, even decades after the introduction of steam:

> Complaints have been made that for some reason there seems to have been a sort of antagonistic feeling between the Engineers and Officers, which has been very hurtful to the Company's interests ... The remark has been made that there are some Chief Engineers who seem to consider themselves sole masters of their departments ... If such ideas exist, they must be at once abandoned.[87]

The coexistence of both traditional and modern maritime labour practices on board the steamer saw the emergence of friction between the two. The rigorously maintained order of the ship was disrupted by a conflict over status, with the idiosyncratically modern industrial labour role of the engineer emerging as an ambiguous one in the space of the ship, in tension with the traditional hierarchies of sail. However, as Albert Hervey's description of the relatively quiet atmosphere of the *Hindostan* attests to, steamship passengers were scarcely exposed to the shipboard labour forms which propelled the vessel. Accounts of the steamship as a historical break are much more preoccupied with steam's facilitation of a shift in the relationship between technology and nature.

A sea change

The steamer's technological limitations did little to dull the effusive veneration of steam's power. Michael Angelo Garvey's book *The Silent Revolution, or, The Future Effects of Steam and Electricity Upon the Condition of Mankind* (1852) provides a forceful example of the bombastic zeal which characterised the discourse surrounding the steamship. A utopian panegyric to the new technologies which were revolutionising nineteenth-century society, Garvey's book eulogises the impact of steam on mobility at sea. Emphasising the steam-powered ship's affinity with industrial production, Garvey stresses that the significant departure presented by steam in the context of maritime transportation lay in its overcoming of nature's force:

> The ocean has now become truly the highway of nations; the gigantic force that animates the factory, and impels the train, has enabled man to dominate the waters also, and to hold on his direct course, without pause or deviation, in the face of adverse winds and tides, steadily and swiftly gliding towards his destined port, his gallant ship scarcely disturbed by the fiercest elemental war.[88]

The vivid picture painted by Garvey delineates a new relationship between the ship and the forces of nature, with the steamship presenting the technological overcoming of the formerly indomitable wildness of the sea. Although Garvey's claims present a healthy instance of the hyperbole which characterised much of the discourse about steam power, steam clearly did constitute a significant historical shift in this regard. Sailing vessels relied on harnessing existing natural conditions; in the age of sail, seasonal trade winds dictated the geographies of global mobility, and rhythms of accumulation were developed in harmony with the fluctuations of nature. Prevailing winds and currents determined the relative ease or difficulty with which a given location could be reached, thus dictating the geographical development of European imperial power. Conversely, steamship routes could take the most direct course, irrespective of the wind's direction, opening up possibilities for new geographies of colonial mobility. In the case of the voyage East, this facilitated a shift which radically shortened the distance travelled – the overland route would have been impossible without the use of steam.

The steam-powered ship, despite its flaws, and its continued use of sails, was capable of propelling itself against the prevailing wind, even in violent storms which would incapacitate a sailing vessel.[89] This ostentatious overcoming of nature's force made the steamer, for many contemporary observers, an exemplary manifestation of the progressive power of modern technology. The notion that human agency (with the aid of technology) could transcend the limitations of nature was a powerful narrative, tied up with the ideas of civilisation, modernity and progress. The steamship provided a persuasive material manifestation of the enlightenment ethos of the emancipation of humanity from nature's power. Garvey's account is indicative of the kinds of discursive excesses which suffuse popular engagements with the steamship. It also emphasises the extent to which steam's impact was not merely functional, but was implicated in the imaginative geographies of maritime space. Garvey's characterisation of the sea as a 'highway' was a widespread trope in the literature of the steamship, and one which was frequently mobilised in the context of the route to India, as Albert Hervey's observation in 1850 confirms. 'The communication by the overland route', Hervey writes, 'has opened a highway by means of which there is a frequency of intercourse between the two countries.'[90] With mobility at sea no longer dictated by natural forces, maritime space was conceptualised as possessing the qualities of terrestrial space, offering unfettered mobility at all times. A sea which presented an isotropic medium of mobility, a 'highway' upon which the ship could move freely and unhindered by the unpredictability of the elements, was inevitably perceived differently from one whose often violent whims were necessarily feared and obeyed.

As we have seen, in Charles Henry Newmarch's overland route narrative, the imperial railway engineer venerated the progressive power of steam. In his account of his 1847 voyage from Aden to Suez on board the *Hindostan*, he provides a representative example of the hubris which underpinned the re-evaluation of maritime space. 'What are now three thousand miles of sea to us,' he writes, 'when instead of forming a complete barrier to our progress, we can cross them in a few days: and what is any distance however great, now that we have steam'.[91] Newmarch was well placed to understand the changes brought about by steam – while the return to England by the overland route concluded his two-volume account of Eastern travel, it had opened with an extensive description of his long voyage to India by sailing ship. For commentators like Newmarch, writing in the first years of the overland route, steam was seen to have effected a shift in not only the logistics of maritime mobility, but in the cultural associations of maritime space. 'The recoding of the sea by modernity begins with the rupture between the age of sail and that of steam', claims Allan Sekula.[92] This shift can be seen in the descriptive means by which overland route passengers attempt to account for their experiences of the sea. With the perceived diminishment of its sovereign force, its threat, the sea underwent a marked aesthetic, representational shift. The anonymous author of an 1858 guidebook to the overland route describes, in technophilic excess, the dramatic shift in the way in which the sea was perceived in relation to the move from sail to steam:

> The Bay of Biscay is now before us, but its crest-white dreaded waves have lost much of their terrors since steam has superseded wind. The calm that now broods upon the deep cannot delay us, as of yore, until a storm burst upon 'our poor devoted bark,' and hurl her, crushed and crippled, into port, or sink her in the brine. No! the ceaseless clank of our throbbing 'heart' goes on, the clear waters are cleft, and a long line of foam marks our swift transit across the Bay.[93]

While the sailing vessel was troubled by calms and storms – both the disabling absence and terrifying excess of nature's force – steam's ability to overcome such limits was placed at the core of a dramatic historical shift in the perception of the sea.

The prominent orientalist and explorer Richard Burton travelled from Southampton to Alexandria in 1853 aboard the *Bengal*, a large iron screw steamer launched that year. In his account of the voyage, Burton emphasises the extent to which the shift from sail to steam was framed in relation to imaginative geographies of the sea:

> Our voyage over the 'summer sea' was eventless. In a steamer of two or three thousand tons you discover the once dreaded, now contemptible, 'stormy waters' only by the band ... performing 'There we lay | All the day | In the Bay of Biscay, O!' The sight of glorious Trafalgar excites none of the sentiments with which a tedious sail used to invest it.[94]

For Burton, the transition from sail to steam was characterised by a marked historical shift in the conceptualisation of ocean space. From a potentially terrifying force of nature, he claims, in a textual rendering more concerned with the banality of the steamship's leisure practices than the gravity associated with seafaring tradition, the sea had become an absence unworthy of consideration. For Burton, this historical departure was tied up with concerns about national identity, representation and the symbolism invested in sail. This can be seen in his disinterest in the view of Trafalgar, site of the famed 1805 British naval victory, and thus a maritime landscape deeply implicated with the tradition of sail and British global dominance at sea.

Philip Steinberg has proposed an understanding of the cultural conception of the sea which reflects wider societal structures and historical shifts. 'During the industrial capitalist era,' he writes, 'the ocean was idealized as the antithesis of land space.'[95] Steinberg suggests that the modern age was characterised by a perception of the sea as a space of nature antithetical to the character of terrestrial civilisation. Given the steamship's characterisation as a distinctly modern form of mobility, one can conceive of its entry into a maritime space which was anything but, as setting up a distinctive binary which had significant cultural, social and perceptual corollaries. The introduction of steam as a motive force was associated with a disenchantment with nature's sovereignty, its authority over human agency. This was construed as a movement away from tradition. Marcus Rediker has suggested that the 'romance of the sea' was intimately tied up with the struggle between humanity and nature at the heart of traditional seafaring – the image of the sailor 'battling the winds, the waves, and the odds', engaged in the 'adventurous, sometimes vicious conquest of nature'.[96] Maritime mobility was disabused of this romance with the introduction of steam power, as the human struggle with the elements was, it appeared, superseded by one between technology and nature, a battle in which the former inevitably came to be seen as the victor. However, the romantic notions of landscape associated with the sea, the sublime or picturesque spectacle of its apparently limitless natural space, continued to play a role in accounts of steamship travel, taking on new meanings in the age of steam.[97]

The symbolic role performed by the technology of the steam engine in the representational shift undergone by the sea is rendered explicit in a letter dated 1858, written by Franklin Kendall while a passenger aboard the *Ripon*, travelling from England to Egypt. This letter relates the steamer's entry into the harbour at Malta during a violent storm. 'If our engines had by any chance given way,' Kendall writes, 'no power on earth could have saved us from being dashed to pieces.'[98] The eventuality of mechanical failure presented, for Kendall, not only the limit of the steamship's ability to overcome the violence of the elements. He considered the technology of the steam engine as precisely the point at which his experience of the sea as a visual spectacle was mediated:

> The sight of the surf breaking on the rocks is immensely grand but when one reflects that the mere breaking of a rope or a piece of iron will send the ship without doubt right onto them, it rather changes the feeling of admiration into one of fear.[99]

For Kendall, the steamship's technological failure was capable of transforming in an instant his perception of nature's wildness from a picturesque spectacle into an object of terror. Kendall's account suggests an understanding of the maritime landscape which appeared almost to have been produced by the technology of the steamship itself. Kendall's aesthetic pleasure was contingent upon a technology whose ability to overcome nature's wildness allowed that wildness to be experienced as picturesque spectacle.

This distinctive aesthetic encounter can again be witnessed in the writings of Archibald Pollok Black, a clergyman travelling aboard the *Euxine* to the

Middle East in 1864. Black describes his experience of a storm encountered while travelling in the Mediterranean. 'A storm at sea is a magnificent spectacle,' he writes, 'and when there is no sense of danger I cannot conceive of anything more sublimely majestic; the billowy giant rolling in massive folds of dark water, curling, foaming and hissing.'[100] In its overcoming of nature the steamship became for Black a vantage point from which he could observe the wildness of the sea in a space of relative comfort. Black's vivid description of the tempestuous sea appears to be a fairly recognisable rendering of the sublime, the pleasure experienced in witnessing the vastness of nature's wildness from a safe vantage point. However, this feeling of safety was in Black's case contingent upon the technology of steam; in a storm, a sailing ship would often be in real danger of being wrecked. What this description presents can rather be seen as an instance of what one might term a 'technicised sublime', an aesthetic encounter whereby the knowledge of superiority over nature was mediated by the technology of steam.[101] Whereas on a sailing vessel, the sea's elemental violence would have presented a danger which would have detracted from the passenger's aesthetic enjoyment of it, on board the steamer the pleasure experienced in viewing the storm was facilitated by the hubristic feeling of safety facilitated by steam.

Nature was tamed not just in a practical sense but as aesthetic experience: with steam's mastering of the elements, the sea's wildness passed from being a restriction on human action to an object of contemplation. This overcoming of the sea was conceived as a fundamentally modern moment, a departure from the traditions associated with the long history of maritime travel. The modern is, however, sometimes haunted by images of the past. The moments at which technology's superiority was challenged, or nature's wildness exceeded the limits of the picturesque thus serve to emphasise the extent to which steam shipping was seen as a departure from tradition. Frederick Walter Simms, a British railway engineer in the service of the East India Company, kept a diary of his journey from England to Calcutta by the overland route in 1845, published some years later by his son. Like many such voyage narratives from the overland route's early years, Simms lauds the new form of mobility made possible by the steamship, recording a wide-eyed amazement at the various experiences he encountered, and at the new environment of the ship itself. In his account, Simms describes his experience of a storm witnessed aboard the *Hindostan* in the Red Sea. Like many passengers, Simms enjoyed watching the spectacle of the sea's violence from the safety of the steamer. 'During the gale', he writes, 'I put my head out at the cabin port to look upon the wild grandeur of the disturbed ocean.' However, Simms's enjoyment of the sea's wildness was soon interrupted by an occurrence which emphasises the extent to which such pleasure was contingent on the aesthetic production of both distance and a feeling of safety:

> The water was not much below the same level at the moment, when, to my astonishment, apparently within a few feet of my face, stood erect the enormous dorsal fin of some giant of the deep; startled with so unexpected an apparition, I drew in my head in double quick time.[102]

For Simms, this encounter with the natural sea occurred at too close a range. The spectacle of nature's wildness, enframed and tamed through its rendering as landscape, was ruptured by the sudden and corporeal emergence of one of the sea's natural occupants.

While such incidents were rare on the overland route, encounters with maritime fauna were more common in accounts of the long sailing voyage around the Cape of Good Hope. Shark fishing, for example, was a particularly popular pastime for passengers on this route.[103] This pursuit provided a diversion during the monotony of a calm, when the sailing vessel's immobility created the still conditions necessary for such sport. The steamship's constant movement thus generally rendered shark fishing impracticable. However, an account from 1861 of a voyage from Suez to Point de Galle aboard the *Candia* recalls how the ship's engine broke down. The pursuit was revived during the delay caused by work to repair the fault. This account relates how a caught shark was 'hauled up on the forecastle, and his fins and tail cut off; his interior taken out, and a capstan bar rammed down his throat. Such was his vitality, however, that he moved even then. After being shown to spectators, he was thrown back into the sea.'[104] This macabre description is at odds with the typically refined, leisured descriptions of life on board the steamship. It evokes the labour-dominated deck of the sailing ship, which was more given to everyday displays of violence and brutality. If steam was seen as a departure from tradition – albeit traditions which persisted in the ongoing cultural life of the sailing vessel – it is notable that its technological failure saw the spectacular re-emergence of cultural practices associated with sail.

Modern myths: The symbolic confrontation of technology and nature

Herapath's Railway Journal of 8 December 1855 relates the presentation of an elaborate service of plate to P&O's chairmen, a gift from the company's shareholders (Figure 1.1). The decorative devices on the service's centrepiece articulate vividly some of the cultural assumptions which held sway over the discourse of the steamship's emergence as a crucial logistical link with the colonial East. Describing the service, the article observes that 'the principal

CENTRE-PIECE OF THE WILCOX AND ANDERSON SERVICES OF PLATE.—(SEE PAGE 14.)

1.1 'Centre-Piece of the Wilcox and Anderson Service of Plate' (*Illustrated London News*, 5 January 1856)

group represents Enterprise, indicating on a chart the routes of the Company's steamers, and the Genius of Steam exhibiting to Neptune … the steam cylinder and the screw as the great agents in the work'.[105] In this configuration, the pre-modern sea – personified in the mythic figure of Neptune – is confronted by a combination of global capitalism and the transformation in the technology of ship propulsion, in the form of steam power and the screw propeller.[106] As a material representation of what was at stake in the new relation with the space of the sea this change brought about, this ostentatious ornament renders visible a certain tension, between a sea whose power had traditionally been feared as an inexorable and often dreadful force, and the innovations in the technological means of overcoming such a power. Steam's newness was expressed in the youth of the figure used to represent it, and the new gods who adorned the service communicated a rational, accumulative world view: the figure who crowned the centrepiece, perched atop the globe, represented commerce. The overcoming of myth and nature, of the spirit of the sea and of maritime tradition, was achieved through a combination of capitalism on the world market and technological innovation. Yet it also discloses the recasting of these principles as new myths – the mythology of progress, rooted in the putative agency of capitalism and technology.

The steamship's symbolic liberation from nature was construed as a departure from tradition and superstition – yet steam's apparent mastery over nature gave rise to its own cultural imaginaries and meanings. Images of the steamship overcoming the destructive power of nature's violence took on a popular appeal in the era of steam. An example from the *Illustrated London News* in 1851 can be seen in Figure 1.2, depicting the *Pekin* in a typhoon encountered while travelling from Hong Kong to Singapore. The periodical published the image accompanied with excerpts from the captain's log documenting the storm. According to an article from the *Edinburgh New Philosophical Journal*, it had been sent to the newspaper by P&O's secretary, 'as a most admirable instance of a typhoon being withstood, and as a glorification of the vessel and its owners'.[107] Representations of ships in storms have of course a much longer pedigree.[108] However, the significance of images such as that of the *Pekin* lay in their representation of a confrontation between the steamer and the elements; in the storm, while the sailing vessel would have been at the mercy of nature's violence, the use of steam saw nature and technology appear to be involved in an elemental struggle for supremacy. As the article in the *Edinburgh New Philosophical Journal* relates, the ship's sails had been blown away early in the storm. 'Had not the vessel been a steamer', the article insists, 'it must have foundered with all on board.'[109] Withstanding the fury of the tropical storm helped illustrate the revolutionary power of steam. The image depicts the vessel keeling over,

THE PENINSULAR AND ORIENTAL COMPANY'S STEAM-SHIP "PEKIN" IN A TYPHOON IN THE CHINA SEA.

1.2 'The Steam-Ship "Pekin" in a Typhoon' (*Illustrated London News*, 6 December 1851)

almost fully submerged, the waves towering above it, emphasising the sheer power of the storm, and the wonder of the machine which was able to defy this power.

Sources which refer to the changed relationship between the steamship and the sea focus not just on the spectacle of nature's wildness; they also often exhibit striking forms of textual expression in describing the ship itself. Again, they can be seen as instances of the 'technological sublime', a hubristic enthusiasm for the logistical spectacle. Archibald Pollock Black, continuing his vivid account of the storm he witnessed in the Mediterranean, moves from his impressions of the sea to that of the steamship *Euxine*. Although by the time of his voyage in 1864 the vessel was already seventeen years old, Black's description is filled with a hubristic technophilia:

> The ship, plunging so fitfully that when a heavy sea strikes her she trembles from stem to stern, as if from fear, the engines snorting and struggling as if oppressed, the storm-tossed craft really like a thing of life, groaning and at times apparently yielding to the unequal struggle, but anon rising, gallantly, defiantly, and triumphantly.[110]

In this encounter, represented as a battle between technology and the elements, the steamship is anthropomorphised, given apparent agency, in a manner not unlike that already seen in the diabolical autonomy attributed to the steamship by Eastern observers. This representational mode was a common one in descriptions of the overland route steamship, and can be seen again in an account by William Walker which describes a voyage from Bombay to Aden in 1851 during the rough weather of the monsoon season on board the *Madras*, an iron screw steamer launched in 1852. Walker relates his experience of the confrontation between technology and nature:

> The *Madras* is the driest sea boat I ever saw, as during the whole passage she never shipped more than the spray tops of seas, although the whole of us (passengers) have been watching a huge wall of sea piled up ten feet above the gunwale, which appeared determined to come on board, but the lively graceful craft would surmount the hill of water, and often hurl a defiant counter buffeting wave from her strong breast as if she laughed Daddy Neptune's efforts to scorn.[111]

Walker's account presents the steamer as the victor in a battle with the violence of the elements, framing the sea's impotence in his mocking invocation of the mythic figure of Neptune. Continuing, Walker accounts for the ship's supremacy specifically in terms of the technological advancement of its means of propulsion. 'The ship derived this power from being a screw-boat', he explains, a reference to the then relatively recent innovation of the screw propeller.[112]

Like Syed Khan's domineering army officer, such a promethean narrative reflected well on the race who had created this technological wonder. Charles Henry Newmarch's 1847 account of his voyage on board the *Hindostan* from Aden to Suez was peppered with references to the progressive, revolutionary impact of steam. Again, Newmarch mobilises the trope of the anthropomorphised steamship to articulate this technophilic jouissance. 'The obedient vessel', he writes, 'was progressing though the water, as if she had been an animate creature endued with the power of moving at pleasure, and waiting only for her master's will to direct her actions.'[113] The earlier examples of Eastern conceptions of the steamship, driven by a hidden diabolical force, find their counterpart in the hubristic fantasies of the modern Western subject. Both emphasise the extent to which the steamship was seen to be propelled by a hidden agency. In such descriptions, technology is endowed with power and agency, employed in the service of a Western master to impose his will on the world. This hubris and projection fuelled an imperialist confidence, informed by a Western conception of self as a superior, enlightened figure unfazed in its global mobility. The mastery of nature finds its counterpart in the enlightenment ideology of taming a similarly 'natural' savage – a subaltern figure who is distinctly absent in these bombastic discussions of the steamship's fantastical mobility.

Agency was attributed to the machine as a power in itself. Accounts of historical change in the cultural history of the overland route steamship overlook labour as the distinguishing factor in coming to terms with this shift, in favour of a hubristic preoccupation with technology and its relation to nature. Labour however, in its apparent absence, in fact remains a key underlying element in the constitution of the perception of this nature–technology relation. This development is manifested in Scottish minister and religious writer John Aiton's narrative of his 1851 tour of what he terms the 'Bible Lands' of the Middle East, which as he notes, the steamship had made vastly more accessible. Opening his account with his voyage aboard the *Ripon* from Southampton to Alexandria, Aiton employs a fanciful conceit in which the stupefied ghost of Julius Caeser is introduced to the wonders of modern Britain – and none more amazing to the classical emperor than the transnational steamship. Aiton describes, in reverent terms, the steamer's

> engine department, so powerful, majestic, and shining like silver. Although it combines and condenses within the space of a breakfast parlour the energies of twelve hundred horses, yet a boy with one hand can stop the vast movement in one moment, and a bucketful of coals and of water carries the whole three thousand tonnes over the stormiest ocean like a thing of nothing.[114]

In this characteristically technophilic passage the overcoming of nature is ascribed to the machine itself, with no mention of the labour practices without which the ship's mobility would have been impossible. With the shift undergone by maritime labour practices in the wake of steam power, and their spatial movement away from a sphere of visibility (on the ship's deck), the technological production of mobility appeared not as a product of social labour, but of the steamship itself. While maritime labour practices were everywhere manifest aboard a sailing vessel, labour on board the steamship was concealed, hidden within the bowels of the ship. This change had consequences beyond the social organisation of labour, helping to facilitate the imaginative investments and modern mythologies of imperial steam. The next chapter engages with this politics of visibility and disappearance, exploring how the invisibilisation and repression of shipboard labour practices was achieved through both spatial discipline and representational practices.

The steamship bore a heavy weight of cultural meaning. A wealth of idiosyncratically modern mythologies were at play in the minds of passengers who were able to forget the labour required to propel the ship, ascribing the power of that labour to the technology itself. In its formative years steam propulsion at sea presented a form of technological innovation which was anything but stable. However, the claims associated with the steamship's modernity provided contemporary observers with a discursive means for framing their understanding of the place of the West in the world. Such notions helped construct a coherent discourse which revolved around technology and difference – and this contributed to an imperial world view, a confident, superior outlook on the world. As they travelled through global space, steamship passengers dwelt upon the imaginative investments in steam power. Encountering these preoccupations in the wealth of literature on the subject, of the heroic, progressive impact of the steamship on the Eastern world, the reader in the metropole was able to construct a coherent narrative of Western superiority and Eastern immaturity.

All these factors contributed to a conception of steam's entry into shipping as a historical break, an incomplete departure which emphasises the extent to which the popular cultural imagination imbued steamships with a more emphatic association with modernity than was perhaps warranted by the material conditions of their mobility. As will be developed in the following chapters, the notions which have animated this chapter were refashioned and contested in the experiences of steamship mobility, through performative, embodied, visual, material, spatial and temporal practices. This chapter's main themes: the texture of shipboard life; the imaginative imperial geographies of global mobility; the British imperial world view; and an attentiveness to historical change continue to inform the preoccupations in the rest of the book. These are expressed in a range of shipboard practices: in the attribution to the steamer of both urban and domestic characteristics, and in the temporalities and rhythms of shipboard life; in the conflicting discourses of a frictionless mobility with the monotony of life in transit, and in the imaginative geographies of empire at the heart of the aesthetic production of panoramic vision; in the sometimes violent labour forms and modes of discipline which governed the space of the ship. Historical change remains the dominant discursive means by which the steamship's mobilities were narrated, particularly as a departure from the still-existent world of sail. Chapter 2 explores these concepts through engaging with the materiality of the shipboard environment, interrogating the social and spatial practices which produced and were produced by this materiality, particularly through a spatial organisation of shipboard bodies which contributed to the invisibility of the new subaltern labour practices of steam.

Notes

1   As On Barak has observed, the use of the slow sailing route round the Cape to send troop reinforcements to India, rather than by the steamship on the

overland route caused a national scandal. Barak, *On Time*, p. 31. See also Lester, Boehme and Mitchell, *Ruling the World*, pp. 236–48.

2 'The Overland Route to India', *Leisure Hour*, 5 November 1857, p. 711.

3 A reference to Theodor Adorno's claim that 'modernity is a qualitative, not a chronological, category'. Theodor Adorno, *Minima Moralia: Reflections on a Damaged Life*, trans. by E.F.N. Jephcott (London: Verso, 2005), p. 218.

4 'The Overland Route to India', p. 711.

5 The gross tonnage of the *Braganza* was 688, compared to the *Bentinck*'s 1,800. Point de Galle, known today as Galle, was the main port of Ceylon (Sri Lanka).

6 Franz Wilhelm Junghuhn, *Terugreis van Java naar Europa, met de Zoogenaamde Engelsche Overlandpost in de Maanden September en October 1848* (Zaltbommel: J. Noman, 1851), p. 40. This, and all subsequent translations of this source are my own.

7 *Ibid.*, pp. 40–1.

8 Walter Benjamin placed the urban crowd at the centre of his theoretical engagement with the quality of shock endemic to urban experience. Walter Benjamin, 'On Some Motifs in Baudelaire' (1939), *Selected Writings: Volume 4, 1938–1940*, trans. by Edmund Jephcott and others, ed. by Howard Eiland and Michael W. Jennings (Cambridge, MA: Harvard University Press, 2003), p. 317.

9 Charles Baudelaire, *The Painter of Modern Life and Other Essays*, trans. and ed. by Jonathan Mayne (New York: Da Capo Press, 1986), p. 13.

10 Georg Simmel, 'The Metropolis and Mental Life' (1903), in *Georg Simmel on Individuality and Social Forms*, trans. and ed. by D. Levine (Chicago: University of Chicago Press, 2011), p. 329.

11 *Ibid.*

12 This has been explored in great depth in the context of steam train mobilities by Wolfgang Schivelbusch, in Schivelbusch, *The Railway Journey*.

13 'Out in Blue Water', *Supplement to the Manchester Weekly Times*, 20 June 1868, p. 196.

14 *Ibid.*

15 Of course, vessels sailing to India around the Cape of Good Hope needed to call at various points to take on supplies (particularly St Helena and Cape Town), especially given the protracted length of time spent in transit. Steam, however, produced a regularised, predictable set of calling points, many of which were located in the populous Mediterranean world. Few passengers would have joined the sailing vessel at its calling points.

16 The nineteenth-century British naming conventions which appear in the primary source materials have generally been employed throughout this book, for the sake of simplicity. Constantinople for Istanbul, Bombay for Mumbai, Ceylon for Sri Lanka, Madras for Chennai, Calcutta for Kolkata, etc.

17 Albert Hervey, *The Ocean and the Desert, by a Madras Officer* (London: T.C. Newby, 1846), pp. 318–19. The book's title is derived from the two landscapes traversed on the overland route.

18 *Ibid.*, pp. 14–15.

19 Janet Oppenheim, *'Shattered Nerves': Doctors, Patients, and Depression in Victorian England* (Oxford: Oxford University Press, 1991), p. 91; Wolfgang Schivelbusch explores the topic of nineteenth-century nervous overstimulation in the context of steam locomotive mobilities in Schivelbusch, *The Railway Journey*, pp. 113–28, 137–49.

20 Hervey, *The Ocean and the Desert*, pp. 4, 20.

21 Ruth M. Coopland, *A Lady's Escape from Gwalior, and Life in the Fort of Agra during the Mutinies of 1857* (London: Smith, Elder, & Co., 1859), pp. 314–15.

22 Richard Lepsius, *Discoveries in Egypt, Ethiopia, and the Peninsula of Sinai, in the Years 1842–1845, During the Mission Sent Out by His Majesty Frederick William IV of Prussia*, trans. and ed. by K.R.H. Mackenzie (London: Richard Bentley, 1852), p. 2.

23 William Makepeace Thackeray, *Notes of a Journey from Cornhill to Grand Cairo by Way of Lisbon, Athens, Constantinople and Jerusalem: Performed in the Steamers of the Peninsular and Oriental Company* (London: Chapman & Hall, 1846), p. 299.

24 This description also illustrates the extent to which the acceleration of mobility could be met with unexpected and protracted moments of stasis, in this case rooted in concerns regarding the mobility of not just people and objects, but also deadly micro-organisms. While P&O's importance to the British Empire meant that it was exempt from the usual quarantine rules for ships arriving in Britain (see Alex Chase-Levenson, *The Yellow Flag: Quarantine and the British Mediterranean World, 1780–1860* (Cambridge: Cambridge University Press, 2020), pp. 256–7), Thackeray had departed from P&O's service at Malta so that he could travel to Naples, returning home via the Continent.

25 Gevers Deynoot, *Herinneringen eener Reis naar Nederlandsch-Indië in 1862* (The Hague: Martinus Nijhoff, 1864), p. 2. Translation my own.

26 *Ibid.*

27 Shelley Baranowski and Ellen Furlough, 'Introduction', in *Being Elsewhere: Tourism, Consumer Culture, and Identity in Modern Europe and North America*, ed. by Shelley Baranowski and Ellen Furlough (Ann Arbor: University of Michigan Press, 2001), pp. 1–31, p. 11.

28 Hervey, *The Ocean and the Desert*, p. 21.

29 Richardson, *The Anglo-Indian Passage*, p. vi. Richardson makes explicit reference here to the Alexander Pope composition which is said to be the origin of the term: 'Ye Gods! annihilate but space and time, | And make two lovers happy.' Alexander Pope, 'Of the Art of Sinking in Poetry', *The Works of Alexander Pope, Esq., Volume VI*, ed. by William Warburton (London: J. and P. Knapton, 1751), p. 235.

30 Richardson, *The Anglo-Indian Passage*, p. vi.

31 See Schivelbusch, *The Railway Journey*, pp. 33–44.

32 'The Bentinck', *Illustrated London News*, 12 August 1843, p. 107.

33 Karl Marx, *Grundrisse: Foundations of the Critique of Political Economy*, trans. by Martin Nicolaus (London: Penguin, 1973), p. 539.

34 David Harvey, *The Condition of Postmodernity: An Enquiry into the Origins of Cultural Change* (Oxford: Blackwell, 1989), p. 240.

35 Richardson, *The Anglo-Indian Passage*, p. vii.

36 'Election Intelligence', *The Times*, 14 July 1866, p. 10.

37 Captain James Barber, *The Court of Directors of the East India Company, Versus Her Majesty's Ministers, the Resolutions of the House of Commons, and the Public of India and England, as Regards a Complete Plan of Steam Communication Between the Two Empires* (London: Smith, Elder & Co., 1839), p. 6.

38 'Reminiscences of Eastern Travel, Chapter XI', *Macphail's Edinburgh Ecclesiastical Journal and Literary Review*, October 1855, p. 143.

39 *Ibid.*.

40 Anthony Giddens, *The Consequences of Modernity* (Cambridge: Polity, 1990), p. 64.

41 Benedict Anderson, *Imagined Communities: Reflections on the Origin and Spread of Nationalism* (London: Verso, 1991), p. 7.

42 Steven Adriaan Buddingh, *Dagboek Mijner Overland-Mail-Reis van Rotterdam naar Java, via Southampton in 1852* (Batavia: Lange & Co., 1852), pp. 46–7.

43 Norman Macleod, *Eastward: Travels in Egypt, Palestine and Syria* (London: Strahan & Co., 1869), p. 11.

44 Norman Macleod, *Peeps at the Far East: A Familiar Account of a Visit to India* (London: Strahan & Co., 1871), p. 14.

45 *Ibid.*

46 Lutfullah, *Autobiography of Lutfullah, a Mohamedan Gentleman and His Transactions with His Fellow-Creatures: Interspersed with Remarks on the Habits, Customs, and Character of the People with Whom He Had to Deal* (London: Smith, Elder, & Co., 1858), p. 363.

47 Jacob van Heerdt, *Mijne Reis met de Landmail van Batavia over Singapore, Ceilon, Aden en Suiz tot Alexandrië in Egypte* (The Hague: K. Führi, 1851), p. 42. This, and all subsequent translations of this source are my own. Wilde was renowned for creating maps which included routes not yet in operation – hence the inclusion in 1840 of as yet projected elements of the overland route.

48 *Ibid.*

49 'The Peninsular and Oriental Company', *Hobart Town Daily Courier*, 30 March 1853, p. 3.

50 *Ibid.*

51 William T. Stead, *Gladstone: A Character Sketch 1809–1898* (London: 'Review of Reviews' Office, 1898), p. 71. Stead attributes this quotation to Cardinal Henry Edward Manning (1808–92).

52 *The Crystal Palace Penny Guide: By Authority of the Directors* (London: Robert K. Burt, 1864), p. 21.

53 Tony Bennett has described a Darwinian exhibitionary order in which the museum has been employed to render the ideology of progress in material form.

Tony Bennett, *The Birth of the Museum: History, Theory, Politics* (London: Routledge, 1995), pp. 179–80.

54 Charles Henry Newmarch, *Five Years in the East, Volume 2* (London: Longman, Brown, Green & Longmans, 1847), pp. 164–5.

55 Susan Buck-Morss, *The Dialectics of Seeing: Walter Benjamin and the Arcades Project* (Cambridge, MA: MIT Press, 1989), p. 91.

56 'Power of the P. and O. Company', *Malta Times*, November 1845, cited in *Singapore Free Press and Mercantile Advertiser*, 15 January 1846, p. 2.

57 van Heerdt, *Mijne Reis met de Landmail van Batavia over Singapore*, p. 21.

58 *Ibid.*, p. 25.

59 Sayyid Ahmad Khan, *The Causes of the Indian Revolt* (Benares: Medical Hall Press, 1873).

60 Syed Ahmed Khan, *A Voyage to Modernism*, trans. and ed. by Mushirul Hasan and Nishat Zaidi (Delhi: Primus Books, 2011), pp. 79–80. This was the first published English translation of Khan's account. The original was in Urdu, and was first published shortly after his return in the *Aligarh Institute Gazette*, the newsletter of the scientific society.

61 *Ibid.*, p. 168. Furthermore, Khan wrote, 'all good things, spiritual and worldly which should be found in man, have been bestowed by the Almighty on Europe, and especially on England'. *Ibid.*, pp. 7–8.

62 Lutfullah, *Autobiography of Lutfullah*, p. 358.

63 David Nye, *American Technological Sublime* (Cambridge, MA: MIT Press, 1994), pp. 54–7.

64 Joachim Stocqueler, 'Overland Trips in General, and a Trip in Particular', *Asiatic Journal and Monthly Register for British and Foreign India China and Australasia, Volume 1.*, May–October 1843, pp. 633–4.

65 Ludwig Moser, *The Caucasus and its People; With a Brief History of their Wars, and a Sketch of the Achievements of the Renowned Chief Schamyl* (London: David Nutt, 1856), pp. iii–iv.

66 Lord William Bentinck, 'Letter from the Governor General to G. Norton Esq., April 11, 1834', in Captain James Barber, *A Letter to the Right Hon. Sir John Cam Hobhouse, Bart. M.P., President of the India Board, etc. etc. etc: On Steam-Navigation with India, and Suggesting the Best Mode of Carrying it into Effect via the Red Sea* (London: Pelham Richardson, 1837), p. 44.

67 Aguiar, *Tracking Modernity*, p. 12.

68 'Panorama of Cairo', *Illustrated London News*, 20 March 1847, p. 181.

69 Richardson, *The Anglo-Indian Passage*, p. vi.

70 *Ibid.*, pp. vi–vii.

71 In 1853, Karl Marx argued that the ideology of progress, which was presented as benevolent and enlightened in the metropole, was laid bare in the colonial world, underpinned by the brutality of imperial violence. Karl Marx, 'The Future Results of British Rule in India', in *Marx Engels Collected Works, Volume 12* (Moscow: Progress Publishers, 1979), pp. 217–22, p. 222.

72 Arthur Anderson, *Communications with India, China, &c.: Observations on the practicability and utility of opening a communication between the Red Sea*

and the Mediterranean, by a ship-canal through the Isthmus of Suez (London: Smith, Elder & Co., 1843), p. v.

73 Thackeray, *Notes of a Journey from Cornhill to Grand Cairo*, p. 94. Robert Fulton was an American engineer and inventor who is often credited with the invention of the steamboat.

74 'Screw Steam Navigation', *The Times*, 19 January 1854, p. 7 .

75 Lester, Boehme and Mitchell, *Ruling the World*, pp. 236–48.

76 J. Willett Spalding, *The Japan Expedition: Japan and Around the World; an Account of Three Visits to the Japanese Empire, with Sketches of Madeira, St. Helena, Cape of Good Hope, Mauritius, Ceylon, Singapore, China, and Loo-Choo* (New York: Redfield, 1855) p. 74. Spalding was no stranger to the power of the steamship as a symbol of national might. He served as clerk to Commodore Matthew Perry on board one of the steamers which became known as the 'Black Ships', on the infamous mission to open Japan politically and economically to the West.

77 Peter Osborne, *The Politics of Time: Modernity and the Avant-Garde* (London: Verso, 1995), p. 17.

78 A notable example concerns Samuel Bentham, noted naval architect (and brother of the philosopher Jeremy Bentham), who is known to have acknowledged the influence of Chinese ship design on his 1795 plans for the pioneering use of watertight bulkheads in Royal Navy ships, a feature which became commonplace in the Nineteenth Century. 'Description of the Great Britain Iron Steam Ship', *The Mechanics' Magazine*, 13 September 1845, p. 186. For Indian innovations employed in the manufacture of sailing vessels used by the British, see also Arnold, *Science, Technology and Medicine in Colonial India*, p. 102.

79 Sarah Seabright, *Steaming East: The Forging of Steamship and Rail Links Between Europe and Asia* (London: Bodley Head, 1991), p. 96; Harcourt, *Flagships of Imperialism*, p. 184.

80 Samuel W. Baker, *Eight Years' Wanderings in Ceylon* (London: Longman, Brown, Green, and Longmans, 1855), p. 349.

81 'Communication with the East', p. 567.

82 See, for example, Lester, Boehme and Mitchell, *Ruling the World*, pp. 168–73.

83 John Tillotson, *The Overland Route to India: Historical, Descriptive and Legendary* (London: J.E. Lloyd, 1859), p. 63.

84 James Vernon, *Distant Strangers: How Britain Became Modern* (Berkeley: University of California Press, 2014), p. 1.

85 Gordon Jackson, 'The Shipping Industry', in *Transport in Victorian Britain*, ed. by Michael J. Freeman and Derek Aldcroft (Manchester: Manchester University Press, 1988), pp. 253–84, p. 274.

86 The history of subaltern labour aboard Western ships is explored in: Balachandran, 'Cultures of Protest in Transnational Contexts'; Ewald, 'Crossers of the Sea'; Ahuja, 'Capital at Sea, Shaitan Below Decks?' In the context of P&O, a document dated 10 July 1848 gives the crew complement of the *Bentinck*. It informs us that, on a ship carrying 102 passengers and 50 passengers' servants,

there was a total crew of 177: the captain, 7 officers, 5 engineers, 62 seamen (39 of which were recorded as 'native'), 71 firemen (67 of whom 'native'), 31 stewards and servants (10 of whom 'native'). This gives a sense of the sheer quantity of labour which made the steamship's mobility possible. It also bears witness to the coexistence on board the steamship of the labour roles of both sail and steam, and to the presence of large numbers of subaltern workers, particularly in the unpleasant and dangerous new labour role of stoking. The considerable number of stewards is also notable, emphasising the importance of maintaining the living standards of the bourgeois passengers. London, National Maritime Museum Archive, P&O Company Records: 'Individual Ships: Bentinck, Miscellaneous Material', 1848, P&O/65/67.

87 London, National Maritime Museum Archive, P&O Company Records: Book of 'Instructions for Chief Engineers', 1867, P&O/9/1, p. 8.

88 Michael Angelo Garvey, *The Silent Revolution, or, The Future Effects of Steam and Electricity Upon the Condition of Mankind* (London: William and Frederick G. Cash, 1852), p. 101.

89 The steamship's reliance on sail could be seen both in terms of the auxiliary means of propulsion they continued to utilise, and the use of sailing vessels to transport the vast amount of coal required to power the steamer's engines to the various coaling stations along the route.

90 Hervey, *Ten Years in India*, p. v.

91 Newmarch, *Five Years in the East*, p. 165.

92 Allan Sekula, *Fish Story* (Düsseldorf: Richter Verlag, 1995), p. 107.

93 *The Overland Route to India and China* (London: Thomas Nelson and Sons, 1858), p. 5.

94 Sir Richard Francis Burton, *Personal Narrative of a Pilgrimage to El Medinah and Meccah, Volume 1* (London: Longman, Brown, Green, Longmans, and Roberts, 1857), pp. 6–7. Coincidentally, both Burton's quoted lyrics and the reference to 'our poor devoted bark' from the previous quotation come from the popular nineteenth-century song 'The Bay of Biscay'.

95 Philip Steinberg, *The Social Construction of the Ocean* (Cambridge: Cambridge University Press, 2001), p. 113.

96 Marcus Rediker, *Between the Devil and the Deep Blue Sea: Merchant Seamen, Pirates, and the Anglo-American Maritime World, 1700–1750* (Cambridge: Cambridge University Press, 1987), p. 3.

97 Steinberg, *The Social Construction of the Ocean*, p. 118.

98 Franklin R. Kendall, 'Letter dated 22 February 1858, aboard the *Ripon*', *Letters* (P&O: 1968), p. 7 (a typed, presumably unique book of letters originally written by F.R. Kendall, P&O employee, produced by P&O in 1968 and held in the Caird Library at the National Maritime Museum, London, reference: 347.792P&O).

99 Kendall, 'Letter dated 22 February 1858, aboard the *Ripon*', *Letters*, p. 7.

100 Archibald Pollok Black, *A Hundred Days in the East: A Diary of a Journey to Egypt, Palestine, Turkey in Europe, Greece, the Isles of the Archipelago, and Italy* (London: J. F. Shaw & Co., 1865), p. 13.

101 I have described this experience as the technicised sublime partially to avoid the term technological sublime, a concept introduced in Leo Marx, *The Machine in the Garden: Technology and the Pastoral Ideal in America* (New York: Oxford University Press, 2000), pp. 195–207 and most extensively developed in Nye, *American Technological Sublime*. While these works document a phenomenon in which the spectacle of technology itself invokes the sublime, in the case of Black's reference, I argue that he describes a fairly typical example of the sublime experience of nature which was mediated by the technology of the steamship.

102 Frederick Walter Simms, *England to Calcutta by the Overland Route in 1845: From a Manuscript Left by F. W. Simms*, ed. by Frederick Simms (London: Harrison and Sons, 1878), p. 117.

103 Joachim Stocqueler, *The Hand-Book of India, a Guide to the Stranger and the Traveller, and a Companion to the Resident* (London: Wm. H. Allen & Co., 1844), p. 165.

104 'From Southampton to Shanghai', *The National Magazine, Volume XII* (London: W. Tweedie, 1862), p. 92.

105 'The Willcox and Anderson Testimonials', *Herapath's Railway Journal*, 8 December 1855, p. 1236.

106 The screw propeller, which replaced the cumbersome and inefficient paddle-wheel, was first used to propel a commercial sea-going ship for Isambard Kingdom Brunel's *Great Britain* in 1845, but wouldn't begin to come into widespread use until the mid-1850s.

107 Charles Piazzi Smyth, 'Meteorological and Astronomical Notices for December 1851', *Edinburgh New Philosophical Journal*, January 1852, p. 174.

108 See Lawrence Otto Goedde, 'Convention, Realism, and the Interpretation of Dutch and Flemish Tempest Painting', *Simiolus*, 16 (1986), 139–49.

109 Smyth, 'Meteorological and Astronomical Notices for December 1851', p. 174.

110 Black, *A Hundred Days in the East*, p. 13.

111 William Walker, *Tom Cringle's Letters on Practical Subjects, Suggested by Experiences in Bombay, Originally Published in the Bombay Daily Newspapers as Letters to the Editors* (Bombay: Education Society's Press, 1863), p. 51.

112 *Ibid.*

113 Newmarch, *Five Years in the East*, p. 164.

114 John Aiton, *The Lands of the Messiah, Mahomet, and the Pope: As Visited in 1851* (London: A. Fullarton & Co., 1854), p. 2.

2

'A turbulent microcosm': Steamship space

Bound for Calcutta in 1845, the British railway engineer Frederick Walter Simms travelled from Southampton to Alexandria on board the *Great Liverpool*. In his account of the voyage, Simms recalls the morning of his first day at sea. 'Many of the company proceeded to the deck,' he writes, 'the gentlemen to talk over, not the affairs of the nation, or the world at large, but those of the small nation and the little world of which we had for a time become a part.'[1] Simms describes the steamer as a world in miniature. During transit, in its isolation at sea, the ship became the sole site of all its occupants' social relations. Simms's account pays close attention to the various spaces of the steamer: to the practices which ordered and disciplined this space, to the social and imaginative investments which lend them their character. Simms was not alone in this regard: accounts of overland route travel exhibit a marked preoccupation with describing this world, an exclusive space of bourgeois leisure and sociality. As this chapter explores, in order to describe the small world of the steamer of which they were a temporary citizen, passengers persistently reached beyond its space, exhibiting distinctive discursive practices which often borrowed from familiar land-based spaces. The choice of these spaces was not arbitrary, but reflected the social, cultural, embodied and imaginative practices passengers employed to engage with the new experiences and anxieties of global travel.

This chapter charts the spatial practices of the various occupants of the steamship (both passengers and crew), and how they inhabited its diverse spaces. The social activities of the steamer's occupants both shaped and were shaped by the ship as an environment. The extensive descriptions of the ship's space describe a new kind of shipboard environment, a distinctly modern space which helped passengers identify with their role as agents of imperialism. Just what sort of space was the overland route steamship? A British space? An imperial space? An amalgam of the two? Those who encountered the steamship were preoccupied with just such questions, characterising the steamship as a novel space which exhibited distinctive social hierarchies rooted in identity and difference. If the steamship was a world in miniature, it was one marked by forms of spatial discipline, both material and discursive, which reflected forms of segregation and exclusion typical of the nineteenth-century imperial world. Yet the steamer did not merely reproduce the wider world: it was a highly distinctive space, which codified imperial hierarchies in novel configurations. At their most extreme, the steamship's spatial politics offer a unique perspective on the barbaric underside of Victorian imperialism.

The steamship as a modern space

In his account of an overland route journey from India to England in 1843, Albert Hervey describes his first impressions of the steamship *Hindostan*. As Chapter 1 explored, Hervey was among a number of early narrators of the overland route, who were particularly attentive to what they saw as the revolutionary impact of steam at sea. For Hervey the *Hindostan*, the first of the two steamships commissioned by the company to serve the Eastern section of the new route, was not merely a novel means of transport: it presented a new realm of experience. Upon boarding the ship, Hervey records a sensation of spatial disorientation: 'These numerous little pigeon holes and corners between decks, with the various passages leading into them, make the whole quite a labyrinth; and it really requires time, patience, and experience, to enable you to find the way to your own dormitory!'[2] The internal space of this new shipboard environment was for Hervey so vast, convoluted and unfamiliar that it proved difficult to navigate. For those who had hitherto experienced only the smaller and less elaborate passenger quarters of the sailing ship the steamship's space was seen as a labyrinthine, complex one.[3] Also aboard the *Hindostan*, travelling from Point de Galle to Suez in 1846, Jacob van Heerdt would experience a similar sense of disorientation. In his account of the voyage, van Heerdt furnished extensive descriptions of the vessel's spatial arrangements. 'The number of cabins, together with its particular arrangement,' he writes, 'may easily lead one who is unfamiliar with the manner of construction of such a steamer to get lost among the meandering passageways, if he wishes to find his cabin unaccompanied.'[4] Those stepping on board the overland route steamship often reported their amazement at what they considered to be a radically new kind of shipboard space. Sources exhibit a preoccupation with describing this space, attempting to textually articulate what they considered a novel environment. The early steamer certainly had a more extensive range of dedicated passenger spaces than most of the sailing vessels that travellers had until that time gone to the East aboard, but what exactly was so novel about this space that it provoked such reactions?

If the steamship was considered modern, it was in part because it was seen to possess spatial characteristics which marked a historical departure from the past. Charles Henry Newmarch also travelled aboard the *Hindostan*, from Aden to Suez in 1847. Chapter 1 made use of several quotations from his account of the voyage, a particularly hubristic paean to the revolutionary power of steam. Again, Newmarch is at pains to articulate the novelty of the steamship's space, which he compares to the *Worcester*, a sailing vessel on which he had travelled round the Cape to India just a few years previously. For Newmarch, in its internal layout, its décor and its size, the steamship was a departure from sail, a modern space:

> This being the first time that we had ever been on board one of these large steamers, we were well occupied for the first hour or two in examining her various departments. When on board the Worcester, which we were told was a fine ship, we found every thing certainly very comfortable, but at the same time there was nothing which differed very widely from our preconceived notions of a vessel; but here, on the contrary, every thing was calculated to surprise us, not only the immense size of the vessel herself, but also the intricacy of her internal arrangements, and above all the magnificence of the saloon.[5]

The characterisation of the steamship as a novel maritime environment was articulated specifically in the extent to which it appeared to differ from the visual, material and spatial culture of sail. The steamer presented a departure from the traditional design and layout of the ship, particularly in exhibiting a bourgeois opulence which is explored in more detail in Chapter 4.

The predecessor of the overland route steamship (and indeed contemporary, given that they continued to sail around the Cape long into the latter half of the nineteenth century) was the East Indiaman. These vessels, in the service of the East India Company, were among the largest merchant sailing ships in the days before steam, although rarely as large as even P&O's first steamers. They travelled slowly and irregularly to the East around the Cape of Good Hope. Passenger space on board an East Indiaman was provided almost as an afterthought to the main purposes of the ship, trade. Unlike the steamer, passage on the East Indiaman was not subject to a fixed fee, but negotiated by an informal process of arbitration. 'The sums paid for cabins', states *The General East India Guide and Vade Mecum* of 1825, 'entirely depend upon the demand, their size, the ship's destination, and the circumstances of the person selling his accommodation'.[6] Furthermore, passenger accommodation was often located in part of the ship which had been allocated to one of the East Indiaman's officers, and was sold by them for passenger use on an informal basis. Even the cabin's dimensions were not fixed, but created by temporary partitions made of either cloth or wood which could be dismantled rapidly if necessary, for example in times of battle.[7] The shift from sail to steam was accompanied by a move from this improvised, indiscriminate engagement to the emergence of dedicated shipboard passenger spaces. The era of the steamship formalised passenger accommodations on the journey to the East, with permanent cabins and a range of other luxurious dedicated passenger spaces: dining saloons, bathrooms, toilets, ladies' dressing rooms, smoking rooms.

Yet space on board the steamer was limited. A number of factors meant that the steamship lacked the space that would have been available aboard a sailing vessel: the industrial machinery of the ship's engines and boilers; the large amounts of coal necessary for the relatively inefficient engines to propel the ship across thousands of miles of sea; the extensive crew required to operate both the ship's engines and its sails, and also to meet the needs of passengers. The size of the passengers' cabins reflected this limitation, a fact that did not go unnoticed in voyage accounts. British politician and diplomat Lord Albert Denison, having boarded the *Tagus* at Southampton in 1848, was particularly aggrieved by the small size of his cabin, which he refers to as 'a curious piece of mechanism', owing to its use of folding beds to create sofas during the day. 'I had the curiosity to measure the standing room with my measuring tape', he writes, 'and found, that three feet by two feet eight inches was allowed for washing, dressing, and undressing for four persons.'[8] The precision of Denison's concern with shipboard space echoes the instrumentalisation of an environment that was no longer subject to the arbitrary apportioning which had prevailed on board the sailing vessel. The overland route provided formalised passenger conditions on the journey to the East, with fixed, permanent cabin space. Passage rates were precisely and methodically applied to the cabins using a standardised system, where larger, more comfortable cabins invoked a premium on the standard cost.

In many ways it is difficult to develop a definitive picture of the distinctive spatial characteristics of the specific steamers which passengers travelled aboard during the period of the overland route, and how, or whether, the environment of the steamship changed over time. Although sources offer extensive descriptions of steamship space, most accounts treat them as more or less generic environments, referring to their saloons, cabins, decks, and so on, as if these were fairly interchangeable spaces. The disorientating experience of steamship space that numerous accounts attest to would have been alleviated by the plans of several of the company's first vessels which were printed in an early guide to the steamship journey East, *The Overland Guide-Book* (1845).[9] These are instructive, providing a detailed illustration of the layout of the passenger spaces. Figure 2.1 depicts the internal space of the identically arranged passenger accommodations of the twin ships *Hindostan* and *Bentinck*. Such plans helped the passenger to navigate the unfamiliar world of the steamship, and offer the historian a useful visual

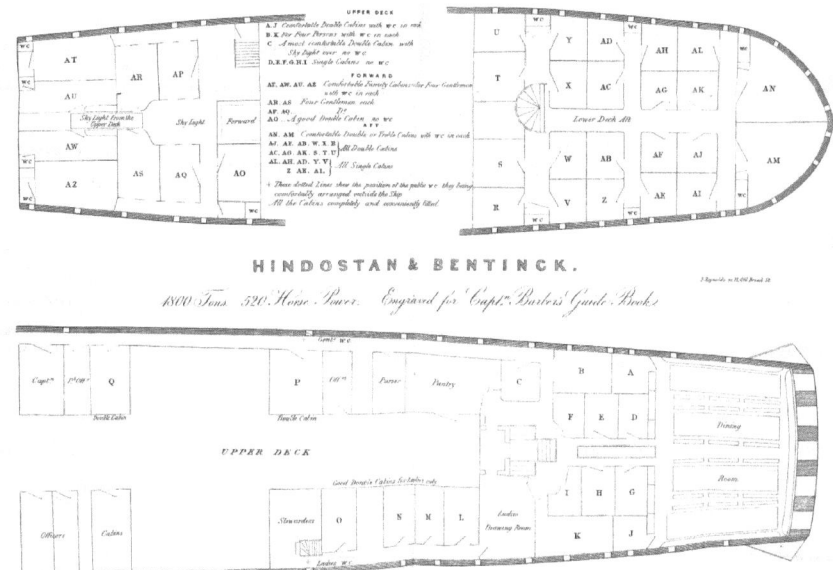

2.1 'Plan of *Hindostan* and *Bentinck*' (Captain James Barber, *The Overland Guide-Book: A Complete Vademecum for the Overland Traveller, to India via Egypt*, 1845)

representation for engaging with the delineations of steamship space. However, no such plans exist for later ships. Furthermore, although numerous articles described the interior décor of the early vessels, such articles almost ceased to be published after the initial novelty of the steamship as a new environment had worn off. There are also surprisingly few images of ships from the period of the overland route – although many vessels are depicted in the 'ship portrait' style, showing their exterior in profile, the internal spaces of the vessels are rarely and only sketchily depicted until well into the period of the Suez Canal.

The overland route's history spanned a period of great innovation in the technology of steam, and steamships were no exception. It saw the shift from paddle wheels and wooden vessels to screw propulsion and iron hulls, and the development of compound engines. Ships became more efficient, and their means of propulsion more compact, meaning that there was more space available for passengers and cargo. In a general sense, however, the shipboard environment seems to have changed little. While histories of technology are often narratives of radical innovation, P&O was a relatively conservative company, preferring reliability to revolution, particularly in Eastern waters where ports were ill-equipped to deal with the new mechanical challenges of steam. They also used their existing vessels for as long as possible.[10] Thus the experience of the overland route was, particularly as time went on, often not an encounter with the latest technological innovations in maritime mobility.

The first vessels which could truly be described as overland route steamers were the four ships acquired by the company to operate the Southampton–Alexandria and Suez–Calcutta services: The *Oriental, Great Liverpool* (both launched 1840), *Hindostan* (1842) and *Bentinck* (1843). As these were the first ships to operate on the overland route, and they were in service for some years, there is much written about them.[11] While the first two ships were acquired through a merger with the (failing) Transatlantic Steam Navigation Company in 1840 to serve on the company's Mediterranean service, the latter two were purpose built for the Eastern section of the route.[12] All four of these vessels were wooden paddle steamers, the common design of steamships at this time.[13] Their internal volume ranged from around 1400–1800 grt (gross tonnage, the measure representing the combined volume of all of a ship's enclosed spaces), and their length 61–66 metres (throughout the period of the overland route, most vessels were around 10–12 metres at their widest point). They all carried around a hundred passengers. In 1846, the company had three iron-hulled steamers built, of a similar size to its existing ships. The hulls of these vessels were better able than wooden ships to withstand the vibrations and warping caused by the ships' propulsion. One of them, the *Haddington*, was the company's first screw-driven ship, featuring a propeller at the rear rather than large paddles at the sides. Through the 1850s, the company purchased a number of iron screw steamers.[14] Although bigger than the first overland steamers, they were not radically so. These vessels ranged from 85 to over 100 metres in length, with tonnages of around 2000–2600 grt. They were generally intended to carry around 130 passengers. The company also acquired much smaller vessels to serve on the lesser used branch lines, such as those in the Far East. Although there were inevitably differences between the larger vessels, there were certain commonalities in the basic internal layout of the passenger spaces throughout the period of the overland route.

Figure 2.2 depicts a classic 'ship's portrait' view of the *Hindostan*, published to commemorate the ship's 1842 departure for India to open up the company's new Suez to Calcutta service. It is possible to map the ship's internal space found in the plan onto the external view. Overland route steamers tended to follow the basic layout found in the plan, with passenger quarters both at the front and rear of the vessel, immediately under the upper deck, and on the level above at the rear of the upper deck, the latter built as a kind of superstructure on the top of the vessel's main open deck space. The upper two decks were used for passengers largely because they were cooler, with

2.2 'The Steam Ship Hindostan departing from Southampton on the 24th Sept 1842, to open the comprehensive plan of Steam Communication with British India' (1843)

better air quality. The front section of the upper deck was generally also enclosed, but used for the ship's functional purposes. The middle section of the upper deck was generally left open, but was enclosed at the sides, providing a relatively sheltered outdoor space. Also in this part of the deck was the bridge, an elevated platform running across the steamship's deck, initially positioned between the paddle boxes to enable the ship's officers to maintain a clear view of both the paddles and the various functions of the steamship. The 'roofs' of the upper deck superstructures also provided open deck space for passenger use, and in Figure 2.2 the small figures seen on the deck are depicted on these raised areas.

The ship's main saloon, which provided passenger dining space and its main social space between meals, was positioned at the ship's rear. As shown in Figure 2.2, the *Hindostan*'s rear features a row of windows admitting light into this area. Although the *Hindostan*'s saloon extended the entire width of the vessel, it was common for saloons to be lined with passenger sleeping cabins at either side. The plan also illustrates the common arrangement for the ship's senior officers' quarters to be in the vicinity of the passenger space, which also included a number of bathrooms and toilets. In the lower decks, which do not feature in the plan, there were more spaces used for the functional operation of the ship, to store cargo, to house the ship's stores, and of course the extensive space required for the vessel's engines, boilers and coal storage. The plan offers a detailed sense of the overland steamer's spatial organisation. Yet, as descriptions of the steamer attest to, they also offer a limited view of the ship's space: as much as encounters with this space were material and corporeal, they were also produced through practices which were discursive and imaginative.

The steamship as an urban space

While the steamship was experienced as possessing a plurality of spatial forms and associated practices, the urban repeatedly emerged as the overwhelmingly predominant spatial metaphor for those who encountered its novel space. The urban is at heart of conceptions of modernity, a space where new spatial formations give rise to new forms of experience. The steamer's identity as a similarly novel environment was in part due to the increasing size of the ships then being built. The P&O ship *Himalaya*, completed in 1854, was the largest steamship then in existence, at 113 metres long and 14 metres at its widest, with capacity for 200 first-class passengers. The *Himalaya*, as an imposing visual manifestation of technological progress and a symbol of British imperial might, became the object of popular attention. Its launch attracted a huge crowd, and a wealth of publications lauded the ship's technological innovation and vast size.[15] The numerous textual responses to the huge vessel provide an illuminating point of reference for engaging with the cultural representation of the novel space of the steamship. Contemporary writers struggled to articulate their response to the enormous ship, relying on a series of representational tropes to describe it.

An 1854 description of the *Himalaya* from the *Illustrated London News* declares that 'combining great and unrivalled speed, with splendid accommodation for passengers, and ample stowage for the largest freight, she resembles more a floating city than a ship'.[16] The trope of the floating city is employed to emphasise the *Himalaya*'s modernity, expressed through its size, technological advancement and luxurious built environment. A more sophisticated imaginative encounter with the *Himalaya*'s spatial characteristics is found in the 1855 article 'Progress in the Size, Form and Power of Ships', from the architectural journal *The Builder*. The article repeatedly defers description onto other forms in an attempt to produce a discursive representation which it considers adequate to the vessel:

> The immense steam-ship *Himalaya* lately completed by the Peninsula [*sic*] and Oriental Company, is 40 feet longer than the leviathan war-steamer, the *Duke of Wellington*. Nine immense boats hang over her sides: the engine-room looks like a large manufactory: the tunnel for the shaft of the screw, in ordinary vessels about big enough for a man to crawl along, is almost as large as a railway tunnel. The ship is as long and wide as a *London street*, and a person

at one end of her cannot, with the utmost powers of his voice, make another hear at the other end. Calshot Castle, the ancient defence of Southampton harbour, might be stowed away in her hold.[17]

This description exhibits a frenetic grasping for novel modes of representation to express the sheer scale and newness of the *Himalaya*. The examples utilised to describe the various parts of the enormous ship – the factory, the railway and the metropolis – are all distinctly modern built forms. In searching for a means of representation adequate to the steamship, the ship was described as a space which encapsulated aspects of other exemplary spaces of industrial capitalism. In its very vastness, the ship exceeded the limits of oral communication. Calshot Castle, the only pre-modern form referred to in the description, is dwarfed by the ground-breaking ship's immensity. Journalistic accounts, while given to hyperbole, emphasised the steamship's modernity – the vessel was deemed to present a departure from the past through its sheer size and spatial novelty.

An 1854 article from the *Hampshire Advertiser* provides an account of the *Himalaya*'s arrival at Southampton. It again frames the ship's huge scale with reference to urban space:

> On stepping on board, her vastness was again evident. She has a flush deck, and is, moreover, nearly as long as Bernard Street (a well-known street in Southampton), which has on one side of it 22 three-storied houses with spacious shops. Her width is as great as many a large metropolitan street.[18]

The urban emerged persistently as a signifier used to express an idea of the steamship's size. As the section concerning bustle in Chapter 1 explored, the urban was a key point of reference in passenger articulations of the steamship as a novel environment. Yet, as also identified in the same chapter, the general absence of bustle – of an atmosphere of commotion and activity – aboard the steamship in transit marked it as a departure from the social character of the city. However, the urban is repeatedly and vividly mobilised as a means of articulating shipboard experience in accounts of the overland route. It is worth dwelling on the complex symbolism of this trope. As well as being a site of frenetic activity, the Victorian city was a boundless modern space, a visual signifier of Western capitalism's wealth and power. It was an ambivalent space: one of limitless possibility and pleasure, a crucial sit of bourgeois leisure practices, but also a space of poverty, often perceived as dirty, noisy and threatening. The city, like the steamship, combined working spaces and spaces of pleasure, the private and the public; it was highly stratified and codified, anarchic but disciplined.

Like Franz Junghuhn, another Dutch traveller, Jacob van Heerdt, recounting his voyage from Point de Galle to Suez on board the *Hindostan* in 1846, also wrote of the steamer's reproduction of the social spaces of the city:

'The whole thing was absolutely equivalent to a full club, or a crowded city coffeehouse, where one would linger on dry land for no more than a few hours on end. Here however, one found oneself there without cease, without pause, without rest.'[19] Van Heerdt, again invoking the figure of the crowd, mobilises the sensations of idiosyncratically urban social spaces as the defining quality of experience on the steamer. It is seen to reproduce the social character of bourgeois leisure spaces on land, a select, exclusive urbanity – yet one from which there was no opportunity for respite. This distinctive character of the steamship crowd is also articulated by Eliot Warburton, describing the spatial dynamics on board the *Oriental* during his 1843 voyage from Southampton to Alexandria. Warburton observes that 'there are nearly two hundred souls on board, yet there is as much order and regularity as in an English hotel'.[20] The crowd is invoked as a disciplined and orderly one, reflecting in the reproduction of another exclusive bourgeois environment that this order was produced through careful management of the ship's social space through the ordering of bodies within this space. While the city persistently emerges as a means of describing the steamship, this was an exclusive, luxury urban space characterised by the discipline and exclusion which exemplified elite nineteenth-century urban social environments.

Passenger comparisons of the steamship with the city were not merely experiential, but also representational and spatial. The modern city was a melting pot where class, gender and race intermingled in ways which the bourgeois subject was often equally threatened and exhilarated by – and also one where spatial discipline managed these various tensions. The burgeoning imperial city was particularly characterised by such spatial forms of social control, manifested in the built environments and infrastructure of imperialism in the cities of British India: company cantonments (permanent British military bases); public buildings; clubs and other leisure facilities for the privileged white elite; railway stations and so on – all these sites emphasised the superiority and ingenuity of the colonising race. Yet this was also a space where a racial Other who outnumbered the colonising population was a constant threat, whose difference had to be kept in check, controlled both through representation, and also through forms of discipline and control which were fundamentally spatial in character. In these sites, the spatial binaries which governed European cities were even more pronounced. As Sara Mills has argued, these forms of spatial separation and control were organised around discourses of racial difference and hygiene.[21] Particularly important was the management of the access and mobility of the racial Other within the cantonment as a British space, a space of leisure for privileged white subjects. As will be explored, such forms of spatial mediation and control can also be witnessed on board the overland route steamship. Yet the steamship did not merely reflect the existing social and spatial configurations of British imperialism: it was a distinct space of its own, characterised by a range of distinctive spatial arrangements, a social imperial world which came to stand in for empire for passengers and the readers of their accounts alike.

Imaginative encounters with shipboard space

Eliot Warburton's fastidious attention to shipboard life was such that his account includes extensive and detailed descriptions of the vessel's various spaces. These exuberant descriptions, which he refers to as 'the details of a modern sea-life', perform a kind of ethnographic survey of this novel space.[22] As his popular account of travel in the Middle East, *The Crescent and the Cross*, was published in 1844, Warburton was one of the first authors to provide such descriptions of the overland route steamship, exposing his many readers to the new form of maritime transportation. His description of the *Oriental* moves down through the vessel's various levels, detailing the inhabitants of each space in turn. Beginning with the ship's upper deck, Warburton describes an environment where one can find 'each inspecting and inspected by his fellow-travellers'.[23] The deck is portrayed as a space of bourgeois social relations, of leisured display and spectatorship. 'Various groups', writes Warburton, 'were scattered over the spacious upper deck, where there was no stain, or interruption to the lady's walk or the sailor's rush.'[24] The binaries of labour and leisure, masculine and feminine, were able to coexist harmoniously in this clean, well-ordered space.

This he contrasts with the area beneath the upper deck, the working space of the ship's crew and its living food supply. If the steamer's deck was a space of social display, polite conversation and bourgeois leisure, going beneath this spectacle revealed the ship's inner workings. The lower deck was alive with the labour activities of the ship's loading:

> Below, the busy, bustling scene was very different. Miss Mitford herself might recognise the lower deck as a complete village. It was a street of cabins, over whose doors you read the names of the doctor, the baker, the butcher, the confectioner, the carpenter, and many others; besides the 'quality at the west end,' in the shape of the officers' quarters. This street terminated in a rural scene, where the smell of new-mown hay, the lowing of cattle, the bleating of sheep, and the crowing of cocks, produced quite a pastoral effect.[25]

In this bucolic depiction Warburton renders the ship's working space as a rustic microcosm. In the era of global sea travel before refrigeration, it was common for ships to carry livestock in order to provide a fresh supply of meat, milk and eggs. However, the limits of this rural analogy as a means for representing the ship's space are soon revealed, as the reader is brought back sharply from the pastoral into the world of industrial modernity. 'Beneath the farm-yard', Warburton writes in a discordant juxtaposition, 'throbbed the iron heart of the gigantic engine.'[26] The reality of mobility at sea's industrial production lay beneath the social spaces of the steamer.

Like numerous accounts of early overland route voyages, the various registers of Warburton's narrative render the character of steamship space as both highly differentiated, and characterised by a variety of social and cultural meanings which accompanied this diversity. Descriptions of the steamship utilise a vast variety of representational and imaginative forms, borrowed from the most diverse of land-based environments: labyrinth, village, city, factory, coffeehouse, hotel. Repeatedly, accounts have recourse to descriptive reference points which reach beyond the space of the ship, imaginatively reproducing familiar land-based spatial and social formations. Few spaces were more subject to such imaginative investments than the steamer's deck. As an important passenger social space, particularly in the warm weather encountered on much of the overland route, the deck became a key focus of passenger accounts. Another passage from Warburton's account of his voyage on board the *Oriental*, describes the upper deck's affinity with elite land-based social practices:

> About ten the sunny deck is alive with inhabitants, not unsuccessfully imitating life on shore. Merry groups of children are playing about as if on a grass-plot. Twos and threes of men are walking the decks for exercise …; a tranquil group of smokers is arched over each paddle-box; ladies are reading, or working worsted monsters under the awning. … The sea is sparkling brightly as we move swiftly but smoothly over it. There is scarcely anything to remind us of our imprisonment; and, except for the silent sailor, at the restless wheel, we might fancy ourselves at the pump-room at Bath, or on the chain-pier at Brighton.[27]

The deck was constituted as a space of leisure through the reproduction of bourgeois social practices, of a modernity which mirrored both fashionable and exclusive locations of upper-class socialisation. The affirmative, urban modernity Warburton describes lay not in the stimulation and dissipation of metropolitan life, however. It owed more to a kind of Regency utopianism rooted in the bourgeois pursuit of a healthy, leisured remedy to such urban excesses. Nevertheless, this discursive reproduction of modern Western spaces reflects a sense of confidence, a reassuringly familiar social milieu in the midst of the passenger's global mobility. The steamship's characterisation as a familiar space of bourgeois leisure helped passengers to identify positively with this mobility, warding off the threatening difference of imperial space.

Only the small trace of traditional maritime labour, the sailor at the wheel, remained to articulate that this was a shipboard space; it also served for Warburton as a reminder of the attendant immobility of these globally mobile subjects, their 'imprisonment' during transit. Bourgeois leisure, a matter of personal choice and taste, was troubled by the enforced immobility of shipboard life.

The deck's new status as a space of bourgeois leisure reflected the shifts in technology and labour in maritime mobility which accompanied the rise of steam. The deck underwent a transition, from the traditional space of maritime labour aboard the sailing vessel into one of bourgeois leisure, due in part to the decline of labour practices in this space afforded by the technology of steam. Despite the continued use of sail as an auxiliary means of propulsion, the deck's use as a space of maritime labour was reduced. This spatial reconfiguration of shipboard labour meant that the arrangement of the steamer's deck presented a departure from tradition, from the culture of sail. The popular shipboard game of deck quoits, a competitive throwing game, flourished on board the steamer, as can be seen in the background of Figure 2.3, a depiction of passengers at leisure on the deck of a steamer in the Indian Ocean, in 1857. Freed from the labour practices of sail, the

2.3 'An Afternoon in the Tropics, Indian Ocean' (*Illustrated London News*, 13 June 1857)

deck provided a space for passenger leisure and sociability. Practices such as smoking, conversing, reading and lounging contributed to the social and cultural production of the ship's deck as a leisured, bourgeois space, epitomising the reproduction of similarly exclusive spaces on land. The prominent journalist William Howard Russell, lauded for his reporting from the Crimean War, travelled to India in 1858 to report on the aftermath of the rebellion. In his account of the voyage from Suez to Calcutta on board the *Nubia*, a large iron screw steamer launched in 1854, Russell again identifies the ship's deck as a distinctively leisured space. 'This deck', he writes, 'is an excellent place whereon to abjure any work of any sort without the smallest danger of being tempted to break one's vows.'[28]

An 1840 article from the *Morning Post* describing the *Oriental* documents the means by which the new steamship's spatial configuration lent itself to the leisured pursuits of passengers:

> The Spar Deck (or upper deck) affords an uninterrupted promenade, 200 feet in length. The gratings occupy little more than the space of a large hatchway, between the mainmast and foremast; and, tarpaulins being provided to place over them in bad weather, the passengers have an opportunity of enjoying a dry walk at all times on the deck below, which is kept clear as much as possible, of central erections for that purpose. The only building on the spar-deck is a neat structure close aft, fronted by a small colonnade of Ionic columns. Here are two commodious smoking-rooms, each with windows on three sides, commanding extensive views.[29]

Liberated, at least in part, from the traditional maritime labour practices of the sailing ship, the steamer's deck was able to provide a space of passenger leisure and social interaction. The open-air promenade emerged particularly as a leisured means for passengers to engage with the vessel's space. As the account documents, steps were taken to ensure that this pastime could take place even despite the unpredictability of the elements. In the warm weather of the tropics, the deck became the main recreational area of the ship.

Strolling on deck provided a means for passengers to reproduce Victorian bourgeois social practices on board the steamer. An 1857 overland route voyage narrative notes the appeal of 'delightful morning walks, and still more delightful evening promenades on deck, enlivened by the presence of the ladies, and by the sweet music which floats away over the glowing waters of the placid sea'.[30] The ship's deck had become a space where the traveller could enjoy strolling in the presence of the opposite sex while the band played and the surrounding maritime landscape was consumed as a natural spectacle. The emergence of this leisure space in a location associated with the tradition of maritime labour was intertwined with the changing labour practices at sea. As Warburton's earlier explorations of the *Oriental* make clear, this was in part due to the differentiation of steamship space – different parts of the ship had distinctive spatial and social roles.

Another passenger account of the lower deck again mobilises the rural to describe the functional, working space of the steamer. In an 1858 letter written aboard the steamship *Pottinger* while travelling from Suez to Bombay, F.R. Kendall writes that 'we have a regular farmyard on board, as in addition to the cows we have about forty sheep and a gazelle, also a goat and a kid'.[31] As Kendall continues, his description takes on the quality of reverie:

> I think of various places in the morning when I wake up, but principally of Shedfield, as the blacksmith's anvil is generally sounding in one's ears at that time and the cocks begin to crow, and the cows low to be milked, the sheep and rabbits and all the animals are making various noises.[32]

Kendall's invocation of the English village reflects his status as an occupationally itinerant individual, drawn into the workings of the British imperial world, whose departure from the familiar spaces of home shaped and mediated their experience of the ship's space. Despite its role in the discursive 'normalising' of steamship space, this incongruous pastoral stands in tension with the steamer's status as a modern environment, a contrast rendered explicit in the *Popular Overland Guide* of 1861.

The guide is a typical example of its genre, providing the prospective passenger with detailed information regarding the route, and useful descriptions of the life met with on board ship, offering advice regarding the etiquette and behaviour appropriate to the overland route traveller. It gives an almost relentlessly positive account of the steamship service. Such publications were intended in part to make the experience of steamship mobility manageable and also meaningful, to narrate the experience of transit in a way that passengers would find consumable. In a section of the guide which acquaints the prospective traveller with the steamer's diverse spaces, the ship's animals are again found near the engine. 'The sight of these inhabitants of the farm-yard, in the midst of the clatter of machinery', the guide notes, 'is extremely curious.'[33] It is here in the engine rooms, the guide declares with technophilic fervour, 'where the wonderful and resistless power which is bearing a small town upon the surface of the deep … can be seen pursuing its unceasing labour'.[34] The figure of the urban is again evoked in the steamer's characterisation as a 'small town', a description which is employed here in relation to its industrial means of propulsion. Like the plan, descriptions of steamship space relied upon certain omissions. The actual labour conditions of the engine and boiler rooms are absent from this description. As will become clear, the steamer could be characterised as a well-ordered reproduction of exclusive land-based spaces only through both discursive and material processes of discipline and exclusion.

Spatial discipline: Class, gender, race

The Popular Overland Guide of 1861 gives an account of boarding a P&O steamer at Southampton. It contrasts the disciplined space of the steamship to the chaos of the adjacent docks, noting 'the perfect order which reigns on board, even amidst the Babel of confusion around'.[35] If the harbour was a chaotic space of frenetic commercial activity, of labour and commotion, the steamer's space presented a distinct contrast: it was ordered, administered and controlled, a space of leisure. This binary was also reproduced in the space of the steamer itself. Frederick Walter Simms, travelling to Alexandria aboard the *Great Liverpool* in 1845, describes the vessel's departure from the Southampton docks. During the ship's loading Simms, along with the majority of the passengers, was standing on the upper deck. This was a space which, he writes 'was but little in disorder'. He contrasts this disciplined space with that of the 'lower deck, where confusion and noise seemed to reign triumphant'.[36] The creation of the upper deck as a discrete leisure space for passengers, removed from the bustle of labour, relied upon the disciplining of shipboard space, the distinct spatial separation of shipboard labour and leisure. Continuing, Simms relates his experience of the steamer's departure:

> It was truly surprising how soon after we had got away from the dock, these piles of boxes, trunks, and packages of all sizes and shapes, square and round, rectangular and cylindrical, vanished down a huge square funnel leading to the regions below, and there disappeared at different depths, through openings or mouths in its sides, and comparative order and quiet were restored.[37]

In Simms's description, the movement of goods exemplified by the space of the harbour was swiftly moved away from, both geographically and materially, as the ship's cargo was ordered, positioned and fixed in space. As explored in Chapter 1, the steamship in transit was often anything but a 'bustling' environment for the passenger. This circumstance was produced through various forms of spatial discipline, which ordered and controlled not only the material uses of shipboard space, but also contributed to the way in which this space was occupied and imagined by the passengers.

An 1857 description of the departure of the *Ripon* from Southampton which appeared in the *Leisure Hour* again depicts the commotion of the ship's final moments before departure, as baggage, freight and passengers were loaded in a state of apparent chaos. This is rendered in stark contrast with the experience of being underway: 'What a change! How quiet the ship seemed! The hissing of the escaping steam was hushed; the crowd of strangers was gone; the deck was all clear for a promenade; every person and everything had, and were occupying, their own place.'[38] The transition from the bustle of departure to the serenity of transit was established through forms of spatial discipline and social practice. Both the ship's human and non-human cargo occupied their proper places; the former performing the spatial practices of shipboard leisure. From apparent chaos, a system of order was quickly established over the various bodies aboard the ship.

The moments at which the steamer's spatial discipline failed to function as intended are revealing of the demarcations which governed shipboard space. The *Law Times* of 5 June 1869 records the case of *Taylor* v. *The Peninsular and Oriental Steam Navigation Company*. The report relates that the plaintiff, a passenger due to travel on board the *Pera*, 'went on board at Southampton the day before the day of sailing to inspect his cabin; and on inquiry for it, and being directed to it, he went along the saloon, and fell down the bullion hatch, which was open in the floor, and sustained severe injury'.[39] This account presents the sudden and corporeal collapsing of the binary which separated the shipboard passenger and cargo spaces. The ship was a working environment, and could become a space of danger for bodies not subject to appropriate spatial discipline. Of course, this was little different to the sailing ship, which had long been subject to strict forms of discipline which were spatial in character.[40] The distinctive spatial character of the early steamship lay in the way in which discipline was used not just to maintain shipboard labour and the functioning of the ship, but as a means of reproducing bourgeois social and cultural norms on board. The steamship was characterised by a stricter separation between the functional and passenger spaces on board, a departure from the more indiscriminate improvisation of passenger space on the sailing vessel. Not only was this intended to prevent the kind of accident described here, but also in order that the passengers be able to maintain forms of bourgeois identity on board, expressed through spatial practices. Separation from the functional space of the ship helped them define themselves as high class, leisured, civilised, superior, in contrast to the spaces of shipboard labour.

The spatial and social contact between passengers and the ship's crew was controlled through sometimes imperceptible codes of spatial discipline. An 1842 account from the *Asiatic Journal and Monthly Register* describes the design of the internal arrangements of the *Hindostan*, emphasising the extent to which the steamer's space – even in the first years of the overland route – governed the movement of the bodies which occupied it. 'Passengers,' the article observes, 'in whatever part of the ship their sleeping-cabins may be, can pass with perfect comfort under shelter to and from the saloon, without going upon deck or mingling with the crew.'[41] The steamer's spatial arrangements were designed to ensure that passengers experienced minimal contact with the vessel's workforce. This is elucidated by the extent to which the relatively new shipboard labour role of the engineer was articulated through spatial practices. In P&O's *Instructions for Chief Engineers* from 1867, a passing observation offers advice to employees regarding their use of shipboard social space: 'He should also be careful not to spend too much of his time in the saloon and on the quarterdeck; matters of this sort are observed and noted more accurately than is perhaps imagined, and ... are not looked on with favour by the managing directors.'[42] Even at a senior level, the ship's labour force was policed in terms of their access to privileged shipboard spaces which were reserved for the leisure practices of passengers. The engineer's ambiguous place in the shipboard staff hierarchy was managed through his access to space.

Shipboard spatial discipline was employed to maintain class hierarchies through separation, ordering, and clearly defined social and spatial roles. Such processes helped maintain the standards which bourgeois passengers were accustomed to, the reproduction of well-to-do social norms on land. Again, the failure to maintain these standards is instructive. In a letter dated 4 November 1853 to Georgina Hogarth, his sister-in-law and housekeeper, Charles Dickens complained of his experience of travelling on board the *Valetta* between Marseille and Naples. The *Valetta* was a relatively small wooden paddle steamer, and was severely overcrowded during Dickens's journey. With an insufficient number of available berths in the cabins, it had been impossible to maintain the usual standards of passenger accommodation:

> We found the steamer more than full of passengers from Marseilles, and in a state of confusion not to be described. We could get no places at the table, got our dinners how we could on deck, had no berths or sleeping accommodation of any kind, and had paid heavy first-class fares!

It is notable that Dickens's complaints were expressed through questions concerning order, access to space, and expectations regarding the money paid for this access. The description he goes on to furnish clarifies the breakdown of a usually carefully maintained social and spatial shipboard order: 'The scene on board beggars description. Ladies on the tables, gentlemen under the tables, and ladies and gentlemen lying indiscriminately on the open deck.'[43] For Dickens, the chaos of the overcrowded steamship was expressed more than anything else by bodies not occupying their proper place. The breaking down of the carefully managed principles of hierarchy and spatial segregation aboard the steamship meant that bourgeois passengers were unable to distinguish themselves from deck passengers who had paid a much lower fare for their passage.

In the first decades of the overland route there was no second-class accommodation on board P&O's steamships in a formalised sense. An unofficial arrangement of reduced-price passages did exist, which tended to involve boarding in the same space as the passengers' servants. In addition, there was also a considerable trade in deck passengers, who were denied access to all but the open space of the deck for the duration of their voyage.[44] The reduced price of passage was manifested in part through restricted access to certain parts of the ship. Jacob van Heerdt, in his detailed descriptions of the *Hindostan*'s various spaces, again emphasises the spatial segregation and discipline which demarcate the passenger and labour spaces: 'Above and below, the whole vessel is occupied at the prow by the crew, servants and second class passengers and at the stern by the travellers of the first class; this separation is strictly observed, the only exception allowed being the servants of travellers during the day.'[45] Access to specific parts of the ship, and movement between and through these spaces, was strictly regulated. Mobility within the ship's opulent passenger spaces was a luxury only available to the privileged passenger. The maintenance of this strict spatial discipline inscribed class hierarchies within the space of the steamer. The only porosity of these boundaries was in the mobility of servitude, of the domestic workers who liberated the bourgeois passengers from the need to perform labour themselves.

Again, the deck was a significant shipboard space in the production of bourgeois identity and leisure practices, and it was subject to the same spatial divisions. 'The fore-part of the upper deck', observes *The Popular Overland Guide* of 1861, 'is devoted to the use of the sailors and second class passengers – the aft being reserved exclusively for first class passengers.'[46] The ship's deck status as a space of passengers' elite leisured social practices was produced through a process of division. This segregation reinforced notions of class superiority on board through the exclusion of unwelcome elements from the passenger section of the deck. The warm climate of the regions traversed by the steamer on its journey between Suez and India meant that the deck was able to replicate exclusive bourgeois leisure spaces on land, with an awning spread to provide shade, and various pieces of furniture for passengers to lounge upon. In marked contrast, the deck passenger, denied access to the ship's internal passenger spaces, had the privilege of neither a bed in a cabin nor a seat at the dining table. As an 1844 article in the *Asiatic Journal and Monthly Miscellany* observes, for such passengers, 'the deck will be at once his *salon* and bedchamber'.[47]

An 1842 article in the *London Saturday Journal* which describes the steamship *Oriental* observes that 'half of the top-gallant forecastle is fitted up for the sheep and pigs, so that, being at the extreme end of the vessel, no disagreeable smell is perceptible by the passengers'.[48] This spatial organisation, in which everything occupied its proper place, reveals a carefully managed shipboard hierarchy which operated both spatially and at the level of representation. The steamer's human – and non-human – occupants were ordered in a spatial arrangement whose materiality was in this case compellingly corporeal. The spatial division of the steamship's deck were not merely functional, but produced identity through the production of shipboard spatial binaries. The cultural associations of this separation are articulated by Sir Syed Ahmed Khan, in the account of his 1869 voyage from Bombay to Suez on board the *Baroda*. Writing of the gratifying serenity of the canopied space of the ship's deck, Khan notes that 'half of the deck is reserved for the first class passengers. In fact, this section is the paradise of the ship. It is very pleasant and airy with a tent over it which is moved in the direction of the sun to avoid the heat ... It is worth the extra money one pays for first class.' Conversely, Khan observes, 'the remaining half of the deck is the ship's hell. It has scavengers, coolies, two kitchens, chickens, sheep, cows and pigs. Deck passengers also stay on that side.'[49] The ship's deck was a socially divided space, in which the poorer deck passengers were brought into close social proximity with both the labour practices of the ship and with the ship's living food supply. The bourgeois portion of the deck was distinguished by an order and purity of spatial character which would not have been possible without this disciplining of bodies in space. A clear tension emerges in voyage narratives between the two sets of shipboard spaces and occupants, with rules, structures and spatial practices designed to ensure that the – largely subaltern – crew members were spatially segregated from privileged passengers.

Even within the bourgeois passenger areas of the ship, forms of spatial division existed, social codes which governed exclusion and access to space. Frederick Walter Simms, travelling to Alexandria aboard the *Great Liverpool* in 1845, observed that in a discreet part of the ship's passenger accommodations there was a cabin which was 'the favourite residence of the young men passengers'. 'This place was called by the lady passengers "Bachelors' Hall",' he writes, 'but by the gentlemen, who perhaps had a shrewder guess as to what transpired in those lower regions, it was called "Crockford's".'[50] This name was an allusion to a popular private club and gambling house in the West End of London.[51] In *The Pursuit of Pleasure*, an examination of the gendered spatial practices of early nineteenth-century London, Jane Rendell has observed that 'removed from everyday life', these all-male spaces to which entry was strictly controlled 'were places of transgression'. The privacy of the men's cabin aboard the *Great Liverpool* acted as a means to conceal the gambling and dissipation of the young male passengers, transposing the spatial characteristics of an all-male private members' club into the steamer's space. Rendell elucidates that these clubs were places where 'male identity was constructed through codes of exclusion and inclusion'.[52] Spatial segregation and discipline were fundamental to the constitution of certain shipboard spaces as spheres of gendered identity.

Gender and spatial discipline

In 1849 a case was brought to England's Central Criminal Court relating to P&O's attempted sale of two newly built steamships, *Bombay* and *Vectis*, to rebels involved in the Sicilian revolution of 1848. P&O stood accused of aiding an aggressor against a sovereign friendly to the British state, an illegal act. Sir Fitzroy Kelly, QC for P&O, rested his defence of the company on the fact that although the ships were fully operational, they were not sold equipped, or 'fitted out' with weapons of warfare. In order to articulate this legal distinction Kelly deployed the familiar metaphor of the ship as a female body:

> A lady was 'fitted up' by having her ears bored, not 'fitted out' till the earrings were actually in their ornamental situation; so here the vessel was 'fitted up,' perhaps, but no guns or other munitions were aboard; so she was not 'fitted out,' in the words of the forbidding law.[53]

Within this legal metaphor lay the insinuation that the vessel's sale was justified through its characterisation as a female body, which circulated as a commodity between (male) owners. During this period, women were beginning to travel globally in larger numbers than they had previously. Anne de Courcy has particularly highlighted the increasingly prevalent practice of young single women travelling to India in order to secure husbands.[54] The apprehension concerning female mobility was to some extent managed and normalised through the assumption that it was only justifiable in terms of the female passengers' relationship to men. William Howard Russell, recalling his 1858 voyage from Marseille to Alexandria on board the *Valetta*, gives an account of the ship's various passengers. He notes that among them were a number 'of wives going to their actual husbands, and of young ladies going to find, if possible, consorts in that land where they hang like flocks of the golden fleece'.[55]

Philip Howard Colomb, a naval officer whose celebrated account of captaining a vessel tasked with suppressing slavery in the Indian ocean, opened the book with his 1868 overland route voyage from Southampton to Alexandria to take up his post. Perhaps due to his military background, and as is increasingly common among later overland route narratives, Colomb presents a distinctly jaded, cynical instance of the genre. Certainly no stranger to shipboard life, specifically the all-male, disciplined world of the naval vessel, Colomb seems keen to illustrate his blasé equanimity in the face of steamship mobilities. An incident which he relates from early in his voyage serves to elucidate the perceived status of the female passenger on the steamer. Colomb refers to the labelling of the chairs in the ship's saloon with passengers' names, a practice employed in light of the social anonymity of steamship travel:

> I opened a mild conversation with a very pretty girl off Finisterre, which ripened into a pleasant acquaintance before we got to the latitude of Lisbon, at which point I became desirous of knowing the name of my fair friend. I accordingly watched my opportunity, and duly marked her down. It was disappointing, although probably true, to learn, on the authority of a blue label at her back, that she was only 'Baggage for Calcutta'.[56]

The anonymous female passenger in Colomb's account was without identity precisely in her objectification as mere cargo. The term baggage was also used pejoratively at the time in reference to a disreputable or artful woman, perhaps an allusion by Colomb to the pursuit of husbands in India.

Feminine normativity was reinforced on board through the reproduction of land-based bourgeois social practices in the ship's space, whose internal layout contributed to the perpetuation of gendered spatial ritual. Just as unchaperoned travel on the overland route was policed through forms of social control, women's mobility within the space of the ship itself was subject to carefully managed spatial practices. The restrictions upon female mobility at the global level were reproduced in microcosm within the space of the steamship. The plans of the *Hindostan* and *Bentinck* in Figure 2.1 detail the existence of discrete female spaces on board the steamship. It is clear that the 'Ladies' Drawing Room', located on the ship's upper deck, acted both as a boundary space between the female cabins (marked O, N, M, L on the plan) and the rest of the steamer's space, and as a point through which movement between these two spaces could be mediated. Furthermore, the space marked as reserved for the stewardess contains a stairway which could be used by the servants to perform duties in the female cabins without having to pass through the ladies' drawing room. The staircase presumably leads to one of the steamer's functional spaces, as it cannot be traced onto another part of the plan. These spaces, superfluous to the bourgeois passengers, are uncharted in the visual representation they used to navigate the steamer.

The abstract spatial demarcation prescribed by the plan was instantiated in the social space of the steamer through the embodied performance of gendered spatial roles. *The Popular Overland Guide* of 1861 informs the reader of the correct spatial etiquette employed aboard the P&O vessel. It describes the ladies' private room as 'a small saloon expressly dedicated to the service of Venus, and here no member of the black-coated fraternity is permitted to enter under any circumstances whatever. Unhappy is the man who ventures into those sacred precincts! Immediate expulsion is inevitable.'[57] The guide describes the shipboard space reserved for female passengers using the trope of the male violation of a chaste interior. Gender divisions were maintained on board through spatial and social protocols. A description of the ladies' saloon aboard the *Hindostan* from the *Morning Post* of 14 September 1842 notes that the 'quiet, peaceful, sequestered nooks ... breathe a harmony and freshness admirably chosen to accord with the retired habits of ladies, and will be a great relief from the noise and bustle of other parts of the ship'.[58] In this account, the gendered spatial ordering of the steamer relies upon an understanding of the ship as a traditionally male space, in which seafaring labour practices rendered it inappropriate as a sphere of female experience. The 'separate spheres' of male and female which were central to bourgeois Victorian society dictated that a woman's place was in the domestic sphere, a private space separate from the public, masculine realm of work.[59] In order to maintain these gendered social divisions on board the steamer, a portion of its passenger accommodations were designated as feminine, domestic space.

The exclusion of female passengers from the labour space of the ship perpetuated social difference, as access to space was mediated by labour practices. *The Popular Overland Guide* of 1861 observes that during the morning ritual of deck washing 'the ladies are compelled to retire to their cabins ... and the gentlemen having the deck to themselves, walk about in the lightest possible clothing, chatting, smoking, reading and enjoying the coolest and pleasantest part of the day.'[60] The labour of shipboard hygiene became an exclusionary practice which perpetuated male spatial dominance aboard the ship. The morning stroll was taken in the company of men, while the women were denied the 'pleasantest part of the day', and confined to the ship's interior, allowed to take only an evening promenade in the presence of a male chaperone.

On the steamer, even the bourgeois female passengers' access to space was subject to discipline, in part because the hierarchies of bourgeois society and the traditional spatial practices of the ship were considered incompatible. Charles H. Allen travelled on the overland route to South Australia and Queensland in 1867 as part of a world tour. Recounting the section of his voyage from Suez to Point de Galle through the Red Sea on board the *Nubia*, he documents the common practice of sleeping on deck, owing to the extreme heat. Although this was a practice generally limited by social decorum to the male passengers, Allen notes that 'on some very hot nights ladies also slept on deck, and then a place was enclosed for them by chairs and benches'.[61] This makeshift process of enclosure, the creation of a physical barrier, marked an attempt to ensure that social and spatial norms could be maintained. This spatial segregation of the women on deck reinforced the notion of a boundary, a threshold between the genders which could not be crossed. These strict forms of spatial control exercised over women's bodies on board the steamer emphasise the extent to which shipboard spatial discipline was motivated by an ideology of purity and exclusion.

Purity, contamination, exclusion

The overland route steamship was a highly disciplined space in which social and spatial practices were maintained to prevent the intermingling of the various shipboard binaries: male and female; rich and poor; leisure and labour; West and East; white and black. Anne McClintock has highlighted the historical significance of such binaries, by which tropes of gender, race and class were acted out in Victorian Britain's cultures of imperialism. She has explored the rituals of hygiene which existed at the boundaries of these distinctions, the policing of their infractions and the maintenance of bourgeois identities. McClintock identifies in imperial mobilities a particular, spatial source of bourgeois anxiety:

> As colonials traveled back and forth across the thresholds of their known world, crisis and boundary confusion were warded off and contained by fetishes, absolution rituals and liminal scenes. Soap and cleaning rituals became central to the demarcation of body boundaries and the policing of social hierarchies.[62]

As the steamship moved through global space, passengers employed such rituals of cleansing to maintain an unambiguous sense of their identity, in the face of the imperial anxieties which threatened to destabilise them.

Albert Hervey's 1845 overland route narrative *The Ocean and the Desert* is particularly attentive to the significant departures from the culture of sail exhibited by the new steam route to India. He observes that on board the slow sailing ships which travelled around the Cape of Good Hope, options for maintaining bourgeois standards of hygiene were limited:

> If you do wish to have a bathe, you are obliged to stand at the break of the poop or gangway, to be soused by all the sailors with water, taken out of a dirty, greasy tub; as for the poor females, they have no such luck, most of them, for the whole voyage; but, in the steamer, every one who wished could enjoy a bath without any hindrance.[63]

In contrast to the makeshift improvisation of the sailing vessel, where passenger hygiene operated in the interstices of shipboard labour practices, the steamship featured dedicated spaces for the purposes of bourgeois cleansing rituals. The steamship, in its identification as a historical departure from the indiscriminate passenger arrangements of sail, a new shipboard environment, is portrayed as a modern space in which all the conveniences of bourgeois domesticity could be found.

Accounts emphasise the steamship's employment of innovative technological solutions to issues of hygiene. Sources frequently refer to the cleanliness of the steamship, drawing attention to innovations in maintaining the shipboard environment according to bourgeois standards of hygiene. This is manifested in a description of the *Oriental* from the *London Saturday Journal*, in 1842: 'The vessel is aired throughout on scientific principles: every state-room has a separate self-acting ventilating pipe; and every lower berth has two pipes to carry the air up to the cabin ceiling to be thence conveyed into the atmosphere by large ventilating pipes.'[64] The provision of clean air and water on board emphasises the use of modern technological solutions to maintain bourgeois social standards. No less than the hubristic claims regarding the steamship's speed and its overcoming of nature, modern methods of sanitation helped the passenger to identify with white, European superiority in the space of the ship.

Dutch writer and colonial servant Jacobus van der Chijs, in his account of a voyage to Alexandria on board the *Bangalore* in 1869, writes that 'in all, the tidiness and cleanliness were greater than I had ever before encountered on an ocean-going vessel; this was accompanied by exemplary order'. This attention to shipboard hygiene van der Chijs found particularly notable in the ship's toilets, which, he writes, was 'worthy of imitation': they were 'kept odourless with a jet of water'.[65] As van der Chijs suggests, hygiene and order were closely connected, emphasising the spatial construction of cleanliness. In the influential thesis proposed by Mary Douglas in *Purity and Danger*, the cultural production of the idea of dirt is a process enacted through difference, specifically as a material ordering principle. For Douglas, dirt is fundamentally 'matter out of place'.[66] This conceptualisation of that which is impure as primarily a spatial concern is useful for thinking about the way that steamship space was ordered and disciplined. This conceptualisation of dirt, Douglas insists, 'implies two conditions: a set of ordered relations and a contravention of that order. Dirt then, is never a unique, isolated event. Where there is dirt there is system.'[67] The creation of spatial order is therefore premised upon the labelling of that which is excluded as the contamination of a purity which is defined in contrast to this excluded Other. The maintenance of bourgeois norms was enacted through complex processes of inclusion and exclusion within and without the space of the steamer – processes which play into pernicious themes of contamination and hygiene; of racial and class purity.

The Popular Overland Guide of 1861 warns prospective passengers against attempting to travel by one of the second-class fares which the company made available on an informal basis. 'As the servants and second-class passengers mess together,' the guide cautions, 'and the latter are not admitted on the quarter-deck, their social status is lowered in public estimation.'[68]

The privilege of wealth was expressed through access to shipboard space and social distance from the lower orders, articulating class hierarchy through spatial practices. Responding to a shareholder at P&O's 1864 Annual General Meeting, who had suggested that the company should offer second-class fares formally and in greater numbers, chairman Arthur Anderson dismissed the suggestion. 'It would be disagreeable', he insisted, 'for the higher class of folks to be elbowed by such vulgar people.'[69] The P&O steamship was conceived of as an exclusive bourgeois social sphere in which it was essential to maintain spatial distance between social class distinctions. 'Mrs John B. Speid' was the pen name of the wife of an East Indian army officer who returned to India by the overland route after a trip to England in 1858. In her account of the journey, she comments on the status and cultural associations attached to P&O. 'It is almost a social distinction', she writes, 'to be admitted on board its gilded vessels.'[70] Although there is a note of sarcasm in Speid's observations, they illustrate the notion of the steamship as an exclusive social sphere, access to which reflected social status.

However, as a limited, discrete space, isolated at sea and filled with a diversity of human and non-human occupants, the steamer was inevitably also a space of social encounters with difference. This distinguishes the steamer as an example of what Mary Louise Pratt has described as imperial 'contact zones'. Pratt defines such zones as 'social spaces where disparate cultures meet, clash, and grapple with each other, often in highly asymmetrical relations of domination and subordination'.[71] Understanding the colonial steamship as an example of such a space clarifies the processes of spatial conflict and control documented in voyage narratives. The steamship was an imperial social sphere in which the diverse groups who peopled its various spaces co-produced their respective identities through the ship's social hierarchies.

As part of her round-the-world voyage, the Austrian travel writer Ida Pfeiffer travelled on board three P&O steamers in 1847. Aboard the *Pekin*, *Braganza* and the *Bentinck*, she travelled from Hong Kong to Calcutta, changing vessels at Singapore and Point de Galle. Exposing a German-speaking public to the world of exotic travel which accompanied imperial expansion, Pfeiffer's work was also translated into English, so wide was its appeal. Although her publications were successful and widely read, and she was from a wealthy background, Pfeiffer tended to travel as cheaply as possible. As one of the few accounts of P&O steamship travel narrated not only by a woman, but also a non-English writer, and the only account by a passenger from this period to travel second-class, Pfeiffer's book offers a unique perspective on the voyage, and particularly on the shipboard rituals which produced the vessel's spatial differentiation. Pfeiffer's travel accounts are often highly critical of European colonialism, and the steamship was just one among many examples of a British imperial space for her at times scathing commentary. As someone who was well-accustomed to travelling on a limited budget, she was struck less by the low standards she encountered on board, and more by the hypocrisy and parsimony of bourgeois privilege.

Acutely sensitive to the demarcations of shipboard space, Pfeiffer's account provides numerous accounts of a shipboard spatial discipline which was governed by hierarchies of gender, class and race. Upon boarding the *Pekin* at Hong Kong, she writes, 'I inquired for the sleeping cabin, and found there was but one for both sexes.'[72] The shipboard spatial discipline which maintained the separate spheres of gender was one apparently reserved only for bourgeois passengers. Access to the exclusive social spaces of the ship was governed not just by the price paid for the passage, but also by rules of social decorum. One of the passengers lodging in the second-class cabin of the *Braganza*, Pfeiffer writes, 'had been removed from the first cabin, because it was asserted that he was somewhat cracked, and did not always know what he said or did'.[73] This passenger's apparent lack of control over his behaviour meant that he was considered unable to sustain bourgeois social norms, and thus was excluded from the space of the privileged passengers. Such instances can be seen as manifestations of the maintenance of the purity of bourgeois identity on board through practices of exclusion. More than any other binary, however, racial difference was at the heart of the social hierarchies which governed access to shipboard space. Pfeiffer relates an incident which occurred on board the *Bentinck* shortly after the ship had called at Madras:

> A native woman came on board with her two children. She had paid second-class fare, and was shown a small dark berth not far from the first cabin place. Her younger child had, unfortunately, a bad cough, which prevented some rich English lady, who had likewise a child with her, from sleeping … The first thing she did on the following morning, was to beg that the captain would transfer mother and children to the deck, which the noble-hearted humane captain immediately did.[74]

The ideology of contamination, of the purity of shipboard racial and class-based spatial segregation was produced in part through social processes of mediation. Social power could be exercised as control over access to shipboard space, maintaining standards of bourgeois domesticity which were troubled by the Other. This is particularly evident in the spatial treatment of deck passengers, who were distinguished from the privileged cabin passengers not only through their segregation on a separate part of the deck but by their spatial association with undesirable elements; just as they were forced into proximity with the dirt and smells of the ship's animal population, the deck passengers also occupied the space of labour, from which the bourgeois passengers were manifestly set apart. The social difference of this shipboard Other was produced and preserved through processes which were enacted through the ship's spatial politics.

The systems of spatial discipline which maintained the clarity of social order on board could be violently reasserted if transgressed. The American journalist Bayard Taylor published an account documenting a trip to India, China and Japan in 1853. Like other American authors of overland route narratives, Taylor was sensitive to the racial cruelties which he witnessed both on board the ship and in the imperial world, a sensitivity which is distinctly lacking in most British accounts. Recounting his voyage from Suez to India on board the steamer *Achilles*, Taylor describes an incident which occurred shortly after the ship's departure from Aden. He relates the story of 'a luckless native, who had fallen asleep in one of the boats and was not observed until we were under way. He was immediately thrown overboard in spite of his entreaties, and left to take his chance of reaching the shore, which was half a mile distant.'[75] Bodies which were 'out of place' on board the steamer could simply be removed, if their racial identity meant that they were afforded little value.

The extent to which the maintenance of shipboard spatial order was implicated in an ideology of racial contamination is elucidated in an account by William Makepeace Thackeray, documenting his 1844 voyage from Constantinople to Alexandria aboard the *Iberia*, a very small steamer used on the company's branch lines. Thackeray describes at length what he considered to be the lack of hygiene among the largely Jewish passengers who lived and slept on the steamer's deck during the voyage.[76] He later writes of the steamer, after its departure from Jaffa (in present-day Israel), that 'in our absence in Syria it had been carefully cleansed and purified … it was cleared of the swarming Jews who had infested the decks all the way from Constantinople'.[77] Thackeray's observations reflect Victorian anxieties about race and class which found expression through their association with contamination from dirt and disease. That which was other to a white, Western, bourgeois, male, leisured identity was perceived as contamination on board the steamer, and subject to rituals of exclusion and purification, both literally, and through the kind of discursive methods employed by Thackeray. The discipline of the steamer was a mode of imposing order upon a space whose identity was remade through its relationship with the racial Other.

The steamship as an imperial space

At the P&O Annual General Meeting of 1863, concerns were raised regarding competition from foreign steamship lines for the company's government mail contracts. One of the company's shareholders, a Mr Jones, was emphatic that the contracts should remain in the company's hands. 'The highways between England and her foreign possessions', he announced, 'should be English ground'.[78] In this context, the ship itself was conceptualised as the extension of British territory into global space – a mobile fragment of terrestrial space. As a space which was neither metropole nor periphery, but which acted as a link between the two, the steamship destabilised the neat binary conceptualisation of imperial space. However, while the steamship's mobility appears to challenge the fixity and stability of territorial space with the dynamic, the fluid, the ship as an environment enacted the reassertion in miniature of the fixity, and boundedness of terrestrial space. Jones's characterisation fits well with the nineteenth-century legal conventions which defined the status of the ship with regard to national jurisdiction. The sea, fluid, non-national, the antithesis to land space, posed something of a challenge to land-based legal structures: 'The open sea, except so far as it is commanded from the land, is exterritorial. It is the domain of no State, and is merely a highway, along which the ships of all nations are entitled to pass.' Yet while the sea was outside of the law of the land, the space of the ship itself reasserted the logic of territoriality: 'The ground of this rule is commonly expressed, for the sake of brevity, in the form of a legal fiction; namely, by saying that a ship is a movable part of the territory of the State whose national flag it bears.'[79] Modern legal structures, in comprehending the sea as a transnational space beyond the sovereign territory of the state, demanded that sovereignty be reasserted in the 'floating structure' of the ship.

Yet, more significant for our understanding of the steamship's characterisation as an extension of British territory are the convolutions of identity and representation that mediated the experience of shipboard space. As we have seen, the steamship was the site of the cultural reproduction of various familiar land-based spaces, produced through the spatial and imaginative practices of its occupants. In many ways, these characterisations of the ship provided passengers with a reassuring sense of normality in the midst of a mobility which could be highly disruptive of their sense of identity and their relation to the metropole. The extent to which the steamer was seen as a Western space is articulated in Norman Macleod's account of his disembarkation from the steamship *Valetta* at Alexandria in 1864: 'As soon as I landed, I realised at once the presence of a totally different world of human beings from any I had seen before. The charm and fascination consisted in the total difference in every respect between East and West.'[80] Macleod's claims of his shocked reaction at the steamer's arrival in Egypt conveys the extent to which the ship operated for him as an extension of British space – the act of disembarkation presented a performative moment of stepping from

West to East. Macleod describes 'the utter chaos, and dilapidation, and confusion ... amid the cries and noise of the mixed multitude who crowded the wharves'.[81] If the steamship was a well-ordered – Western – space in which bodies and objects occupied their proper place, the docks at Alexandria provided a marked material departure from this spatial logic. The steamship, in replicating familiar land-based spaces, exaggerated for Macleod the alterity of the East, mediating his experience of national difference.

The British army officer and colonial administrator William Tyrone Power returned from New Zealand to England via the overland route in 1847. The characterisation of the steamer as the antithesis of Eastern space is again articulated by Power, travelling in the opposite direction to Macleod, from India to Europe. 'From the moment one leaves the harbour of Alexandria,' he observes, 'the homeward voyage is divested of all its Orientalism.' Power attributed this change particularly to the nationality of the ship's labour force. In the Mediterranean steamer, he writes, 'English tars take the place of Lascars.'[82] If the steamer he had travelled aboard on the eastern side of the Isthmus of Suez had been 'oriental', Power presumably considered it so because of its subaltern crew. William Delafield Arnold, in his 1856 account of an overland journey to the East, again describes the impact on passengers of the experience of disembarking at Alexandria:

> They have marked the wonderful contrast by which they passed in five minutes from the Peninsular and Oriental Steamer with its English crew, its English stewards, its English system, its English four meals a day, to streets down which was pouring the high tide of Oriental life, marked by Oriental complexion, manners and language.

Again, the steamship is characterised as a replication of the social life of the metropole, and again this serves to emphasise the difference between West and East. However, Arnold continues, upon boarding the steamship on the other side of Egypt, passengers were struck by the Eastern character of the vessel: 'in the punkahs – in the native servants, in the Lascar crew, in the iced water, in the hot curries, they receive a foretaste of their coming life'.[83]

If the P&O steamship in the Mediterranean could be characterised as an extension of British territory, the vessel which was used to implement the Eastern portion of the journey was considered to replicate the social character of India. However, these accounts make it clear that this was very much a British imperial India, the India of white supremacy and bourgeois affluence. This was, in part, a logistical concern, as it was easier for the company to maintain crews made up of subaltern workers on the Eastern side of the route, where the ships had no contact with Western ports. George Buist, editor of the *Bombay Times*, returned to India by the overland route in 1845. His account provides a vivid description of the character of the transition to the ship on the Eastern side of the route: 'The traveller towards the East, who has been dragging by each remove a lengthening chain – who has found semi-tropical Europe at Gibraltar and Malta, and fairly tasted of the Orient in Egypt – at length finds a floating fragment of India before him at Suez.'[84] The process of the voyage is described by Buist as a series of geographical disjunctures, as the passenger's experience of nearing the East was mediated by the terrestrial locations at which the ship called. Upon boarding the steamship which served the Eastern side of the route however, its replication of British Indian life is seen to anticipate the passenger's arrival in the East itself. The steamship as a space was seen to narrate the journey between metropole and periphery. Such a sentiment is again expressed by the British journalist Sidney Laman Blanchard in 1863 in an article describing his voyage on board the *Nemesis* from Suez to India. 'It is not until we get once more on ship-board, in the Red Sea,' he writes, 'that we feel ourselves really in the East.'[85] Blanchard suggests that the steamship was possessed of a more idiosyncratically 'Eastern' character than the space of Egypt which the overland route travellers had traversed. However, this was very much a British East, reproducing the logic of imperial hierarchy and control.

The extent to which life aboard the steamship was seen to reproduce the social relations of colonial India is clarified by Norman Macleod, recounting his voyage down the Red Sea from Suez to Bombay aboard the *Rangoon* in 1867. While he had described his 1864 disembarkation at Alexandria as a sudden departure from the Western space of the steamer, Macleod encountered a distinctively imperial social milieu on board the *Rangoon*. He notes 'the strange way in which, as I afterwards found, the Indian society in the steamer represented India [*sic*] society in general'.[86] For Macleod, the steamship again seemed to anticipate the passenger's arrival in the East. Yet the India he refers to was one encapsulated the bourgeois sociality of white imperialists, a colonised, hierarchical India, and one that not all passengers saw as a desirable shipboard environment. This tension is present in George Francis Train's account of his voyage from Madras to Suez aboard the *Nubia* in 1856. An American, Train shares the perspective of the outsider which other non-British passengers manifest. He expresses his consternation at the formality he encountered in the social manners of the British colonial passengers he shared the voyage with. 'You must take passage in the P. and O. to get a taste of official life in Calcutta', he observes. For Train the ship reproduced the rigid social relations of imperial India. 'Most of them are servants of the Company, from the highest to the lowest, each vain of his position', he remarks of the East India Company employees who made up the occupants of the steamer, where, he continues 'you are frozen with the dignity of office'.[87] The social hierarchies of the British colonial administration were deep-rooted, and were reproduced at a microcosmic scale in the space of the steamer. This was a hierarchy which, Train lamented, seemed to prize wealth more than anything else. 'Education or refinement', he writes, 'seems to have little to do with the barriers of society – money – salaries – pay – is what is most thought of.'[88]

The steamer's identity as an imperial space, already hinted at in the accounts which have detailed the movements and exclusions of bodies whose identity fell outside a narrow criterion of white, Western normativity, was seen as an expression of the cosmopolitan character of the ship's occupants. The journalist William Howard Russell's book documenting his trip to India in 1858 to report on the aftermath of the rebellion proved popular with a public eager for information regarding an imperial world which had featured so prominently and traumatically in the British press. Providing a detailed account of the social life of colonial India, Russell opened the book with an extensive narrative of his overland route voyage. This did not merely document the means by which British soldiers were able to rapidly travel to India to reassert control there, and with whom Russell shared the journey. The overland route steamship formed for Russell a significant extension of the imperial world he was eager to document. Russell's book provides a somewhat jaded, humorous, yet highly incisive account of the steamship as a social space, and not one without a certain critical awareness of the contradictions of the British imperial project. Despite the outrage with which the Rebellion's violence had provoked, Russell was sensitive to the shortcomings of British rule – his account is at times intensely critical of British imperialism, although at others it tends to reproduce its dominant rhetorics.

Recounting his 1858 voyage from Marseille to Alexandria on board the *Valetta*, Russell employs the familiar trope of the ship as a world in miniature. 'The little steamer', he writes, 'was a turbulent microcosm'.[89] For Russell, the geographically heterogeneous character of the various destinations of the steamship's occupants meant that it appeared to reproduce the wider world. Russell's identification of the global character of shipboard social relations was rooted in the European imperial project:

> To trace the destinations of our fellow-passengers from Malta would be to cover the East with a wide-spreading fan. There were men for Australia, for China, the dominions of the Rajah of Sarawak, for Penang, Singapore, Hong Kong, Java, Lahore, Aden, Bombay, Calcutta, Ceylon, Pondicherry, and many unknown places beyond the seas.[90]

Russell's image of a fan unfurled over the colonised geography of the East presents a distinctly topographical rendering of the nineteenth-century imperial world. It narrates the European production of global space specifically as imperial space. That this geographical depiction spread out from the mobile individuals who shared the space of the ship is significant in comprehending Russell's designation of the steamer as a microcosm. Steamship passengers saw themselves as part of a far-reaching imperial network which was embodied in their persons. As Russell suggests, the overland route steamship did not merely reproduce metropole or periphery, but one was a space in which diasporic, hybrid identities were formed. Furthermore, it was not simply a reflection of the social worlds of empire, but rather presented a distinctive environment in which new social arrangements were played out – and none more fractious than those which concerned the ship's subaltern labour force.

Subaltern labour in shipboard space

The steamer was a community with an ever-shifting, nomadic population. If the destinations of the steamer's – predominantly white – passengers hinted at the geographies of European imperialism, the steamship's labour practices created a shipboard community with a racially heterogeneous population. For many passengers, the steamer's subaltern labour force was at the heart of their characterisation of the ship as an imperial space. Bayard Taylor describes the diversity of the crew of the *Achilles* in his account of a voyage from Suez to Bombay in 1852. 'The stewards were mostly Hindoos,' he writes, 'the sailors the same, the cooks two Portuguese and a Chinaman, and the firemen ... negroes from Mozambique.' For Taylor, this range of racial backgrounds exhibited by the crew contributed to his identification of the ship as an Eastern space:

> Amid such a motley gathering of character and nationalities there was no lack of diversion. For myself, when I drank Bombay water, ate real curry, hailed the waiter as 'khitmudgar!' and was addressed by him as 'sahib!' I felt that I was already in India.[91]

Indeed, this description evokes an environment far from the everyday social and cultural norms of the West. As an American, Taylor was more critical of British imperialism in India than most authors of the time. Particularly, his account possesses an attention to subaltern shipboard labour which is notably absent from those by British passengers. Indeed, very few British accounts contain anything other than passing references to the crew members – most of the detailed descriptions of the steamship's racialised labour forms which this section draws upon are from American and Dutch passengers. However, the Indian world which Taylor claims to have encountered on board was defined as specifically a British, colonial one. This imperial hierarchy was articulated through the performative interactions of passenger and crew, particularly through the language employed: 'khitmudgar' (khitmatgar, a male servant with the responsibility of waiting at table) on the one hand identifying the named as a figure of servility and 'sahib' on the other, one who was due respect, the master.

Another American, the prominent merchant and shipper Robert Bowne Minturn, travelled from Bombay to Suez on the *Ganges* in 1857. He also noted the ethnically diverse population of the vessel's labour force:

> The crew were Lascars, except the secunnies, or steersmen, who were from Manilla. The duty of steering the ship was shared by the Chinese crew of the captain's gig. The servants were Parsees or Moosulmans, and the stokers were stalwart negroes from the African coast.[92]

The steamer is presented as a space in which the delineation of ethnic 'types' could be performed. The division of labour roles on board was organised along racial lines, naturalising the various roles and hierarchies on board. This is elaborated in a drawing, reproduced in Figure 2.4, by the Dutch traveller Jacob van Heerdt, featuring two members of the *Hindostan*'s crew, a stoker and a figure he refers to as a 'sweeper'.[93] These subaltern labourers

2.4 Jacob Carel Frederik van Heerdt, 'Vuurstoker aan boord van de Hindostan (Laskar)' and 'De veeger aan boord van de Hindostan (Klinger)' (*Mijne Reis met de Landmail van Batavia over Singapore, Ceilon, Aden en Suiz tot Alexandrië in Egypte,* 1851)

are represented as racial types, exemplified by the work they performed on board, which is conveyed by the tools of their trade, a shovel and a brush. They are not unsympathetic portraits – there is a certain pensive dignity about the figures depicted, and certainly this representation affords the workers a greater sense of identity than written sources tend to ascribe to the subaltern maritime workforce. Yet, just as the landscape sketched at the right of the ship, with its wispy palm trees and dhow-like sailing vessel, functions as a stand-in for a generic 'Eastern' scene, these workers are intended to stand in for specific shipboard 'types'. Minturn, concluding his account of the *Ganges*' crew, observes that 'this great variety of nationalities gave the quarter-deck a very picturesque appearance'.[94] Through this aestheticisation of the subaltern crew's diversity, the shipboard labour activities which took place within view of the bourgeois leisure space of the deck could be encountered by passengers as a pleasing ethnographic spectacle.

Persistently, the racial diversity of the crew, a social relation which was produced by the conditions of European imperialism, was experienced by the steamer's passengers as a superficial surface display. This is made explicit in an observation made by the Austrian Ida Pfeiffer, recalling her journey from Singapore to Point de Galle on board the *Braganza* in 1847. Pfeiffer furnished a description of the scenery she viewed during the ship's passage through the Straits of Malacca, the narrow stretch of water between the Malay Peninsula and the Indonesian island of Sumatra. She was, however, unimpressed by the view. 'If the scenery around us was not remarkable,' she writes, 'the spectacle on board the vessel itself was highly interesting. The crew was composed of seventy-nine persons, comprising Chinese, Malays, Cingalese [*sic*], Bengalese, Hindostanese, and Europeans.'[95] For Pfeiffer, the racially diverse population of the steamer's crew provided a spectacle more stimulating than the Eastern landscape. Not all of the subaltern crew appealed to Pfeiffer's aesthetic sensibilities, however. She complained that her appetite was ruined by the appearance of one of the crew members who waited on the second-class table, 'a mulatto servant … afflicted with elephantiasis'.[96] Generally, though, Pfeiffer was sensitive to the violence of the shipboard racial hierarchies she encountered. Her account laments that 'the manner in which all these poor coloured people were treated was certainly not in accordance with Christian principles. No one ever addressed them but in the roughest manner, and they were kicked and cuffed about on every occasion.'[97]

The anonymous account of an 1853 overland route voyage to China published in the *Southern Literary Messenger* catered for an American audience less familiar with the imperial world made increasingly accessible by the steamship. Travelling on board the *Haddington* from Suez to Point de Galle, like other American passengers, the piece's author exhibits a keener interested in the culture of British imperialism than the preoccupation with the wonders of steam common to so many other accounts. Again, the article is possessed of an ethnographic interest in the ship's racially diverse crew. It notes the Indian sailors, 'degenerate beings [who] reminded me not a little of the scenes of savage life'. Despite conforming to hierarchical conceptions of race, like Pfeiffer the account condemns the physical and verbal abuse these crew members were subjected to: 'I regretted to see some of the minor officers of the vessel exercising a petty despotism over these poor and despised creatures, losing no opportunity to bestow upon them a volley of abusive epithets, delivered in no very choice Hindostanee, at other times kicking and cuffing them.'[98] There is a marked ambivalence in many of these accounts to the racialised power relations they encountered on board. The violence this author witnessed didn't fit into a benevolent vision of empire in which while the native was inferior, even primitive, they were the beneficiary of the Christian kindness of a more enlightened race.

The steamship's purported reproduction of the imperial East which numerous accounts have attested to was not limited to its conglomeration of diverse racial groups – as these sources illustrate, the everyday violence of empire was normalised on board the ship. Furthermore, the overland route steamship can be understood as a mobile imperial space in which the colonial sensibilities and moral codes of the passenger were developed. As Douglas Burgess has suggested, for a great deal of Western imperial actors, the overland route was a significant formative experience:

> It conditioned them to the mores, rituals, and even language of the world they would soon inhabit and reinforced their conviction in the rightness of their task. They were not the same people who embarked in England. In a few short weeks, it made them imperials.[99]

The overland route journey can be seen as a process of normalisation, acclimatising imperial actors not just to the cruelty of racial social relations, but also to the social codes and behaviours of the British Empire more generally. An anonymous author recounts his 1861 overland voyage from Southampton to Shanghai, in an account published in *The National Magazine* the following year. The journey's progression is narrated as a series of letters sent from points along the route, and thus exhibits a processual character. In the letter from 6 November 1861, the author bemoans the violence of the ship's white officers toward the subaltern crew, protesting that they 'knock the natives about shamefully'. However, in the following letter, from 20 November, he writes: 'I was too compassionate for the natives when I last wrote; they are the laziest and filthiest people I ever saw.'[100] This passenger's account confirms the significance of imperial mobilities as a formative process, mediated by the embodied shipboard performance of racial hierarchies. The constitution of imperial identity and subjectivity could take place in the process of global mobility.

A notable example of the way in which the social world of the overland route steamship provided an environment for the promulgation of imperial imaginative geographies and social relations is exhibited in the story of the eminent orientalist Richard Burton's journey from Southampton to Alexandria on board the *Bengal* in 1853. Burton infamously disguised himself as an Arab pilgrim in order to covertly perform the Islamic Hajj, recorded in his celebrated book *A Personal Narrative of a Pilgrimage to Al-Medinah and Meccah*. This imperial masquerade was in fact staged first of all aboard the P&O steamship.[101] Burton donned his disguise at the outset of the voyage, and remained in 'character' throughout its duration, the *Bengal* affording him a space in which he was able to rehearse the performance of his orientalist façade. While Burton provides an extreme example, the overland route steamship provided passengers with a space in which to rehearse their engagement with the Eastern world, and their place in it. As has been explored in Chapter 1, the regularised, predictable circuits of global communication facilitated by the steamship allowed for the conception of Victorian imperial space as an integrated totality, in which the metropole was imaginatively linked to the peripheral space of empire by a bureaucratic logistical system. This integration had a significant impact on imperial social relations, and the space of the steamship itself was no exception – for many passengers the steamship appeared to reproduce the social relations of empire at the microcosmic level.

'I have called the steamer a world of planks, and not unjustly so', writes the Dutch missionary and scholar of Javanese culture Jan Brumund, in the account of his 1858 voyage from Point de Galle to Suez, also on board the *Bengal*. For Brumund, like many other passengers, the small world of the steamer mirrored the wider world precisely in the diversity of racial groups which populated its space. Brumund's is a highly curious, detailed and insightful account of life in transit, attentive to the social relations, to the quality of shipboard experience, to the steamship as a distinctive environment – above all, he is acutely sensitive to the hierarchy and demarcations of steamship space. His perspective is very much that of an outsider, exploring a British imperial space which was ordered along different lines from the Dutch colonial world he was familiar with. As with other Dutch passengers, Brumund's account is full of enthusiasm and admiration for steamship mobilities, yet betrays an ambivalence towards Britain and the British Empire. Although Brumund's account bears the hallmarks of the ideological racism of his day, like other non-British passengers he is attentive to race and difference. If

British capitalism had achieved a technological supremacy, for Brumund, the social and cultural world of imperialism's global infrastructure was in many ways found lacking.

Brumund continues his ethnographic description of the microcosm of the steamer, emphasising that this was a world governed by spatial demarcations on racial lines:

> A well-known writer, strange as it may sound, it is quite true, has made his overland mail journey especially and fruitfully subservient to geological investigations. If another would then perhaps devote his time to anthropological and linguistic studies, I can assure him of an even richer and at the same time easier harvest. On the Bengal are Chinese, Africans, Arabs, and individuals of various Indian peoples, together with those of Europe. What different worlds, that which is behind – and that before the companion hatch! – Here civilised Europe with its habits, manners and languages; there, the not yet, or only half-civilised world represented by about two hundred people. Just a few steps, and from the middle of Europe you have entered into the heart of Asia and Africa; a diversity of peoples with a greater confusion of language than that at Babel.[102]

Brumund's striking narrative emphasises the extent to which spatial and material shipboard practices were mediated by representation and the imagination. In reiterating the idea of the steamer as microcosm, a globe in miniature, Brumund emphasises the division and difference which emerged around Western and non-Western shipboard ethnicities, expressed specifically in spatial terms.

In Brumund's evocative account, during the ship's journey through global space the passenger could re-enact in miniature the movement from metropole to periphery, in a walk across the ship's deck which took only moments to perform; the steamship's compression of global space was accomplished not merely in its mobility, but in a performative journey through the space of the ship itself. The two strictly delineated 'worlds' of the ship, segregated through spatial discipline, were also seen to occupy different stages of historical development, as the teleology of Western civilisation served to underscore the perceived retrograde nature of the non-Western world. In transit, the passenger's modernity could be conveniently posited against an Other, yet one constructed by the hierarchies and discipline of shipboard social relations. The identity of steamship space was produced in opposition to what Tim Mitchell has termed, in the context of the colonial city, its 'constitutive outside'. 'In order to determine itself as the place of order, reason, propriety, cleanliness, civilisation and power,' he writes, the city 'must represent outside itself what is irrational, disordered, dirty, libidinous, barbarian and cowed'.[103] As has already been explored, steamship space was constituted through the production of a series of such binaries, within the space of the ship itself.

The disciplining of shipboard space allowed this Other to be encountered in a specific way, emphasising their difference, their inferiority, their belonging but not belonging to the world of the ship, their location outside of the modern. The deck's spatial separation can thus be seen as an articulation in microcosm of the spatial politics of imperialism – an imperial world view which reproduced the imaginative relationship between metropole and periphery in the ship itself. Yet the steamship-as-microcosm was not merely a reproduction of imperial spaces and hierarchies, but presented a unique environment whose racialised organisation of bodies in space has much to tell us about the imperial project.

Brumund's description goes on to articulate the racial exploitation at the heart of the imperial world he encountered on the ship. 'Africa's soot-black sons', he observes, 'particularly attract our attention'.[104] Brumund's racial typology represents the subaltern worker's body through an association with the coal that formed the object of their labour, and the source of the steamer's mobility. What follows is one of only a few descriptions of the new labour practices which underpin the steamship's mobility:

> They share with a few Bangladeshis the stoking work there in the depths, where through the iron latticework three floors below deck, they pitch coal into the open ovens, burning with rage and the fires of hell. Three iron ladders lead from this Tartarus to the world above. A few stokers climb up from there. They look as if they have come from a bath. What man will not tolerate to earn a piece of bread or a bowl of rice. It seems to me their fate is worse than that of a slave.[105]

Again the steamer's space is delineated as distinct and separate 'zones', with roles and occupants attached to specific spaces. In attempting to portray the social relations of the most modern forms of industrial maritime labour practices, this description reaches back into the archaic, the mythic, articulating the hellish reality which sustained imperial mobilities at sea. Brumund depicts the obscure world below the steamship's deck as Tartarus, the deep abyss in Greek mythology far beneath Hades where Sisyphus performed a labour whose repetition, suffering and perpetuity was echoed by modern work conditions.

The labour of the subaltern industrial seaman was repeatedly represented by passengers using this discursive trope, echoing the belief in the steamship's diabolical agency attributed to Eastern observers. This was, however, a widespread discursive response to the industrial, perhaps most famously expressed in Blake's oft-quoted reference to 'dark satanic mills'.[106] There is a sense that passenger references to this trope pinpoint a deeply problematic aspect of the – imperial – modern they encountered on the steamship. Brumund's unfavourable comparison of shipboard labour to slavery exhibits an unease with the labour conditions of British imperial modernity. As the Netherlands' exposure to industrialisation came considerably later than in Britain, such conditions would have been relatively unfamiliar to the Dutch. However, rather than recognising this exploitation as internal to the logic of modernity, sources ascribe to it a mythic ancientness. The subaltern labour of the stokers is not defined as even pre-modern, but rather mythological – external to the modern both spatially and temporally.

The stoker's labour took place in a part of the ship far below the passenger space. This spatial arrangement limited passenger exposure to these conditions, and indeed allowed for the fantasies regarding the ship's illusory autonomy – seen in Chapter 1 – free reign. As that chapter explored, the transition from sail to steam meant that new kinds of maritime labour conditions emerged; new ways of arranging labourers on ship socially and spatially. On the overland route steamer, this was accompanied by a shift from an often predominantly white sailing crew to a multi-ethnic labour force working in factory-like conditions, for lower pay than their white counterparts.[107] In these labour conditions, the imperial and the industrial met, recodifying imperial hierarchies. It is this uneasy juxtaposition that these accounts are responses to.

In its reconfiguring of shipboard labour, steam was responsible for new conditions of racialised exploitation – new spatial, representational, embodied power relations. For the passengers, and for those who read their accounts, the mobile space travelling between metropole and periphery presented a sphere of experience which itself manifested a re-shaping of imperial and British social relations. Alfred Barton, a doctor in the company's service travelling aboard the *Erin* from Aden to Suez in 1855 describes xhis exposure to the steamer's labour conditions in a diary entry. 'Down they dive to their infernal cavern', he writes, again mobilising the diabolical as a mode of representing the concealed space of the ship's engine rooms. 'Nothing is heard but the shovel, the intense vibration of machinery, the blowing off of superabundant steam.'[108] In contrast to the sailing vessel, where the labour of mobility was everywhere evident, here there were only the abstract signs of labour, the noises, sensations and sights of new industrial forms of technology giving expression to concealed labour practices.

There is a politics of visibility at play in these descriptions: the invisibility of these labour practices was not merely spatial and material, outside the sphere of passenger experience, but also discursive and subjective. It is worth noting that, of the four descriptions of the labour conditions of the stoker cited here, not one is from an English language account published during the period of the overland route.[109] The many accounts of overland route travel by British passengers would thus appear to exhibit an impressive dedication to not noticing race. Figure 2.5 provides a rare representation

STOKEHOLE OF A STEAM-SHIP ON THE RED SEA.   BRIDGE OF A STEAM-SHIP ON THE RED SEA.

2.5 'Stokehole of a Steam-ship on the Red Sea' and 'Bridge of a Steam-ship on the Red Sea' (*Illustrated London News*, 9 November 1872)

of a stoker from this period. It juxtaposes two shipboard labour spaces unique to the steamer – the stokehole and the bridge. The two images set up an instructive series of binaries regarding the new labour practices of steam, and their spatial configurations: one white, one black; one concerned with the logic of sight, the other with that of disappearance; one largely intellectual, the other brutally corporeal. Occupying the space of the same ship, these two visions are worlds apart. The technology of steam itself contributed to shipboard spatial demarcations, which exaggerated and normalised racial difference. The 1872 *Illustrated London News* article which these images are taken from, 'The Voyage to China', provides a compellingly corporeal account of the stoker's labour conditions:

> The poor wretches who are doomed to this work ... when it is so hot as it often is in the Red Sea, have to be carried up in a fainting condition, and are restored to animation by dashing buckets of water over them as they lie on deck.[110]

The labour conditions which produced the imperial steamship's mobility consumed and destroyed the body of the subaltern worker. Despite the relative scarcity of references to shipboard labour, and the proximity and distance, concealment and visibility produced by steam's spatial configurations, such accounts suggest that passengers were often well aware that the steamship's mobility was predicated upon exploitation, and able to recognise its deeply racialised nature. They exhibit at times a palpable unease with the conditions of modern mobility's production.

This hardship is again articulated by Arthur Lloyd Clay, a member of the Indian civil service who, in a diary entry of his time in the East, describes his outward voyage in the heat of the Red Sea aboard the *Nubia* in 1862. Clay observes that

> the stokers are 'Seedee boys,' full blooded African negroes, who can endure heat better than most people. But even these have to be relieved at intervals, and seeing them come on deck, their half-naked bodies dripping with perspiration, one can realise what an inferno it must be below.[111]

Steamship labour conditions were inscribed upon the subaltern body, a key site at which imperial power was exerted and codified – the crew's bodies appear to have exerted a kind of fascination for these passengers, concerned with their disappearance and visibility. This was a body which emerged from the hidden internal space of the ship's boiler rooms, articulating the barbaric extremes of imperialist social relations, only to disappear once again. Implicated in the representability of the new labour practices of steam, this moment of visibility emphasises that the extensive disciplining of shipboard space explored in this chapter was, in part concerned with the very possibility of such a representation. While the overland route steamship united a racially diverse group of people in shipboard space, its space was also marked by the production of social distance.

Inevitably, overland route travellers, and the readers of their accounts, were frequently exposed to a range of labour forms, both on and off the ship. They would have been particularly aware of the servitude which allowed them to sustain many of the trappings of the bourgeois lifestyle even in transit. However, the specific labour of the production of mobility moved with steam away from a position of prominence, to one of concealment. Unsurprisingly there is not a single account of this labour itself, or of the interior of the boiler room. There was little to connect the sweating bodies on deck with the ship's movement through space. For the passengers, these workers were pre-modern curios, who had little to do with modern mobility. However, these workers' mobility, the unrecorded biographies of their diasporic existences, which could only be traced upon their bodies, plying between Africa, Arabia, India, the Far East, speaks of the very networked nature of British imperialism at this time. Paying attention to the logistics of mobility foregrounds such imperial actors, centring in the narrative of imperialism figures who are often play a peripheral role in this history.

Passenger accounts of steamship space reflect what Marian Aguiar, writing about the Indian railway, has referred to as 'the contradiction embedded in mobility – namely that the vehicle that expresses freedom through movement also rigidifies what might otherwise be fluid'.[112] Simultaneously as it performed the breaking down of spatial barriers, producing the dynamism of global mobility, the steamer was itself experienced as an environment characterised by spatial fixity, as forms of ordering and discipline delineated the space of the steamer, naturalising racial difference and exploitation. As Gopalan Balachandran has written, 'in the era of steam, political, racial, and cultural barriers to some extent replaced barriers falling to technology or human ingenuity'.[113] Balachandran draws attention to the inequalities between the passengers of steamships and their crew, which are at the heart of maritime mobility, and the ways in which this disparity came to be expressed materially. Global mobilities were met with microcosmic immobilities in the small world of the steamship. The figurative annihilation of space and time was facilitated through labour practices which literally annihilated the subaltern bodies that made that mobility possible. This violence exhibited by modern labour practices on the steamer was merely the most explicit iteration of the imperial violence which underpinned the disciplining of subaltern bodies on board.

Not only was the steamer implicated in the reconfiguration of global space and time, but the age of steam bore witness to the reconstitution of shipboard space – a space whose modernity was deeply tied up with the materiality and geographical imaginaries of imperialism. The steamship was a spatial environment which structured and regulated the behaviour of the people who occupied its space. The diversity of spatial functions and imaginative practices in its space gave rise to associated forms of behaviour, to modes of perceiving and experiencing the ship as an environment. While the steamship presented for many passengers the re-creation of Western elite spaces, during its passage a temporary community came into being which embodied the contradictions at the heart of the imperial project. If the plan of the steamer could be taken as an idealised representation of the passengers' engagements with shipboard space, the various spaces of the ship which are absent from this representation could be said to recreate in visual form the gaps in the passengers' knowledge of the ship's other 'spaces', particularly those in which shipboard labour took place. The plan can thus be seen as a chart of an imperial space in which the imperial Other is not documented.

The overland route can be seen as a significant formative environment experience for the imperial subject. It constructed new configurations of the social, organised around labour, class, gender and race. Not only were passengers exposed to this imperial world in miniature, but given the ubiquity of the narratives which describe its distinctive spatial manifestations, it exposed readers in the metropole to an emergent literary culture organised around the model of the steamship as an idealised imperial space. In its very mobility (and placeless-ness), the steamship destabilised the binary between metropole and periphery. Yet this binary was reasserted through social practices in the space of the ship itself. Steamship space was distinguished not only by practical changes, but was invested by passengers with the practices and associations of other – specifically modern – spaces from beyond the ship. These projections helped passengers to engage positively with their mobility, aiding the construction of a coherent narrative. Yet they also relied upon shipboard spatial rituals of hygiene, discipline and exclusion, which obscured the realities of the production of steam's mobilities, and ensured that the shipboard Other was encountered in a distinctly unequal relationality. By seeing the vessel as a mobile, floating part of Western space, passengers perpetuated forms of identity and difference which helped them to identify as modern. Some of the central means by which such identification was achieved was through shipboard temporality and the production of domesticity, themes explored in the next two chapters.

Notes

1 Simms, *England to Calcutta by the Overland Route in 1845*, p. 26.

2 Hervey, *The Ocean and the Desert*, pp. 6–7.

3 The *Hindostan* had 60 passenger cabins, arranged over two decks, designed to carry over 100 passengers, in addition to which 50 servants could travel. As noted, the identical ship *Bentinck* carried 177 crew members. The vessel was around 66 m long, 11 m wide and 9 m deep. While it may have been that, as these accounts tend to focus on the *Hindostan*, it featured a particularly unusual layout in its passenger space, this can only add to claims of its novelty. It is also notable that the *Bentinck*, which arrived on the line the following year, was subject to no such claims.

4 Van Heerdt, *Mijne Reis met de Landmail van Batavia over Singapore*, p. 23.

5 Newmarch, *Five Years in the East*, pp. 165–6.

6 John Borthwick Gilchrist, *The General East India Guide and Vade Mecum: For the Public Functionary, Government Officer, Private Agent, Trader or Foreign Sojourner, in British India, and the Adjacent Parts of Asia Immediately Connected with the Honourable the East India Company* (London: Kingsbury, Parbury, & Allen, 1825), p. 21.

7 Cyril Northcote Parkinson, *Trade in the Eastern Seas, 1793–1813* (Cambridge: Cambridge University Press, 1937), p. 264.

8 Lord Albert Denison, *Wanderings in Search of Health* (London: Printed for private circulation, 1849), pp. 2–3.

9 Captain James Barber, *The Overland Guide-Book: A Complete Vademecum for the Overland Traveller, to India via Egypt* (London: W.H. Allen & Co., 1845) .

10 The *Haddington* and the *Ripon* for example, both built in 1846, remained in service until 1870, the year after the opening of the Suez Canal.

11 Although the *Great Liverpool* was wrecked off the coast of Spain in 1846, the other three were only taken out of service from 1860.

12 Such steamers had to travel round the Cape on their first voyages in order to ply the Eastern waters.

13 Isambard Kingdom Brunel's famed iron-hulled screw steamer the *Great Britain*, launched in 1843, was well ahead of its time.

14 The *Delta*, built in 1859, was an incongruously anachronistic paddle steamer.

15 'Launch of the "Himalaya" Screw Steam-Ship', *Illustrated London News*, 28 May 1853, p. 412.

16 'Alexandria – The "Himalaya" Steam-Ship', *Illustrated London News*, 18 February 1854, p. 141.

17 'Progress in the Size, Form and Power of Ships, etc.', from *The Builder*, no. 575, cited in *The Year-Book of Facts in Science and Art: Exhibiting the Most Important Discoveries and Improvements of the Past Year*, ed. by John Timbs (London: David Bogue, 1855), p. 33.

18 From the *Hampshire Advertiser*, 14 January 1854, cited in 'The "Himalaya" Screw Steamer: The Largest Ship Afloat', *Kidd's Own Journal; for Inter-Communications on Natural History, Popular Science, and Things in General*, Volume 5, January–June 1854, p. 45.

19 Van Heerdt, *Mijne Reis met de Landmail van Batavia over Singapore*, pp. 29–30.

20 Warburton, *The Crescent and the Cross*, p. 7.

21 Sara Mills, *Gender and Colonial Space* (Manchester: Manchester University Press, 2005), pp. 107–8.

22 Warburton, *The Crescent and the Cross*, p. 9.

23 *Ibid.*, p. 2.

24 *Ibid.*, p. 3.

25 *Ibid.* Warburton makes reference to Mary Russell Mitford, author of *Our Village: Sketches of Rural Character and Scenery*, a popular series of observations of English rural life originally published in the 1820s and 1930s.

26 *Ibid.*

27 *Ibid.*, p. 7.

28 Russell, *My Diary in India*, p. 46.

29 'The Oriental Steam-Ship', *Morning Post*, 26 August 1840, p. 2.

30 'Our Tea Table', *Titan: A Monthly Magazine*, vol. 24, January–June 1857, p. 244.

31 Kendall, 'Letter dated March 9, 1858, aboard the Pottinger', *Letters*, p. 23.

32 *Ibid.* Shedfield is a village in Hampshire.

33 *The Popular Overland Guide, Hints to Travellers by the Overland Route to India, Australia, and China* (London: Ward and Lock, 1861), p. 22.

34 *Ibid.*

35 *Ibid.*, p. 17.

36 Simms, *England to Calcutta by the Overland Route in 1845*, p. 20.

37 *Ibid.*

38 'The Overland Route to India', p. 712.

39 'Court of Queen's Bench', *Law Times*, 5 June 1869, p. 108.

40 Greg Dening performs an extensive exploration of spatial discipline on the sailing ship in his masterful study of the mutiny on the bounty. 'Space and the language to describe it make a ship', he writes. 'Space was inseparable from the authority it displayed and the relationships it enclosed.' Greg Dening, *Mr Bligh's Bad Language: Passion, Power and Theatre on the Bounty* (Cambridge: Cambridge University Press, 1992), p. 19. The spatial discipline of the sailing ship is also extensively discussed in Richard Guy, 'Calamitous Voyages: The Social Space of Shipwreck and Mutiny Narratives in the Dutch East India Company', *Itinerario*, 39 (2015), 117–40.

41 'Miscellaneous', *Asiatic Journal and Monthly Register for British and Foreign India China and Australasia, Volume 39*, September–December 1842, p. 253.

42 London, National Maritime Museum Archive, 'Instructions for Chief Engineers', 1867, P&O/9/1, p. 8.

43 Charles Dickens, 'Letter to Georgina Hogarth, 4 November 1853', *Letters of Charles Dickens: 1833–1870*, ed. by Georgina Hogarth and Mary Dickens (Cambridge: Cambridge University Press, 2011), p. 308.

44 Ida Pfeiffer, *A Woman's Journey Round the World: From Vienna to Brazil, Chili, Tahiti, China, Hindostan, Persia, and Asia Minor* (London: Ingram, Cooke & Co., 1852), p. 116. See also Harcourt, *Flagships of Imperialism*, pp. 70, 206.

45 Van Heerdt, *Mijne Reis met de Landmail van Batavia over Singapore*, p. 23.

46 *The Popular Overland Guide*, p. 21.

47 'A Homeward Trip', *Asiatic Journal and Monthly Miscellany, Volume 2*, November–1844, p. 56.

48 'The "Oriental" Steam-Ship', *London Saturday Journal*, 9 April 1842, p. 170.

49 Khan, *A Voyage to Modernism*, pp. 71–2.

50 Simms, *England to Calcutta by the Overland Route in 1845*, p. 24.

51 Jane Rendell, *The Pursuit of Pleasure: Gender, Space and Architecture in Regency London* (London: Athlone Press, 2002), p. 66.

52 *Ibid.*, pp. 78, 72.

53 'The Sicilian Insurrection', *Annual Register, Or, A View of the History and Politics of the Year 1849* (London: F. & J. Rivington, 1850), p. 71.

54 Anne de Courcy, *The Fishing Fleet: Husband-Hunting in the Raj* (London: Weidenfeld & Nicolson, 2012).

55 Russell, *My Diary in India*, p. 4.

56 Philip Howard Colomb, *Slave-catching in the Indian Ocean: A Record of Naval Experiences* (London: Longmans & Co., 1873), p. 6.

57 *The Popular Overland Guide*, p. 20.

58 'The Hindostan Steam-Ship', *Morning Post*, 14 September 1842, unpaginated.

59 Mary Lyndon Shanley, *Feminism, Marriage, and the Law in Victorian England* (Princeton: Princeton University Press, 1993), p. 5.

60 *The Popular Overland Guide*, pp. 23–4.

61 Charles Harris Allen, *A Visit to Queensland and Her Goldfields* (London: Chapman & Hall, 1870), p. 28.

62 Anne McClintock, *Imperial Leather: Race, Gender and Sexuality in the Colonial Contest* (New York and London: Routledge, 1995), p. 33.

63 Hervey, *The Ocean and the Desert*, p. 19.

64 'The "Oriental" Steam-Ship', p. 170.

65 Jacobus van der Chijs, *Mijne reis naar Java in 1869 en terugkeer over Engelsch-Indié, Palestina enz. in 1870* (Utrecht: C. Van Der Post Jr, 1874), p. 11. Translation my own.

66 Mary Douglas, *Purity and Danger: An Analysis of Concepts of Pollution and Taboo* (London: Routledge, 2013), p. 36.

67 *Ibid.*

68 *The Popular Overland Guide*, p. 5.

69 'Peninsular and Oriental Steam Navigation', *Herapath's Railway Journal*, 10 December 1864, p. 1397.

70 Mrs. John B. Speid, *Our Last Years in India* (London: Smith, Elder & Co., 1862), p. 14.

71 Pratt, *Imperial Eyes*, p. 4.

72 Pfeiffer, *A Woman's Journey Round the World*, p. 116.

73 *Ibid.*, p. 128.

74 *Ibid.*, p. 140.

75 Bayard Taylor, *A Visit to India, China, and Japan: In the Year 1853* (New York: G.P. Putnam & Co., 1855), p. 31.

76 Thackeray, *Notes of a Journey from Cornhill to Grand Cairo*, pp. 136–7.

77 *Ibid.*, p. 238.

78 'Report', *Herapath's Railway Journal*, 5 December 1863, p. 1282.

79 Sir George Cornewall Lewis, *On Foreign Jurisdiction and the Extradition of Criminals* (London: John W. Parker and Son, 1859), p. 10.

80 Macleod, *Eastward*, pp. 13–14.

81 *Ibid.*, p. 14.

82 William Tyrone Power, *Sketches in New Zealand: With Pen and Pencil* (London: Longman, Brown, Green, and Longmans, 1849), p. 270.

83 Arnold, 'An Overland Mail Adventure', p. 113.

84 Eastwick, *A Handbook for India*, p. l.

85 Sidney Laman Blanchard, 'Yesterday and Today in India', *All the Year Round*, 17 October 1863, p. 185.

86 Macleod, *Peeps at the Far East*, p. 9.

87 George Francis Train, *An American Merchant in Europe, Asia and Australia: A Series of Letters from Java, Singapore, China, Bengal, Egypt, and the Holy Land, etc.* (New York: G.P. Putnam & Co., 1857), p. 269. Train, a shipping magnate and keen traveller, was a possible inspiration for Phileas Fogg, the fictional protagonist of Jules Verne's *Around the World in Eighty Days* (1872) and the Victorian global traveller par excellence, whose voyage around the world involved passage on three separate P&O steamships. Stephen Kern, *The Culture of Time and Space, 1880–1918* (Cambridge, MA: Harvard University Press, 2003), p. 212.

88 Train, *An American Merchant in Europe, Asia and Australia*, pp. 261, 267.

89 Russell, *My Diary in India*, p. 4.

90 *Ibid*. The Raj of Sarawak was located on the northwest coast of the island of Borneo.

91 Taylor, *A Visit to India, China, and Japan*, pp. 21–2. The elision in the first quotation omits Taylor's use of racist language to describe the stokers.

92 Robert B. Minturn, *From New York to Delhi by way of Rio de Janeiro, Australia and China* (London: Longman, Brown, Green, Longmans and Roberts, 1858), p. 403.

93 'Vuurstoker' and 'veeger' in the image, the latter possibly a reference to a Hindu of the Dalit caste, sometimes referred to as 'sweepers'.

94 Minturn, *From New York to Delhi*, p. 403.

95 Pfeiffer, *A Woman's Journey Round the World*, p. 128.

96 *Ibid*.

97 *Ibid*., p. 129.

98 'En Route; Or, Notes of the Overland Journey to the East', p. 152.

99 Burgess, *Engines of Empire*, p. 232.

100 'From Southampton to Shanghai', pp. 90, 92.

101 Burton, *Personal Narrative of a Pilgrimage to Al Medinah and Meccah*, p. 5.

102 Jan Frederik Gerrit Brumund, *Schetsen eener Mail-Reize van Batavia naar Maastricht op Reis en Thuis* (Amsterdam: 1862), p. 119. This, and all subsequent translations of this source are my own. In his Preface to the book, Brumund emphasises his keenness to expose his reader to vicarious encounters with both distant lands, and also with shipboard life: 'As for my readers,' he writes, 'I hope that the sketches may move them aboard and ashore, to see, hear, and even perhaps also feel what I saw, heard and felt there.' *Ibid*., p. iii. Brumund's first words are presumably a reference to Franz Junghuhn's book.

103 Timothy Mitchell, *Colonising Egypt* (Cambridge: Cambridge University Press, 1988), p. 165.

104 Brumund, *Schetsen eener Mail-Reize van Batavia naar Maastricht*, pp. 119–20.

105 *Ibid*., p. 120.

106 The use of this classical trope in the context of capitalist labour conditions will be recognisable to those familiar with an oft-cited passage which appears in Engels' *The Condition of the Working Class in England*, and which Marx himself quotes in *Capital*, Volume I: 'The miserable routine of endless drudgery and toil in which the same mechanical process is gone through over and over again, is like the labour of Sisyphus. The burden of labour, like the rock, keeps ever falling back on the worn-out labourer.' Marx, *Capital*, Volume I, p. 467. (The original can be found in James Phillips Kay, *The Moral and Physical Condition of the Working Classes Employed in the Cotton Manufacture in Manchester* (London: James Ridgway, 1832), p. 8.)

107 Jonathan Hyslop, 'Steamship Empire: Asian, African and British Sailors in the Merchant Marine c.1880–1945', *Journal of Asian and African Studies*, 44 (2009), 49–67, p. 50.

108 London, Wellcome Archives, Alfred Barton, *Journal of further voyages for the P.&O. Company between Bombay, Singapore and Hong Kong, and on*

a return voyage to England, August 1854–June 1855, MS.5959, p. 151 (15 May 1855).

109 One was published in Dutch; two are from diaries, only one of which was published, but not until 1896. The *Illustrated London News* article was published in 1872, three years after the opening of the Suez Canal.

110 'The Voyage to China', *Illustrated London News*, 9 November 1872, p. 438. The article states that the temperature in the stokehole during the passage down the Red Sea in August was 145° Fahrenheit (63° Celsius).

111 Arthur Lloyd Clay, *Leaves from a Diary in Lower Bengal* (London: Macmillan, 1896), p. 7. Seedee is probably a reference to the term 'Siddi', used to refer to ethnic Africans who lived in South Asia and who tended to be employed in shipping.

112 Aguiar, *Tracking Modernity*, p. 29.

113 Balachandran, 'Indefinite Transits', p. 188.

3

'The diurnal economy of these steamers': Steamship temporalities

> In the old Indiamen the usual amusement of the passengers was making love and quarrelling, the most charming and most odious of pursuits; but in these days of steam there is not much time for either.[1]
>
> Matthew Henry Marsh, *Overland from Southampton to Queensland*, 1867

An article discussing the relative merits of sail and steam for the journey between England and India appeared in the *Indian Medical Gazette* of 1 September 1868. 'Of course,' the article insists, 'where *time* is a *paramount* object, the overland route must be adopted *coûte qui coûte* [at all costs].'[2] For the imperial traveller, the overland route offered a radical reduction in the journey's duration: time, for the purposes of comprehending steam's introduction to the voyage East, is needless to say a paramount object of concern. Steam's impact on the voyage East – the annihilation of space by time which was a key trope in the discursive production of the steamship voyage – was a fundamentally temporal one. On Barak has explored the entangled means by which modern technologies of transportation and communication – steamships, railways and the telegraph – introduced a contested and fractious conception of time into nineteenth-century Egyptian society. For Barak, steamships were the bearers of an idiosyncratically Western temporality, which clashed and intermingled with existing Egyptian temporalities.[3] This chapter focuses on a striking concern found in the archive of the overland route with the steamship's temporality: on passengers' preoccupations with the passage of time, with temporal precision, and with the rhythms of shipboard life. Whether time appeared to pass slowly, fast, or even to stand still, passenger accounts are saturated with claims regarding the shipboard experience of time.

Temporality is at the centre of understandings of the modern world: not only has the modern been persistently characterised as the historically new, a temporal departure from the past, but the subjective perception and sensation of time is fundamental to the experience of modern life. Michael Adas has explored the extent to which Western identities have been historically rooted in temporal beliefs and practices. Time was at the core of the Western imperial sense of self – rituals of saving, disciplining and measuring time provided European actors with a means for identifying with the norms and conventions of the metropole. In the midst of an imperial world which they considered to be temporally retrograde, these practices also convinced them of the inferiority and difference of the East.[4] As Giordano Nanni has insisted, timekeeping practices were at the heart of the Western conquest of the globe. 'The project', he writes, 'to incorporate the globe within a matrix of hours, minutes and seconds demands recognition as one of the most significant manifestations of Europe's universalising will.'[5] Such conceptions of time provided a key means of narrating the West's civilising mission, as the exporting of modernity and capitalism to a primitive East. Modern technologies of mobility subjugated distance to time, plotting precise timetables on the vastness and heterogeneity of global space. Such temporalities emphasised the difference between metropole and periphery, West and East, white and black, modernity and its Other.

Disciplining the temporality of imperial mobilities

So regular are the weekly arrival and despatch of the Peninsular and Oriental steamers, that the general public cease to look with any degree of surprise on the marvellous precision and speed with which the mails to and from the East and the far-off Australian Continent are now delivered.[6]
    Charles H. Allen, *A Visit to Queensland and Her Goldfields*, 1870

In the section dealing with 'credit and fictitious capital' in Volume III of *Capital*, Karl Marx reproduced a long passage from the *Manchester Guardian* of 24 November 1847. This quotation pertained to one of a number of practices of what Marx termed 'fabricating fictitious capital' (generally meaning stocks and securities). This practice involved the use of timed bankers' drafts, documents whose value could be redeemed only upon the arrival of the shipments of goods they had been used to purchase some time before.[7] The Indian house of a trading company was able to use these drafts to defer payment on goods purchased in India until they were sold upon their arrival in Britain. The goods were transported around the Cape of Good Hope by sailing vessel, which could often take many months to complete their journey. However, companies began to send the shipping documents to England by steamships on the overland route, which could thus be used to pawn the goods, then still in transit, with a London bank well in advance of the draft's payment becoming due.[8] Not only does this story emphasise that complex financial instruments were often rooted in the material movements of goods – it illustrates the extent to which the era of the overland route was marked by the simultaneous existence of two heterogeneous temporalities of maritime mobility.

The temporality of steamship mobilities was markedly distinct to that of the sailing vessel, which essentially still operated according to the traditional, seasonal circulatory rhythms which had long characterised mercantile capitalism. However, this shift, from the temporality of sail to that of steam, was more complex than a simplistic increase in speed or decrease in duration. An 1843 article from the *Asiatic Journal and Monthly Register* entitled 'Communication with the East' emphasises the centrality of temporal discipline to the emergent mobilities of the overland route:

> Steam navigation, mighty as its progress has been during the last ten years, is yet in its infancy. In the perfection of the machinery; in the diminution of the expense of the locomotive power; in the prevention of accidents, there is much scope for improvements which science, acting upon experience, will in time devise and accomplish. But one of the most indispensable conditions of this new mode of communication is that it shall be secure and regular, not liable to disturbance or interruption, which is more immediately essential to it than its acceleration. It is undoubtedly of great moment that the arrival of the inward mail, both in Europe and in India, should precede the despatch of the outward by a sufficient interval to allow a return of correspondence; but this object is obtainable only by such a degree of regularity as will permit of the arrivals being calculated upon with some degree of precision.[9]

Regular repetition and temporal discipline, the article insists, were the fundamental principles of the steamship's global mobilities revolution, over and above the quality which is more often considered to be the prime factor in this shift, a straightforward increase in velocity.[10] With the introduction of steam as a means of propulsion, the sea voyage to India was shortened from a matter of months to one of weeks, achieving the annihilation of space and time which was at the heart of discourses concerning modern mobilities. This was achieved, however, not through the acceleration which typifies that narrative, but rather through the means of regularity and rigorous bureaucratic administration. As steamships were no longer constrained by the contingency of the elements which delimited the mobility of sailing vessels, for the first-time, sea voyages could be made predictable and run to established, regular schedules. While the speed at which they travelled was in fact not dissimilar to that of a sailing vessel, steamships were distinguished by their ability to both advertise a precise departure time and date and specify their voyage's duration. This state of affairs was unprecedented in maritime transportation. Sailing ships obeyed seasonal rhythms of circulation, often had to remain in harbour for days awaiting a favourable wind, and their voyage's duration varied wildly, due to its dependence upon frequently unpredictable conditions.[11]

Speed was thus very much secondary as a mode of effecting more efficient global transport and communications, subordinate to the facilitation of predictable recurrence. The temporality of maritime mobilities was subject to modern forms of bureaucratic rationalisation which were both made possible by steam but which can also be seen part of a wider drive of the capitalist system toward an integrated global communications network. Much has been said of the standardisation of time effected on land by the proliferation of the steam locomotive.[12] As Anyaa Anim-Addo has argued in the context of the nineteenth-century Caribbean, the transnational steamship was responsible in an analogous manner for imposing new temporal rhythms on colonial space. 'A focus on the rhythms of steamship travel', she insists, 'helps to nuance our understanding of speed and communication in colonial contexts, and highlights that this was more complex an historical process than a linear trajectory towards annihilating distance with speed.'[13]

The extent to which speed in itself remained marginal to P&O's global mobilities revolution is attested to in an 1861 article in the *Illustrated London News*:

> The Peninsular and Oriental Company pay annually nearly a million sterling for coals, and their efforts, therefore, have been constantly directed to the encouragement and development of machines that will do the most work with the least consumption of fuel. Speed in ships with great power is always attainable; but the cost of an extra knot on a seagoing steamer is something enormous, and companies have found that, like other things, speed may therefore be bought too dear.[14]

In the production of new imperial geographies of mobility at sea, time was money. Particularly in the early years of steam navigation, the inefficiency of marine steam engines meant that a relatively minor increase in speed was an expensive luxury. This expense was in part rooted in the materiality of coal and colonial logistical geographies: the vast quantities of European coal consumed by steamships operating in the East had to be transported around the Cape of Good Hope by sailing vessels. Any claims regarding steam as a radical historical break thus need to be tempered by its continued reliance upon the logistics of sail.[15] Nevertheless, the circulatory patterns of merchant capitalism had been rooted in natural rhythms of circulation, particularly the seasonal trade winds and currents which were restricted to certain times of year. Industrial capitalism employed steam to overcome these rhythms, in order to impose its own regularised temporal patterns on global transportation networks. Steam facilitated scheduled, regular departures at a precise time, which could run throughout the year. This innovation has to be understood as part of the larger developments in time discipline at the core of modern industrial capitalism. These shifts occurred not merely in the sphere of labour, but increasingly permeated all aspects of social life.[16]

In the context of nineteenth-century mobilities, the apotheosis of this new bureaucratic temporality was the schedule. P&O were able to publish detailed information about the duration of their ships' voyages and their departure times. A schedule published by the company in 1849 details the length of time taken by passengers on their steamships to travel from Southampton to the various calling points on the overland route: 8 days to Gibraltar; 11 to Malta; Alexandria 16; Suez 19; Aden 27; Bombay 35; Ceylon 41; Madras 45; Calcutta 48. On the company's Far Eastern branch line, 46 days to Penang; 49 to Singapore; 55 to Hong Kong. Passengers wishing to travel to these locations were advised that the steamer would depart from Southampton harbour on the '20th of every month, at 1.30 pm'.[17] Prospective travellers could plan their journey with the knowledge of the exact day on which they would arrive at their destination, marking a complete departure from the temporal logic of sail. In an 1863 article, resident of Calcutta Sidney Laman Blanchard documents the contrasting temporalities of steam and sailing ship arrivals in the city. He describes 'Peninsular and Oriental ship-loads arriving once a fortnight, and long-sea ship-loads arriving whenever they can'.[18] Even in the first decade of its operation, On Barak has observed, the overland voyage's duration was beginning to be calculated with a precision whose exactitude was measured by the minute.[19]

An article from 1852 in *Household Words* relates the departure of the *Bentinck* from Southampton. It emphasises the meticulous approach toward temporal precision with which the movements of P&O vessels were administered:

> Every point of the ten thousand four hundred miles which lie between South-ampton and Hong Kong, is as rigidly timed as if it were a station upon a short line of railway. The accuracy and punctuality with which each single mile is performed out or home, operates upon the punctual delivery of the mails in China or in London. The Bentinck must, therefore, start at two.[20]

This description plots the rigid temporal framework of the railway timetable over the contingency of global maritime space. The reliance of emerging global communication networks upon a rigorous predictability injected into shipping a new sense of temporal urgency; it was imperative that the steamship began its journey at the time predetermined, precisely because it had entered into a network of relations which were global in character. Spatial distance was subsumed under time not merely as an increase in velocity, as the discourse of the annihilation of space and time had it. Steam facilitated the quantification of vast stretches of maritime space, expressed as a precise temporal measurement.

Only through such precise disciplining of steamship temporalities could P&O maintain the circulatory rhythms required of it by British imperial capitalism. The extent to which this temporal precision and predictability was at the heart of discourses concerning the nineteenth century's increasingly interlinked global system is articulated in an account of the 1860 shipwreck of the *Malabar* in the harbour at Point de Galle.[21] The British and French ambassadors, Lord Elgin and Baron Gros, were travelling to China on board the steamer as envoys to the Chinese state, towards the close of the Second Opium War. While there were no casualties, the wreck, the article claims, resulted in 'the detention of two important personages, on whom depended the question of peace or war to half the human race'.[22] The transcontinental steamship was caught up in a web of global social and political relations which relied upon the strict temporal discipline and predictability it was able to provide. The interruption of this temporal discipline, through what the article refers to as the 'undervaluation of contingencies', could lead to far-reaching geopolitical consequences.

The steamship's regularity was not simply the result of private capital operating on the free market; nineteenth-century laissez-faire capitalism was perhaps too anarchic to create such conditions alone. This temporal discipline was produced through the British imperial state's intervention in the temporal rhythms of global maritime mobility, through subsidy. P&O operated under Royal Charter, funded by a number of government mail contracts which demanded precision and punctuality.[23] The findings of an 1853 parliamentary inquiry into P&O's service found that in little over a decade the company had come to provide a global transport and communications network invaluable to the British imperial apparatus: 'The ocean has been traversed with a precision and regularity hitherto deemed impossible – commerce and civilization have been extended – the colonies have been brought more closely into connection with the Home Government.'[24] Again, the notion of steam as a break with the past is invoked, and specifically as a temporal concern, rooted in the administration and disciplining of maritime mobilities. The company's relation to the nation state was a temporal one, serving the bureaucratic needs of capitalist imperialism. In turn, this temporal precision was seen not just as a means to an end, but as a signifier of civilisation in itself.

These imperial cultural associations with which steam's temporalities were imbued can be seen again in an 1867 parliamentary debate, in which ministers discussed the possibility of routes which had until then been operated exclusively by P&O being put out to tender. Regarding the potential of this move to result in the routes' implementation by the French shipping line

Messageries Impériales, the Member of Parliament for Wick, Samuel Laing, expressed misgivings. Notably, Laing's concerns were articulated specifically in terms of temporal discipline. 'There is nothing, I am satisfied,' he declared, 'that tends so surely to keep up the name and the influence of England in the East as the sight of those splendid steamers coming and going with the regularity of clock-work.'[25] For Laing, temporal precision lay at the heart of the steamship's functioning as a spectacle of British imperialism and global status. The notion of clock time underpinned the Western logic of an industrial capitalism characterised by the precise disciplining of time. The steamship was seen to project the temporality of Western modernity into imperial space, which was characterised as timeless, external to the temporal logic of modernity.

Historical claims of a binary opposition contrasting Western temporal rigour with an Eastern entropy should of course be viewed with circumspection. An anecdote related by the Victorian novelist and civil servant Anthony Trollope gives the lie to such simplistic narratives. Employed by the Post Office, Trollope was sent in 1858 to negotiate with the Egyptian government the conditions of the transfer of mails from Alexandria to Suez. His Egyptian counterpart was adamant that 48 hours should be allowed for the transfer, rather than the 24 hours desired by the Post Office. Trollope initially attributed this friction to the opposition between what he termed 'British energy' and 'oriental tranquillity'.[26] However, it transpired that the reluctance of the Egyptian government to accede to the British demands for expediency was in fact due to the needs of Western enterprise, rather than any stereotyped Eastern lassitude. 'The Peninsular and Oriental Steamship Company', writes Trollope in his account of the negotiations, 'had conceived that forty-eight hours would suit the purposes of their traffic better than twenty-four'. Trollope went on to surmise that 'as they [P&O] were the great paymasters on the railway, the Minister of the Egyptian State, who managed the railway, might probably wish to accommodate them'.[27] Temporal expediency, at the heart of British imperial identity, was not always in P&O's interests.

Disciplining shipboard temporalities

Passengers were well aware of the idiosyncratic temporalities of steamship mobilities. A traveller who went by the name of 'Mrs John B. Speid' opens her account of an 1858 overland journey to India by emphasising the temporal precision which governed the route:

> Embarked on board the steamer *Ripon*, at Southampton, at twelve o'clock, and by two we were steaming down the river, with almost the accurate punctuality of an express train; a punctuality reflected in the exacting expectations of

the Indian public, who scold when a mail is overdue, as only the consciously accurate have a right to do.[28]

Again mobilising the trope of the railway's punctuality, Speid emphasises that the temporal disciplining of mobilities at sea had to be understood in a global, imperial context. The time of departure from England was part of an overarching schedule which governed the entirety of the route, linking metropole and periphery in a distinctly temporal relation.

British businessman William Adamson travelled from England to Egypt aboard the *Himalaya* in 1854. An entry in his diary from 28 January, made while travelling East in the Mediterranean, reveals a distinct preoccupation with numerical precision:

> The day is hot but not unpleasantly so – sea very calm and quiet – ship going sweetly through the water at 14½ knots per hour – Thermometer at 60 degrees in the shade and 100 degrees in the sun. Our clocks now require to be put forward about ½ an hour every day.[29]

Adamson's diary entry records timekeeping rituals which formed part of a series of numerical measuring practices which he employed to engage with the ship's mobility. Notably, this was achieved through an engagement with the mechanics of temporal change which reflected a desire to maintain British chronological standards even in transit through global space. Such rituals helped to sustain a sense of self during the voyage, a precise, ordered Western subjectivity. Western perceptions of temporality emphasised the difference between metropole and periphery. The steamship in transit was suspended between two heterogeneous temporalities, both real and imagined – that of a modern, industrial-capitalist Britain and the imperial East, perceived as slow, retrograde and undisciplined.[30] As we will see, this dislocation contributed to the sensation for many passengers of being 'outside' the passage of time in the modern world. Shipboard temporal practices contributed to the perpetuation of Western identity in the flux and temporal homogeneity of life at sea, by helping to produce a sense of temporal simultaneity with the metropole.[31]

As Adamson's practices suggest, shipboard life reflected the same temporal logic which steam had instilled into maritime mobility – the quantifiable, clock time of the schedule. While this is not to imply a simplistic causal relationship between the rhythms of steamship mobility and passenger experience, they both existed within the larger administration and disciplining of time which governed the modern capitalist world. Correspondingly, they also intersected with the same set of cultural associations with time. The temporal claims regarding the steamship – with its speed, its saving of time, its machinic capacity for precision – permeate the ubiquitous passenger engagements with the temporal qualities of shipboard life. As explored in

Chapter 1, the steamship's mobility was conceived as a specifically temporal process: as the reduction of the time taken to travel from one point to another effectively reduced the influence of spatial distance, space was increasingly measured in terms of the period of time taken to traverse it. This was not merely an abstract idea, however, but a social process which mediated the subjective experience of distance. A quotation from Charles Henry Newmarch's 1847 account of his voyage from Aden to Suez aboard the *Hindostan*, clarifies how this conceptualisation of mobility was experienced on the overland route. 'On our road home,' he writes, 'we reckoned the distance, not by the miles, but by the number of days which must elapse before we reached it.'[32] In providing a predictable, measurable form of mobility, the steamship was seen to subordinate space to time.

Precisely timetabled, the sea voyage by steamship became essentially reproducible, and thus lost something of the uniqueness and romantic associations which had attended the spatiotemporal unpredictability of travel by sail.[33] This can be witnessed in an episode related by John Aiton, travelling aboard the *Ripon* from Southampton to Alexandria in 1851. Aiton narrates an incident towards the end of the voyage when, nearing Egypt, land was sighted. He describes the passengers' view of a 'shore with hills rising up behind, and then a fine lake of water … and trees growing on its banks'.[34] However, as Aiton went on to relate, the ship's passengers who gathered on deck in anticipation of the journey's imminent end were to be disappointed; the landscape they observed was in fact a Fata Morgana, a marine optical illusion which causes distant objects, which would under normal circumstances be out of sight, to appear on the horizon.[35] While the phenomenon was historically associated with provoking confusion and astonishment in seafarers, Aiton observes that the *Ripon*'s officers were unmoved by this apparent sighting of land. Remaining below deck, they dismissed the passengers' claims, merely remarking 'that Egypt would not be seen for two hours'.[36] That which had once played a role in the mythology of seafaring was experienced instead as a mere temporal discrepancy, an illusory deviation from the timetable's precision.

The new temporal precision of mobility at sea was rooted in the steam engine's overcoming of the ship's reliance upon natural rhythms. The engine itself manifested this precision and repetition through the metronomic rhythms of machine time, referred to in a description of a P&O steamer in an article from 1868 in the *Manchester Times*. 'On board a screw-steamer,' it remarks, 'even in the calmest weather, the perpetual "tremolo" is most irritating.'[37] While the ever-present labour practices aboard the sailing ship operated according to rhythms dictated by the vagaries of the elements, on the steamer the passenger's sensation of mobility's production was characterised instead by the pervasive mechanical rhythm of the engine. 'The engine-room is full of life and motion', remarks Arthur Lloyd Clay of his voyage from Suez to Point de Galle on board the *Nubia* in 1862. 'The regular beat of the engines,' he continues, 'like monotonous dance-music, mingles with the throb of the propeller.'[38]

This machinic rhythm presented for the passenger one of the few sensory manifestations of the production of steamship mobilities. The 'porous' temporality of traditional shipboard labour, as Marcus Rediker has described it, was one 'marked by periods of intensity and inactivity', contingent upon the inconsistency of the wind. This was replaced aboard the steamer by a 'continuity, uniformity, regularity, order [and] intensity', which were rooted in the distinctive temporalities of steam power.[39] As Chapter 2 documented, for the subaltern worker who shovelled coal in the ship's boiler rooms, the experience of the temporality of steamship mobility was of the hellish, Sisyphean repetition of industrial labour. As noted, the passengers' exposure to these labour practices was limited. However, conceptions of shipboard labour's machinic temporalities can be seen even in forms of service which facilitated passenger comfort. William Howard Russell, in his 1858 account of a voyage from Suez to Calcutta on board the *Nubia*, refers to the subaltern child labour employed in punkah-pulling, working the ceiling-mounted fans used to keep passengers cool in the tropics. He describes 'a row of animated machines sitting crouched down on the floor of the cabin, swaying listlessly to and fro as they pull the punkahs'.[40] For these workers, shipboard temporality was experienced in the monotonous repetition of the labour practices which made passenger leisure possible.

'I will now briefly describe the diurnal economy of these steamers, which in regularity of system cannot possibly be surpassed', declares *The Popular Overland Guide* of 1861.[41] The guide goes on to explicate a precise structure of shipboard temporal discipline and uniformity, governed by a system of bells and bugle calls which were used to dictate the rhythms of passengers' movements and behaviour. The ship's bell, a long-standing feature of traditional maritime labour practices, found a new role with increasing passenger traffic. The strict temporality of the naval watch passed into the temporal discipline of passenger life. The extent to which this temporal discipline regulated the movement and behaviour of bodies on board is vividly expressed in the management of the time at which passengers dined. A colourful description of this practice is provided by Philip Colomb, a naval captain who travelled on board an unnamed P&O steamer from Southampton to Alexandria in 1868:

> I dreaded the sound of the bell when I first heard it, and I dread the thought of it now. It began at 9.00 a.m. when you fell to at a strong breakfast. At noon you were rung to lunch, just heavy enough to spoil your appetite for

dinner, whose knell sounded at 3.00. At 6.00 the bell attacked you for tea; and if it let you alone to take or avoid 'biscuits and grog' at 9.00 it was probably because your digestion was thought to be pretty well done up by that time. Those who have not travelled P & O will probably say, 'How very weak you must be to allow yourself to be commanded by the bell to eat when you know it is not good for you!' Those who have travelled will not make such a remark.[42]

Although Colomb's description is clearly intended to offer a wry commentary on steamer life, it highlights the passivity of the passenger in the face of a rigorously regulated, clockwork structure of shipboard time-discipline.

The temporal repetition of shipboard life again finds expression in the 1853 article narrating the overland route from the American journal the *Southern Literary Messenger*, in its account of the voyage from Suez to Point de Galle aboard the *Haddington*. 'How then shall I describe our shipboard existence', its author laments, 'when one day so nearly reflected the former and so faithfully presaged the one to come?'[43] This passenger struggled to articulate the experience of steamship mobility precisely on account of the unvarying character of life in transit. Persistently, the sensations of speed and acceleration are lacking from overland route narratives, descriptions of life at the cutting edge of modern global mobility. Instead, it was often characterised by a temporality so homogeneous that time itself appeared almost to stand still. Indeed, the very possibility of narrating the experience of steamship mobility was for this passenger at stake in the homogeneity of the steamer's repetitious temporality, its 'diurnal economy'.

Lost time: Imperial boredom at sea

At the best, a voyage in one of these vessels is a period of endurance; and the only consolation a passenger experiences is, that it will soon come to an end.[44]
Indian Medical Gazette, 1 September 1868

'The monotony of a sea voyage is awful', lamented the English travel writer and entertainer Albert Smith in his account of the journey from Suez to Point de Galle aboard the *Bentinck* in 1858.[45] Smith was one of the most celebrated travel writers of his day, and regularly filled halls in London with customers eager to hear about his various adventures – the overland route narrative from which this quotation is drawn, *To China and Back*, was available to purchase at his performances of the entertainment inspired by his journey. Given that his business was to promote the exciting, exotic aspects of the new world which steam was opening up, it is perhaps surprising that Smith dedicated so much of his account to complaints regarding the monotony of the voyage. Like many popular Victorian travel writers, Smith subscribed to a sardonic style, which was perhaps employed to emphasise his well-travelled, worldly perspective. Nevertheless, the steamship as an environment itself clearly provided little of the excitement associated with foreign travel which was Smith's stock and trade. Such a characterisation of overland route travel was a widespread one, a sentiment in marked tension with the radical shortening of the duration of the journey to the East which steam had made possible. As already noted, steamships in transit were not considered bustling environments of frenetic activity, but were characterised rather by order and calm serenity. Despite steam's facilitation of both the radical abbreviation and temporal predictability of the sea voyage between Europe and the East, references to monotony and the passage of time saturate accounts of travel on the overland route.

Jeffrey Auerbach has highlighted the significance of boredom as a foundational experience of life in Britain's Victorian empire. Notably, he demonstrates that for many of those whose imperial lives lacked the romance and excitement which was often associated with empire, this encounter with 'imperial boredom' began with the sailing ship voyage to the East. As Auerbach suggests, the increasing safety, regimentation and repetition of nineteenth-century sea travel meant that the adventure and novelty which had characterised many narratives of sea voyages in the age of exploration were conspicuous by their absence.[46] However, this claim is rooted in a set of material conditions specific to the voyage by sailing ship around the Cape of Good Hope: 'by the nineteenth century', Auerbach writes, 'voyages to the East were generally made nonstop and out of sight of land for almost the entire distance'.[47] Certainly, as Auerbach suggests, for even the most resourceful passenger a sailing voyage of many months featuring little contact with land and with only the open sea to gaze upon would inevitably be a monotonous experience. Yet persistently, accounts of the overland route are no less filled with descriptions of the boredom suffered during the voyage than those of sail. Considering the many emphatic claims regarding steam as a revolutionary departure from sail, this would seem surprising. Why, with its relative brevity, regular stops, passage through Egypt, and frequent travel within sight of land, was overland route travel so frequently characterised as boring? The answer has to do with the question of time, specifically cultural attitudes to temporality in the modern era.

An 1867 narrative of an overland route voyage from Suez to Bombay from *The Morning Post* gives a representative account of the boredom experienced during transit. 'To kill time', it states, 'is the only aim and object of every soul on board.'[48] References in overland route narratives to boredom exhibit a distinctive preoccupation with time, with a temporality which appeared to undergo significant experiential shifts: time was seen to speed up and slow down; it was eradicated, measured, saved, wasted, repeated. Few passengers experienced the steamship's vaunted 'annihilation of space and time' in the terms familiar to the narrative of the flux and dynamism of modern life. Descriptions of steamship temporality frequently bear out this contradiction. Richard Burton's narrative of his voyage from Southampton to Alexandria on board the *Bengal* in 1853 exhibits a typical concern with the duration and temporality of steamship mobility. This concern extends to Burton's description of his transition from the steamship to the villa where he lodged upon his arrival at Alexandria. He characterises this move as a 'sudden change from presto to adagio life'.[49] This marked shift in tempo, from the steamer's celerity to the leisurely pace of Egyptian life, is not, however, reflected in his descriptions of temporality during the voyage: the 'journey was a monotonous one', he writes; 'the voyage lasted long enough, but not too long'.[50]

However, the ubiquitous references to monotony found in overland route narratives should not be seen as being *in spite* of the hubristic claims surrounding the steamship as a revolutionary break with the past, a technological wonder which had eradicated the distance between East and West. Rather, the boredom of the steamship voyage was produced in light of these claims. Although this appears to contradict Auerbach's instance that the monotony of the voyage East was rooted in the logistics of sail, his wider thesis is instructive: for Auerbach, imperial boredom was rooted in the reality of life in the British Empire falling far short of the mythologies associated with it – the rhetoric of adventure and romance which typified the dominant discourses of empire. Analogously, life on board the steamer could never live up to the mythology surrounding the overland route, particularly the claims of radical newness, speed and power explored in Chapter 1.[51] Passengers found the steamship voyage boring in part because the quotidian banality of shipboard life was other to their perception of themselves as modern, superior beings, traversing the globe in the most advanced of technological marvels. Instead, it was encountered as a temporal departure from modern life.

Philip Howard Colomb, who had bemoaned the strict temporal regulation of life on board the steamer during his 1868 voyage from Southampton to Alexandria, found overland route travel tedious in the extreme. Like many other passengers, he articulates his experiences of the voyage's monotony in distinctly temporal terms:

> A great deal is said of the delight of a P&O voyage in fine weather; to me it only seems an absolute and unavoidable waste of time. You see nothing, hear nothing and do nothing. If one could be rendered torpid at Southampton and be restored at Alexandria, it would be better, and then one would save wear and tear; but as it is, one gets through so much life without living it.[52]

Able to perform the voyage to a fixed schedule and in a radically reduced period of time, the steamship was nevertheless described by Colomb as characterised by a monotony whereby it was precisely time which appeared to be a wasted, unproductive resource. Colomb describes an experience of time's passage during the voyage, which in its very homogeneity and repetition, was external to lived experience, the everyday passage of time on land. The absence of sensory stimulation is at the heart of what was for Colomb both an embodied and psychic experience of time. He goes on to describe his desire to 'substitute active feeling of some kind for the sort of vegetable discomfort in which I live', complaining of 'the monotony into which my thoughts seemed hardening'.[53] Given that Colomb was himself a ship's captain (on his way to command a naval vessel engaged in the suppression of the slave trade in the Indian Ocean) it is unsurprising that he should have found inactivity in a shipboard context vexing. However, the subtle textures of passenger descriptions of boredom give voice to cultural associations and wider social attitudes regarding the place of time in modern life. Like Colomb, passengers persistently characterised the voyage as a departure from lived time, framed in relation to the absence of sensory stimulation and the repetitious homogeneity of life on board.

The sensation, related in numerous narratives of overland route travel, of a departure from the everyday passage of time was often associated in these accounts with the space of the open sea. As has already been explored, the steamship in transit was characterised by a conspicuous absence of the bustle and activity which is associated with modern life. As the vessel departed from the shore and was surrounded by the emptiness of the maritime landscape the passenger felt cut off from the experience of time's passing associated with their life on land.[54] The maritime landscape was perceived less often as a wild spectacle of nature than simply as an absence. The Australian writer and politician William Westgarth travelled from India to Suez on board the *Simla* in 1857. His characteristic description of the voyage associates the boredom he experienced with the open sea. 'The voyage is', he writes, 'one of monotony, almost unrelieved by a single object beyond the heavens above and the waters below us.'[55] Gazing out of the cabin's porthole at the undulating sea, Westgarth reflected on this relationship: 'What would be deemed trifles amongst the world of objects ashore', he writes, 'are noticeable in the comparative blank of sea life'.[56] This characterisation of time spent at sea as an absence is again manifested in David Lester Richardson's account of his voyage from Calcutta to Suez on board the steamer *Hindostan* in 1843. Given Richardson's imperialist veneration of the steamship's revolutionary ramifications (see the Introduction and Chapter 1), it is perhaps surprising that his description of the voyage itself should bear witness to none of this technophilic fervour: 'Travellers', he writes, 'are never so willing to be entertained as when suffering from the *objectlessness* of existence on board a ship. A long sea voyage is usually so much time of a man's life lost.'[57] The time of the steamship voyage is again described as a wasted resource, outside of the passage of time on land.

For both passengers the monotony of the voyage was associated with the absence of stimulation at sea. Philip Steinberg has suggested that the characterisation of the sea as an empty space, the inversion of land-based civilisation, came to dominate conceptions of maritime space in the modern age. 'In the industrial capitalist era,' he writes, 'the deep sea became defined as a great void, idealized as outside society, a wild space of nature that was antithetical to the social places on land.'[58] As a means for overcoming nature's wildness, the steamship was implicated in this conception of the sea as an absence. An ocean that was equally navigable in any direction could be characterised as a topological, featureless void, an abstract space to be overcome by the industrial production of mobility. The heterogeneity of maritime space was subsumed under the abstract measure of the time it took to traverse it. In its characterisation as a vast, wild, incomprehensible absence, the sea functioned as the exemplary anti-modern space. It is thus unsurprising that the characterisation of the voyage as a departure from the temporality of modern life on land was associated with the monotony of the open sea.

Steamship passengers on the overland route characterised the monotony of the open sea as the inversion of a terrestrial modernity distinguished by meaningful activity and sensory stimulation. In actuality, however, steamship passengers suffered only relatively brief periods of travel through the space of the open sea compared to those who travelled the Cape route by sail. Rather, the production of the sea as an absence can be seen in relation to the overland route's imperial geographies of steam. Owing to the vessel's frequent contact with land, steamship mobilities emphasised the monotony of the open sea. As Philip Steinberg has suggested, the capitalist drive to make maritime mobility as 'friction-free' as possible lay behind the characterisation of 'the ocean as an empty surface between the terrestrial places that "mattered"'.[59] The anonymous author of the aforementioned account from the *Southern Literary Messenger*, for whom the voyage over the Indian Ocean, far from land, was distinguished by its repetitive homogeneity, expressed this sameness specifically in relation to the sea's characterisation as absence. The homogeneous temporality of the voyage, which the author termed 'sea life's ... dearth of variety', was marked by 'the usual succession of uneventful days'. This account roots this homogeneity in the sea's visual uniformity, 'a smooth surface of ultra marine, whose provoking placidity was only equalled by the unbroken azure of the sky above'. Again, the climatic conditions at sea feature prominently in the passenger's articulation of shipboard monotony:

> *The weather*, that universal topic of conversation when all else fails, was so changeless … In such a state of things, a rainy day would have been a relief, and a storm at sea a positive blessing – to rouse us from the apathy which affected our little company.[60]

If the storm at sea was for the sailing vessel a contingent factor in its mobility, a source of disruption and danger, in the context of steam, this account suggests, it is reduced to the status of a distraction from the monotony and repetition of life in transit. Freed from the restrictions of nature and thus temporally predictable, the steamship voyage was characterised for its passengers by an acute awareness of time's passing. The preoccupation with the monotony of the voyage reflected the sea's continued presence as an intractable material space which still had to be traversed, even given the revolutionary impact of steam on maritime mobility. Colomb's wish to be rendered unconsciousness for the duration of the voyage can be seen as the desire for the overcoming of this barrier, for an ever-increasing annihilation of space by time.

Long-distance travel at sea is inevitably characterised by dislocation: from the land, from social interaction, from the familiarity and continuity of everyday life.[61] Analysing accounts of the protracted voyage to Australia by sailing ship in the mid-nineteenth century, Tamson Pietsch has emphasised the extent to which passengers experienced these voyages as an interruption in the continuity of their everyday lives. These accounts, she writes, 'show just how unsettling of established expectations and practices the experience of sea travel could be'.[62] Despite its abbreviation of the time spent in transit, steamship passengers experienced an analogous sense of the voyage as a departure from the everyday. As Pietsch insists, the experience of shipboard time has to be understood in light of the wider temporal and societal changes which were occurring in the nineteenth century. 'The processes of industrialization', she writes, 'were reshaping patterns of time and work in British cities. With the growth of the factory and wage labour, time was increasingly measured in hours and units.'[63] As Pietsch points out, steam played a decisive role in such disciplining of temporality in a land-based context, not least in the regularity of the steam train's timetable and in its consequent influence in standardising time across geographical space. 'The individual experience of time', she writes, 'began to be regularized and segmented as the patterns of everyday life were refashioned by the growth of modern social and economic institutions.'[64] Shipboard temporality was culturally, socially and performatively produced in the context of these wider temporal shifts in Western society.

Rationalising steamship time

No less than on land, steam in its maritime context facilitated the instrumentalisation of time; in its rationalisation and disciplining of the temporality of global mobility, the steamship brought time and money into a direct structure of equivalence. *Grindlay and Co.'s Overland Circular* (1847) a guide to travel to India published by the prominent colonial bank, includes a tabular comparison of the relative costs and duration of the voyage by sail and steam. This table states that the journey to Bombay by the overland route would take 35 days and cost around £120 per person, while the sailing ship voyage lasted 90 days and cost £70 to £90 per person.[65] Although both the length of time spent in transit (in the case of sail) and the expense varied in practice, this gives a graphic representation of the interconnection of time and money in the public understanding of the voyage East. Not only were passengers willing to pay more for the saving of time and the predictability that the steamship afforded – this saving could be explicitly plotted in terms of the relationship between time and money. David Lester Richardson, discussing the overland route specifically as a departure from sail, characterised steam as effecting the revolutionary transformation of the journey between imperial metropole and periphery. Expressing this in temporal terms, he describes the voyage as 'so short and cheap, as to present few difficulties to the home-sick British Indian'. Qualifying this statement in light of the greater expense of the overland route, he notes that 'in speaking of its cheapness I include many considerations, amongst them … the saving of money by the saving of time'.[66] Again, time and money are positioned as interchangeable resources.

This equivalence forms part of the context in which 'wasted' or 'lost' time presented a source of anxiety for the passenger. Time was increasingly seen in modern capitalist society as a valuable resource, and one which needed to be productive. As suggested, the temporalities of overland route mobility can be understood in the light of a range of concerns which animated the temporal culture of the modern world: among them efficiency, rational calculation and spatio-temporal discipline. The bureaucratic rationality exhibited in the temporality of steamship mobilities can be seen as an exemplar of Max Weber's influential account of modernity. Weber rooted the constitution of modern life in an instrumental reason characterised by the reduction of all contingency to the logic of value-based calculation.[67] Developing these concepts, Zygmunt Bauman has argued that the modern era was characterised by the application of this rationalisation to the intensification of the time-saving capacity of innovations in mobility:

> The 'conquest of space' came to mean faster machines. Accelerated movement meant larger space, and accelerating the moves was the sole means of enlarging

the space. In this chase, spatial expansion was the name of the game and space was the stake; space was value, time was the tool. To maximize the value, it was necessary to sharpen the instruments: much of the 'instrumental rationality' which, as Max Weber suggested, was the operative principle of modern civilization, focused on designing ways to perform tasks faster, while eliminating 'unproductive', idle, empty, and so wasted time.[68]

The strict temporal discipline by which steamship mobilities were managed can be understood as part of the wider drive toward an ideology of rationalisation which privileged an instrumentalised conception of time. In this utilitarian age, steamship mobilities were rationalised as part of a wider Western preoccupation with maximising the quantity of productive activity which could be performed in a given time.

The centrality of this perspective in the discourse of steamship mobilities is foregrounded in a passage from the *Asiatic Journal and Monthly Register*. This appeared in the aforementioned 1843 article which emphasised the importance of temporal regularity and predictability for P&O's steamship service. The article's speculations regarding this transition's timesaving ramifications play into an increasingly instrumentalised understanding of lived time:

> If we regard life merely as a space of time within which a certain number of things may be done or suffered, it is obvious that the acceleration and multiplication of those operations in which we are agents and patients, may, in a certain sense, be said to lengthen life. If the facilities of communication between remote countries are so increased that their intercourse, which required twelve months, can be performed in two, six times as much can be done of those things which depended upon that intercourse ... This is to make the space assigned to human life the measure of a greater number of acts and of gratifications than formerly, and what is this but a virtual increase of that space?[69]

Steamship temporality is framed in this striking passage in an explicit relationship with lived time. Time is rendered as a spatial dimension, reflecting its measurability and homogeneity. Lived time is expressed within the structural logic of temporal instrumentalisation, in which human life is measured solely in terms of the number of activities which can be performed or experienced in a given period of time. Such a perspective reflects the rationalisation of time internal to the logic of modern capitalism. Further elucidating this connection, the article clarifies that among the consequences of the steamship's radical temporal abbreviation of the voyage, 'the merchant can transact six times as much business'.[70]

However, despite its unprecedented saving of time, the monotony ubiquitous to accounts of the overland route frames the time of steamship mobility as wasted, empty, unproductive time. Just as time was rationalised, developments in the technological means to save time, to minimise the time spent in unproductive activity, contributed to the identification of time as specifically a resource to be filled with productive activity: as the time in transit was reduced, so its identity as unproductive time was emphasised. This association between lived time and productive activity reflects the instrumentalised conception of time at the heart of Michael Adas's account of Western temporal rationalisation. 'Time', he writes, 'came to be ... viewed as a commodity to be economized or squandered.'[71] This perspective informed the transactional nature with which the relationship between steamship mobilities and time was viewed. William Howard Russell's 1858 account of a voyage from Suez to Calcutta on board the *Nubia* presents a typically transactional account of the voyage's monotony. 'If the sea be the great highway of nations', he writes, 'certainly those who traffic on it pay toll in the shape of patience.'[72]

Experiences of shipboard time were informed by wider conceptualisations of temporality which reflect specifically modern, Western, capitalist conceptions of identity. As Miles Ogborn has observed, 'capitalism, bureaucracy, imperialism and disciplinary power all remake time and give content to understandings of what is historically new'.[73] Yet overland route narratives are permeated with a sense of dislocation from a temporal simultaneity with the lived time of the modern world. Eliot Warburton, recounting his voyage to Egypt aboard the *Oriental* in 1843, emphasises his sense of separation from the day-to-day experience of social relations on land:

> Our time flows on smoothly and pleasantly enough; its course is so monotonous and even, that it seems rapid. The minds of sea-going men enjoy entire freedom from the daily cares that fever ordinary life; there is no wealth to be lost or gained, no letters to disturb into joy or sorrow, no intrusive visitors.[74]

Monotony here finds expression as a category of pleasure in the apparent compression of duration it facilitated. Time passed faster for Warburton, he claims, because it appeared hardly to pass at all. This passage again exhibits an association between the experience of shipboard temporality and the dislocation from the lived time of life on land. The fact that this is expressed in terms of monetary transactions and the receipt of letters and visitors makes it abundantly clear just what kind of life the passenger was separated from. It describes the social relations typical to the modern, bourgeois individual, for whom productive activity was the measure and *raison d'être* of life. As Tamson Pietsch has suggested, claims regarding boredom on long ship passages in the nineteenth century can be understood in light of wider frameworks of cultural attitudes toward time. 'Being bored', she writes, 'implied a *desire* to work or be active, shifting the moral weight of responsibility for inactivity from the individual to the constraints of the environment.'[75]

Norman Macleod, recalling his 1864 voyage from Southampton to Alexandria on board the *Valetta*, provides an even more emphatic characterisation of the voyage as a separation from this social reality. His language emphasises the extent to which the space of the sea was perceived as a vast emptiness which intervened between the passenger and the temporality of modern life:

> A mighty gulf of deep water separates us from the world of letters, business, calls, meetings, appointments, committees, visits, and all like disturbers of selfish ease ... The brain and memory empty themselves so completely of all that has troubled or occupied them during previous periods of existence.[76]

Macleod describes an intensely psychic sensation of separation from the distractions of modern life. Modernity assumes a sense of temporal simultaneity with other 'moderns', the feeling of living in the 'same time' as other Western subjects. Time at sea removed the passenger from this sense of being simultaneous with the Western world.[77] Unsurprisingly, complaints of boredom tend to be more prevalent in accounts of the Eastern section of the route. By the mid-nineteenth century, travel had become associated in bourgeois society with a complex set of cultural meanings: enjoyment, escape, education.[78] Met with the repetition, familiarity and blankness of shipboard life, passengers sometimes struggled to narrate their time in transit as an appropriately edifying experience. The steamship voyage's temporal repeatability meant that it was very clear to the passenger that despite their global mobility, they were experiencing a standardised, predictable form of travel. While the steamship provided an industrially produced form of global mobility, the passenger was essentially little more than a passive consumer of this commodity.

Stimulation and the imperial geographies of steamship mobility

'Got bored upon deck, and went to my cabin', recalls Albert Smith of his wearisome 1858 voyage from Suez to Point de Galle aboard the *Bentinck*: 'got bored there, and came upon deck again, and wished I was anywhere else'.[79] Smith's shipboard perambulations manifest a desire for stimulation, specifically for a change in environment which the mobile space of the steamer was unable to provide. 'I come down to tea every night simply because it is *something to do*', he writes. 'I am really getting terribly bored ... and am only thinking of home.'[80] The passenger's separation from land, and all the comforts, familiarity and activity of home, was expressed as a need for stimulation. Despite the steamship's innovations in mobility, life during transit could itself be stultifyingly unchanging. Jan Brumund, recounting his 1858 voyage from Point de Galle to Suez on board the *Bengal*, paints a representative picture of the tedium of the overland route voyage. His description presents an image of steamship mobility which resembles more a journey into a state of somnambulism than one taken on board the most advanced technology of global transportation:

> The conversation was rarely animated. There was more reading and sleeping in the chairs than talking; but the rocking of the boat brings you so imperceptibly into a sweet slumber, and the sharp bright light is soporific. A few times in the evening for a moment I heard the soft tones of a gentleman or woman's voice. But the song soon died away and it was as still again as darkness around me.[81]

Like numerous other passenger accounts, the striking description of shipboard life furnished by Brumund emphasises the homogeneous quality of the time spent in transit. This dreamlike depiction, juxtaposed with an incident Brumund describes from a few days later in the journey, graphically illustrates the extent to which the boredom experienced by passengers was rooted in their dislocation from the social life of land. In this passage, Brumund relates the sudden and unanticipated appearance, during the journey up the Red Sea, of another P&O steamship, an event which provokes a spontaneous and profound transformation of the mood on board. The passengers' emotional state shifts from stupefied boredom to one which would not be out of place in descriptions of the overstimulation and novelty which typify accounts of the modern city:

> Toward nightfall a steamship appeared unexpectedly on the distant horizon, the mail boat from Suez. Soon she was at our side. A repeated 'hurrah!' went up from both decks, where passengers and crew were crowded against the bulwarks. The stewards of the other boat had taken up positions on the side of the paddle box. They waved tablecloths and raised dishes. What a sudden, profound change at such an encounter! All who were just recently so quiet and calm, are now full of fire, ignited in enthusiasm. Those repeated cries; that face full of expression; those beautiful eyes, some filled with tears! But could it be otherwise? Could you remain cold, indifferent? Behold, they are drawing near, just a little too close they shoot past each other, for a moment they are deck to deck – these two boats, each of which rushes to a completely opposite end of the earth. The travellers just a moment ago invisible to each other now see each other face to face, exchanging a word, a cry, a wink, but everything just for a moment, in the next once again they have forever vanished from each other's eyes.[82]

This vivid scene, the fleeting contact of two atomised groups of travellers in the midst of their global mobility, is described by Brumund as 'a reunion and farewell, in the same moment!'[83] The passengers experienced a spontaneous shift from social atomisation to a fleeting sense of connection with the global network of imperial actors of which they were part. This ephemeral encounter was marked by a frenetic energy which appeared almost to jump like a spark between the two steamships. Immediately following this scene of bustle and commotion however, Brumund recounts a return to the unreality of steamship life he had previously described. 'With redoubled force', he writes, 'the two steamers chase past each other. It is to us like an apparition. We see, hear, rejoice and yet it is to us as a fantasy, but a fantasy of profound impression.'[84] If the monotony of shipboard life was rooted in the passengers' disconnection from a sense of temporal simultaneity with other 'moderns', then this story appears to narrate the passengers' sudden and fleeting reconnection with that temporal logic. The passengers' spontaneous re-engagement with the social relations from which they had been separated by the vast void of the sea prompted a form of experience analogous to the feverish bustle typically associated with modern life.

Not all passengers, however, complained of boredom during the passage. Albert Hervey's account of his 1843 overland route voyage lauded the new means of communication with the East over the Cape route by sailing ship. This privileging was framed not merely in terms of the radical reduction in the journey's duration. While, as I explored in Chapter 1, Hervey had described the steamer itself as an oasis of calm, the various calling points along the route provided ample distraction and stimulation. Although the overland route was marginally more expensive than the alternative by sail, Hervey considered its benefits in distinctly transactional terms: 'all that the traveller sees', he writes, 'amply compensates for any extra outlay of money for the passage'. He goes on to express his delight at the stimulating experience of the voyage from Madras to Suez on board the *Hindostan*:

> Our life, on board the Hindustan [*sic*], was a very joyous one; plenty to eat and drink; many ways of amusement; many methods of killing time, which flew by us as fast as did our ship through the immense space of water ... Our pace was so rapid that we could not help coming upon some novelty on each coming day.[85]

The monotony which characterises so many accounts of the overland route was for Hervey dispelled by the novelty of the experience of mobility. In his account, the ship's progress through maritime space was intimately connected to the passage of time during the voyage. Admittedly, Hervey travelled scarcely a year after the overland route's inauguration, and inevitably compared the novel steam route with his interminable, uneventful four-month voyage to India by sail of a decade before.[86] For Hervey, the experience of sensory stimulation was provided by both the steamship's mobility and the various shipboard forms of distraction.

William Makepeace Thackeray also described his 1844 steamship excursion as one rich with experience, again rendered in distinctly transactional terms. The trip was what he termed a 'profitable' one, precisely because, he writes, 'it leaves such a store of pleasant recollections'.[87] Thackeray's experience of the overland route, however, was as an intensive sightseeing tour of the Mediterranean. The pleasures he recollects refer less to shipboard life itself, but rather to the rich diversity of locations he visited during his trip: Vigo, Lisbon, Cadiz, Gibraltar, Malta, Athens, Smyrna, Constantinople, Rhodes, Beirut, Jaffa, Jerusalem, Alexandria, Cairo – all seen in a period of two months. It was this profusion of geographical locations, contingent upon the steamship's mobility, that left Thackeray grateful for the respite from sensory stimulation offered by his time spent in quarantine in Malta.[88]

For David Lester Richardson, the new means of transportation to India provided by the steamship contrasted favourably with the voyage by sail. Although he had lamented the 'objectlessness' of steamship travel, Richardson considered steam to be a decisive departure from sail. This he expressed not only in steam's practical shortening of the voyage, but in an altered conception of the voyage's duration. This experiential shift Richardson attributed to a stimulating series of distractions which punctuated the voyage's continuity: 'From the dull monotony of the voyage to India by the Cape of Good Hope, the way seems longer than it really is, while the varying aspects and many points of lively interest in the Overland Route, make a short trip seem shorter still.'[89] Again an alteration in the sensation of time's passing is invoked, framed by Richardson as a binary contrast of unvarying tedium and exhilarating change which characterised the experience of the sail and steam voyage respectively. Significantly, his identification of the overland route as a departure from the pelagic monotony of the Cape voyage refers not to shipboard life itself, but again to the time the steamship spent away from the open sea. While the 'varying aspects' which Richardson refers to denote the diverse and changing scenery viewed from the ship, the 'points of interest' were provided by the various locations which the steamer called at on its route. These stops provided brief touristic interludes in the voyage, with all overland route journeys from England to India calling at least at Gibraltar and Malta in the Mediterranean and Aden and Point de Galle on the Eastern side of Egypt. The middle part of the route, the overland section from Alexandria to Suez, itself provided ample opportunity for distraction and sightseeing. Indeed, as On Barak has argued, the overland route was itself instrumental in the production and popularisation of Egyptian tourism in the mid-nineteenth century.[90]

Joachim Stocqueler, in his 1844 travel guide *The Hand-Book of India*, discusses the relative benefits of the sailing voyage and the new steam route. The former, he writes, compared unfavourably with steam for many passengers, owing to the duration of the voyage and the dearth of stimulation during the passage. Stocqueler describes 'the prospect of an imprisonment on board a ship for three or four months, with no more agreeable view, externally, than a vast expanse of sea and sky'. Passengers, he writes, anticipate 'a wearisome and monotonous existence'. Perhaps unsurprisingly, the overland route compared favourably with this protracted period of time at sea:

> It has the advantage of being an infinitely more expeditious method of reaching India, and of being less wearisome by reason of the perpetual change of scene which it presents between England, passing the coast of Spain, Gibraltar, Malta, Egypt, Aden (and if bound to Calcutta), Ceylon and the continent of India.[91]

The overland route steamship presented both a faster means of transport, and benefited from a succession of stimulating diversions, offering the passenger distraction and respite from the boredom of life at sea. Although there is little remarkable in Stocqueler's claim, it appears to run contrary to the widespread characterisation of the overland route as itself a monotonous experience. However, again the claims regarding steamship mobilities refer not the experience of shipboard life itself, but to the variety of different locations encountered on the route.

If the experience of life on board the steamer at sea was described as almost akin to a state of unconsciousness, every location at which the ship landed was marked by a sensation analogous to Brumund's account of the two ships meeting in the Red Sea, a spontaneous and exhilarating awakening. Eliot Warburton had described his voyage aboard the *Oriental* in 1843 as one characterised by a monotony rooted in the passenger's separation from life on land. The listless equanimity of the passage produced in him a desire for stimulation: 'In the care-free idleness of our voyage', he writes, 'every trifle becomes a matter of interest.'[92] In distinct contrast to this familiar characterisation of shipboard life, Warburton describes the ship's arrival at Alexandria:

> Amid a deafening din of voices and a pestilential effluvia from dead fish and living Arabs, you fight your way ashore: and if you had just awakened from a sleep of ages, you could scarcely open your eyes upon a scene more different from those you have just left.[93]

The movement from the ship to the shore is portrayed as a transition from sleep to waking, a spontaneous explosion of overwhelming sensory excess. Warburton's description of the spontaneous reconnection with the activity and bustle of life on land is in stark contrast to the sense of ontological absence which pervades accounts of steamship travel. However, Warburton subscribed to the widespread orientalist conceit that while the West was characterised by a dynamic temporality of change and frenetic activity, the

East was frozen in time, retrograde, unchanging and serene. He describes the marked contrast between what he calls the 'tumult and fever of European life with the silence and repose of the East'.[94] The dead time of life in transit thus sat ill with claims regarding the steamship's modernity.

As the continuity of the overland route was punctuated with numerous interruptions of the kind described by Warburton, the overland route passenger was in a constant state of anticipation – for the next sighting of land, the next shore visit, of joining the flow of time on land once more. The rhythm of mobility experienced in the punctuation of the steamer's ports of call appears, for many passengers, to have compensated for the sensation of a departure from lived time while on board the ship itself. However, while the ship's various calling points provided passengers with a welcome respite from the monotony of life on board, the stimulation they provided itself only served, for many, to emphasise the empty homogeneity of the time spent in transit. Charles H. Allen's account of travelling on the *Tanjore* from Marseille to Alexandria in 1867 suggests that the sense of anticipation he felt for the ship's next calling point was experienced as an idiosyncratically temporal concern. Despite the relative brevity of the voyage, and what he refers to as the 'marvellous precision and speed' of steamship mobilities, Allen characterised the voyage's duration as itself merely a period occupied with waiting for the journey's end. 'The moment you sail', he writes, 'you commence looking forward eagerly to the hour and day when you are due at the next place of call.'[95] Voyage narratives often framed the ship's calling points as touristic breaks in the monotony of the voyage, which provided the pleasure of sensory stimulation and distraction. These carefully spaced pauses along the steamship's route were of course contingent upon the steamship's means of propulsion – they provided coaling stops used to replenish the vast fuel supplies required by the ship's engines. Through the punctuation of these interruptions, the temporal logic of steam travel was inscribed on the consciousness of the passenger, experienced as touristic leisure.

For Allen, the sensation of temporal emptiness he experienced in transit was such that any distraction was greeted as a moment of stimulation. 'The great feature on board steamers', he writes, 'is the meal hour. There is a break in the monotony whenever the bell rings for eating.'[96] Like the ship's contact with land, bourgeois leisure activities and polite sociality played an analogous role, offering a precisely timed interruption of the homogeneous temporality of transit. It was only in the reproduction of social relations on land that steamship travel could become less conducive to boredom (as explored in detail in Chapter 4). This is articulated in Allen's description of his voyage aboard the *Nubia* in the Red Sea: 'Life on board ship is necessarily very monotonous and wearisome. On the Peninsular and Oriental steamers there are always plenty of passengers to afford pleasant intercourse, and there is no doubt less *ennui* than where there are but few persons on board.'[97] The recreation of bourgeois social relations on the steamer presented for Allen a remedy to the monotony of the voyage, creating the sensation of the continuation of lived time, rather than its absence. Above all, this continuity was expressed through the practices of bourgeois leisure.

Leisure time: Consuming mobility

Steven Adriaan Buddingh, the Dutch pastor whose 1852 overland route narrative features in Chapter 1, also published an account of his return journey from the Dutch East Indies in 1857. Buddingh's second account lacks the exuberant enthusiasm which the Dutch often expressed for the British imperial logistical revolution. His description, from the later book, of the voyage from Singapore to Point de Galle aboard the *Aden* features a familiar description of the apathetic sensation of monotony experienced by many passengers – and like these other accounts, Buddingh expressed this shipboard experience as a specifically temporal concern. 'Dinner ends at 5,' he writes, 'and so there are 5 long tedious hours up to 10 o'clock that one does not know how to spend. The passengers are already dozing on deck by 7 and sometimes sleeping soundly.'[98] For Buddingh, his 1857 voyage compared unfavourably with the overland route journey he had undertaken five years previously:

> On the occasion of my last overland mail voyage in 1852 the saloon was bright with oil lamps in the evening and some passengers engaged in whist, ombre, chess, backgammon etc. There were piano and guitar players, and singers. A band of musicians and usually a dance on the deck enlivened the monotonous sea voyage. Now there is nothing.[99]

The monotony described by Buddingh had apparently been mitigated on his previous trip by the distractions of leisure activities, which reproduced the conditions of bourgeois social life on land. As the consumer of an expensive, exclusive form of mobility, the bourgeois passengers' expectations regarding the standards of living on board were high.

Buddingh articulates his experience of the second portion of his disappointing 1857 journey, from Point de Galle to Suez on board the *Bengal*, specifically in terms of the absence of the trappings of the bourgeois lifestyle he had encountered on his 1852 voyage:

> Here one finds no oil lamps in the evening, but weak and very sparsely distributed candles. The champagne has been abolished; napkins are never provided. Everything has changed greatly since 1852. There is even just a cracked cymbal used on board the 'Bengal', to give the signals for the dinner etc. The salons are not so richly decorated. In a word, it is to be hoped that another Company

(preferably not an English one) will establish a second undertaking for the Overland passage to India. Then shall the present P. and O. S. N. Company be taught to treat passengers no longer as mail or goods.[100]

Buddingh's criticisms were perhaps in part motivated by an element, found in even enthusiastic Dutch accounts, of a keenness to find fault with the infrastructure of British imperialism. While it was clear that the Dutch had been far surpassed in their formerly significant imperial power, there was perhaps some consolation in finding fault with the relatively insignificant minutiae of British imperialism's cultural life. For example, in Buddingh's description of Singapore, an important port of call on his homeward route, he registers his disapproval of the British management of the formerly Dutch imperial possession: 'It is still the same melancholy place', he writes, 'as all the English possessions are in Asia. The English do not understand life in tropical regions. Everything looks shabby and uncomfortable, and the famous English *Comfort* is nowhere to be found.'[101] As Chapter 4 will explore, comfort was a hotly contested concept around which the experience of overland route mobility was negotiated, and one that went to the heart of conceptions of bourgeois leisure in transit.

The absence of comfort on board the *Bengal* which Buddingh describes is revealing, specifically expressed in terms of a series of signifiers of mid-nineteenth century bourgeois status and culture: décor, lighting, entertainment, social etiquette, fine dining. These material, social and performative elements of shipboard life clearly served as a means to ward off the monotony of mobility at sea. Buddingh compares this lack of shipboard luxury and distraction to being treated as cargo – an object of the mobility process rather than the consumer of an expensive commodity. With this association, Buddingh's criticisms articulate a widespread apprehension concerning emergent industrial forms of transportation in the nineteenth century. Wolfgang Schivelbusch has explored this characterisation of the passenger experience in the context of the steam train:

> This form of travel transformed the traveler into a parcel. The realization that one no longer felt like a person but like a commodity indicates some awareness that one had been assimilated not only by physically accelerated speed but also by the generally accelerated process of the circulation of goods.[102]

Owing to their limited freight capacities, early P&O steam vessels sought to carry low-volume, high-value cargo such as specie (money in the form of coins) or silk, in addition to the mail consignment. The wealthy colonial traveller was among these cargoes, those who were able to pay high prices for the temporal compression and precision of the journey the steamship provided. The boredom during transit was frequently expressed in passenger accounts as an absence of agency, thought and action: as noted, the passenger's identity as a passive consumer of mobility was problematic, identifying the time spent in transit as the inversion of the productive, busy time of modern bourgeois life on land. As Buddingh's observations suggest, the façade of luxury and distraction on the ship served to insulate the passenger somewhat from this experience. This phenomenon will be explored in depth in Chapter 4, specifically in terms of the embodied, performative social practices associated with the domestic. As we shall see, these practices helped passengers to associate the overland route voyage with the perpetuation, rather than antithesis, of time on land. They warded off the sense that the passenger travelled merely as any other cargo would. The failure of this differentiation highlighted for passengers their status as passive consumers of mobility, rather than privileged patrons of bourgeois leisure.

One distinctive and contentious high-value cargo carried by P&O steamships operating in East Asian waters illustrates the extent to which the dividing line between passenger and cargo could be ill-defined – and the consequences of such a failure in demarcation. The artist and travel writer Robert Elwes, in his 1854 account of a voyage aboard the *Lady Mary Wood* from Hong Kong to Shanghai, recalls a shipboard encounter with opium smoking. 'One of the passengers was a well-educated and rich Chinese', he writes. 'He always dined with us, and then retired to his cabin to smoke opium, an indulgence in which we sometimes joined him.' However, Elwes continues, 'as the cargo of the "Lady Mary Wood" was opium, an odour of it filled the whole ship without any smoking'.[103] P&O had commenced shipping the drug from Bombay to China in 1847, the first company to transport opium by steamship. As a high-value, low-volume freight, opium presented a superlative cargo for the steamship, which was able to perpetuate the trade during periods when seasonal variations in the weather meant that the sail-driven clipper ships which dominated the market were rendered ineffective. P&O's involvement in this trade was significant, introducing reliable, predictable supplies of the drug with the use of steam. Between 1847 and 1858 they shipped 642,000 chests of opium to China.[104] This illegal, yet state-administered trade in the drug was a measure by which the British state forced opium – which had been produced cheaply by exploiting its Indian growers – onto the Chinese market, thus rebalancing a colossal deficit in silver which had been brought about by the extensive imports of Chinese tea and other luxury commodities into Britain over the previous decades.[105] This trade, forcing millions into addiction and poverty, was performed against the wishes of the Chinese state, and enforced by the imperialist violence of the Opium Wars.

The vapours of the opium cargo permeated the passenger quarters, blurring the lines between the two distinct shipboard spaces. Opium's imperial mobilities highlight the sometimes poorly defined boundary between passengers and cargo on the steamer, presenting a very literal iteration of the more general sense in which the texture of shipboard experience intersected with the logistical, the economic, the geopolitical. In his account of a voyage from Singapore to Hong Kong aboard the *Madras* in 1855, George Francis Train found that the porosity of this boundary was such that sometimes the opium cargo even came to occupy space on the steamer which was intended for passengers. 'I was disquieted', he writes, 'to find that the agent at Bombay had filled several of the cabin state-rooms with opium, which accounted for the passengers all being huddled together three or four in a state-room.' As boundaries blurred, with passengers and cargo occupying the same shipboard space, passengers inevitably became involuntary consumers of the drug. Train complains that the ship was filled with 'the sickening smell of the drug'. The opium permeated the shipboard experience of the passengers:

> Go where you would you could not escape its stupefying influence, down below or on deck, in your state-room or at the dinner-table, the continual nauseating smell of opium gave you a headache and the blues, to say nothing of keeping your eyes half closed when you did not care to sleep.[106]

The intangible shipboard presence of the drug mediated the experience of travel, producing a psychic state not dissimilar to the sensation of apathy and blankness which is a ubiquitous feature of overland route narratives. It also highlights the extent to which the broader politics of the imperial economy could find expression (in unexpected ways) within the ship itself, even permeating the embodied experience of travel.

Albert Smith's 1859 account of his voyage from Point de Galle to Shanghai aboard the *Norna* again records the proximity of the ship's passengers to the drug. 'Some of the people', he writes, 'say that the smell of the opium cargo, which is very strong, makes them drowsy. The other passengers did not read, or do anything; they would sit for hours looking at the sea.'[107] However, there is little to distinguish such claims regarding the sensory impact of the opium cargo from Smith's extensive remarks detailing the dull monotony of life at sea. The anonymous author of the 1853 *Southern Literary Messenger* article documenting an overland route voyage from England to China furnished extensive descriptions of the temporal homogeneity and tedium of the voyage on board the *Haddington*, travelling from Suez to Point de Galle. Despite these claims, the *Haddington* had been carrying almost 200 passengers, and upon boarding the *Ganges* at the latter port, bound for Hong Kong with just fifteen passengers, the author notes a marked shift in the atmosphere on board:

> To the unusual quiet which prevailed, after the bustle of shipboard to which we had been accustomed, we were at first inclined to attribute our somnorific

tendencies by day and prolonged deep sleep at night; but we soon discovered that this was owing to a far different cause. Snugly stowed away below was a goodly freight of opium, and the odour from this narcotic drug stole through the bulk-heads and pervaded the air of the cabins.[108]

Again, there was little to distinguish the drug-induced torpor from the widespread mood of apathy and inertia which reigned on board the steamship.

Like the effects of opium, this passivity and detachment infused even the forms of distraction available to the passenger. Narrating his voyage from Southampton to Alexandria on board the *Valetta* in 1864, Norman Macleod had described the profound sensation of separation from the distractions and obligations of a busy bourgeois life, which underpinned the pervasive mood of apathy he experienced. 'On ship-board,' he writes, 'pleasure and necessity are one. We cannot help being idle. We may possibly exert ourselves to play draughts or backgammon, but not chess – that requires thought.'[109] Undemanding games and other leisure activities provided a significant respite for passengers from the monotony of the voyage. These leisured social practices provided not just a means to 'fill' the unproductive time of transit with distraction – they allowed for the bourgeois passengers' identification of the voyage as a period of leisured enjoyment, rather than merely the dead time of transit. As Carol Harrison has written, leisure was at the heart of the emergent nineteenth-century bourgeois identity. 'Indulgence in leisure was crucial to bourgeois status', she writes. 'It represented bourgeois emancipation from the demands corporate society placed on an individual's time.'[110] Indulging in bourgeois leisure pursuits allowed passengers to identify the empty homogeneity of the steamship voyage as a relaxing escape from the demands of work and social obligation, rather than an enforced departure from the temporality of life on land.

As Gregory Votolato has suggested, the popularity of shipboard leisure pursuits was intimately related to the separation of the passenger from everyday life and productive activity:

> The passenger ship more typically remains a cocoon from the world of enterprise and industry, and it demands a relaxation of the productive urge in favour of time spent on pleasant and diverting activities. Thus, from the earliest steamships to today's floating theme parks, games have had a particular importance at sea. In addition to gambling, be it organized gaming such as roulette, or simple card games, whist or poker, the wager has always been a compelling shipboard pastime.[111]

On the overland route, games of chance provided a particularly popular means of diversion. *The Popular Overland Guide* of 1861, a companion for those making the journey, warns against the temptations of gambling during the passage. 'The want of occupation which naturally exists at sea', the guide cautions, 'will probably lead to an invitation to join a card-party.' Gambling presented a tempting corrective to the monotony of life at sea. However, the guide warns, engaging in such practices could leave the passenger 'under obligations to strangers with whom it may not be desirable hereafter to consort'.[112] Engaging in such shipboard pursuits could result in unwelcome social relations beyond the confines of the ship and the duration of the voyage.

Gambling on board the steamship was not merely a means to fill the empty time of the voyage, but was often itself suffused with the temporal logic of steamship mobility. As a number of accounts of steamship travel attest to, the passenger's preoccupation with the voyage's temporality was often tied to the moment of the ship's arrival at its various ports of call, moments which provided an interruption in the monotony of waiting. A description of a variety of gambling popular on board overland route steamers, from an article in *Fraser's Magazine* reveals the way in which games of chance, a means of passing time, themselves became fixated upon the temporal specificity of the ship's geographical movement:

> That form of gambling which is most general on board these steamers, is that of lotteries. An hour or the day of twelve hours is divided into parts equal in number to the number of subscribers to the lottery: each subscriber draws a ticket, having written upon it one of these fractional periods, and he who draws the time at which the anchor falls or the engine stops at the next port, wins the sweep. As the steamer approaches the next port a good deal of excitement exists among the sporting community as to the determination of the question of time.[113]

Gambling on board the steamer existed in a relation of tension with 'the question of time', as passengers laid bets on the insignificant interstices of temporal contingency which existed within the precise discipline of the ship's schedule. Once steam had liberated the sea voyage from the contingency of nature, the time of arrival no longer varied by days, weeks and months, but by seconds, minutes and hours. In a description of a similar but distinct form of gambling, *The Popular Overland Guide* of 1861 observes the passengers' interest in 'the distance run from noon the previous day, which is always noted on a board by the captain, and forms the subject of many bets among the "sporting" passengers'.[114] This game of chance, which again marked the passing into leisure practices of the temporality of the ship's mobility, was part of a broader preoccupation with steamship time, with its measurement, its flow and its repetition. The gambler reinscribed as social experience the steamship's production of a predictable and repeatable arrival time. Such shipboard rituals provided passengers with a mode of identification with the steamship's temporally regimented global mobility.

In many regards steamship mobility was an idiosyncratically temporal affair – passengers tracked the ship's movement through various numerical and temporal practices. These shipboard rituals helped passengers engage with their journey through what was often perceived as a blank, threatening landscape, which provided little sensation of their global mobility. For many passengers however, the reality of overland route travel fell short of the often bombastic claims which surrounded the steamship. Between the percussive moments of stimulation experienced at the ship's calling points, an experience of mobility produced by the technology of steam, the voyage was often deadeningly mundane, and life at sea produced an acute sense of separation from the passing of time in the metropole.

The characterisation of the steamship voyage as time spent outside the continuity of modern life emphasises the extent to which the temporality of transit was mediated by wider developments in the social and cultural uses and understandings of time: the rationalisation of time meant that it was reduced to a simplistic binary, in which it was experienced as either productive or unproductive. Various forms of distraction, both on board and during the numerous touristic interludes at the vessels calling points, helped passengers identify the 'unproductive' time of the voyage with the social rituals of bourgeois leisure. Chapter 4 explores the extent to which an idiosyncratic shipboard domesticity contributed to this characterisation of the voyage, producing in passengers a sense of continuity and normalisation antithetical to the temporal dislocation of steamship mobilities charted in this chapter.

Notes

1 Matthew Henry Marsh, *Overland from Southampton to Queensland* (London: Edward Stanford, 1867), p. 13.
2 'To the Neilgherries and Back', *Indian Medical Gazette*, 1 September 1868, p. 211.
3 Barak, *On Time*, pp. 21–52.
4 Adas, *Machines as the Measure of Men*, pp. 241–58.
5 Giordano Nanni, *The Colonisation of Time: Ritual, Routine and Resistance in the British Empire* (Manchester: Manchester University Press, 2012), p. 2.
6 Allen, *A Visit to Queensland and Her Goldfields*, p. 1.
7 Karl Marx, 'Capital, Volume III', *Marx Engels Collected Works, Volume 37*, trans. by Ernest Untermann and others (Moscow: Progress Publishers, 1998), p. 407.
8 This practice was able to flourish from the time of the inception of the overland route until the completion of the Suez Canal which – as Engels points out in a note to the text – through the standardisation of maritime traffic between Britain and India would render it impracticable.

9 'Communication with the East', p. 567.

10 Barney Warf's discussion of 'shrinking waters with the steamship' is an example of the emphasis upon increased speed in the discourse of the steamship's history, to the detriment of temporal precision and predictability. Barney Warf, *Time–Space Compression: Historical Geographies* (Oxford: Routledge, 2008), pp. 103–10.

11 Lester, Boehme and Mitchell, *Ruling the World*, pp. 15, 168. The Black Ball Line had introduced scheduled departure dates for sailing packets in 1818. However, this was performed on the relatively simple transatlantic service, and the duration of the voyages varied considerably.

12 See, for example, Schivelbusch, *The Railway Journey*, pp. 42–4.

13 Anim-Addo, 'The Great Event of the Fortnight', p. 371.

14 'Peninsular and Oriental Company's Steamship Mooltan', *Illustrated London News*, 3 August 1861, p. 106.

15 As the example provided by Volume III of *Capital* suggests, steam's mobility regime was not simply the supersession of the existing system, but one which ran in parallel to the use of sail, simultaneous but nonsynchronous. It would not be until the latter part of the nineteenth century that steam vessels were able to provide a viable means of carrying anything other than high-value, low-volume freight. Bulky cargo which demanded little urgency thus remained the domain of the sailing ship, which travelled between Britain and the East irregularly and was based upon demand.

16 E.P. Thompson, 'Time, Work-Discipline, and Industrial Capitalism', *Past & Present*, 38 (1967), 56–97. See also Nanni, *The Colonisation of Time*.

17 *Hand Book of Information for Passengers and Shippers by the Peninsular & Oriental Steam Navigation Company's Steamers* (London: Peninsular and Oriental Steam Navigation Company, 1849), pp. 4–5.

18 Sidney Laman Blanchard, 'Housekeeping in India', *All the Year Round*, 31 January 1863, p. 91.

19 Barak, *On Time*, p. 25.

20 'For India Direct', *Household Words*, 1 May 1852, p. 144.

21 This was particularly so in the days before the global telegraph network's expansion to the East in the 1870s allowed for near-instantaneous global communications.

22 'Wreck of the "Malabar"', *Annual Register*, May 1860, p. 74.

23 As Freda Harcourt points out, the company were beholden to 'the unbreakable shackles of a mail contractor's timetable'. Harcourt, *Flagships of Imperialism*, p. 2.

24 Thomas Rainey, *Ocean Steam Navigation and the Ocean Post* (New York: D. Appleton & Company, 1858), p. 173.

25 'Supply – Civil Service Estimates' (1 August 1867), *Hansard's Parliamentary Debates, Third Series, Vol. 189* (London: Hansard, 1867), p. 693.

26 Anthony Trollope, *An Autobiography, Volume 1* (New York: Harper & Brothers, 1883), p. 112.

27 *Ibid.*, p. 113.

28 Speid, *Our Last Years in India*, p. 1.
29 London, National Maritime Museum Archive, P&O Company Records: 'Diary kept by William Adamson (later a Director of P&O) on a voyage to Singapore in the Himalaya and Oriental, in the form of letters to his father, plus a typescript copy', January–March 1854, P&O/92/1, p. 10 (28 January 1854).
30 Adas, *Machines as the Measure of Men*, pp. 246–8. The imposition of Western conceptions of temporality upon colonised populations as a facet of colonialism is explored in great detail in Nanni, *The Colonisation of Time*.
31 See Adas, *Machines as the Measure of Men*, p. 245. 'For European travelers,' he writes, 'time-keeping devices were also tangible links to the more "advanced" societies they had left behind.'
32 Newmarch, *Five Years in the East*, pp. 161–2.
33 For a discussion of the sense of romance and adventure which attended the eighteenth-century sailing ship voyage, see Auerbach, *Imperial Boredom*, pp. 42–3.
34 Aiton, *The Lands of the Messiah, Mahomet, and the Pope*, p. 40.
35 Maria Warner, *Phantasmagoria: Spirit Visions, Metaphors, and Media into the Twenty-first Century* (Oxford: Oxford University Press, 2006), pp. 95–104.
36 Aiton, *The Lands of the Messiah, Mahomet, and the Pope*, p. 40.
37 'Out in Blue Water', p. 196.
38 Clay, *Leaves from a Diary in Lower Bengal*, p. 15.
39 Rediker, *Between the Devil and the Deep Blue Sea*, p. 114.
40 Russell, *My Diary in India*, p. 29.
41 *The Popular Overland Guide*, p. 23.
42 Colomb, *Slave-catching in the Indian Ocean*, pp. 3–4.
43 'En Route; Or, Notes of the Overland Journey to the East', *Southern Literary Messenger: Devoted to Every Department of Literature and the Fine Arts*, March 1854, p. 156.
44 'To the Neilgherries and Back', p. 211.
45 Albert Smith, *To China and Back: Being a Diary Kept, Out and Home* (London: Chapman & Hall, 1859), p. 7.
46 Auerbach, *Imperial Boredom*, p. 12. Tamson Pietsch also explores shifts in the experience of time aboard nineteenth-century sailing ships during voyages to Australia. Pietsch 'Bodies at Sea', pp. 214–15.
47 Auerbach, *Imperial Boredom*, p. 12.
48 'En Route to Abyssinia', *The Morning Post*, 5 November 1867, p. 2.
49 Burton, *Personal Narrative of a Pilgrimage to Al Medinah and Meccah*, p. 12.
50 *Ibid.*, p. 10.
51 For explorations of the culture of speed and acceleration which prevails as one of the dominant discourses of Western modernity, see, for example: Kern, *The Culture of Time and Space*; Hartmut Rosa, *Social Acceleration: A New Theory of Modernity* (New York: Columbia University Press, 2013); John Tomlinson, *The Culture of Speed: The Coming of Immediacy* (London: Sage, 2007).
52 Colomb, *Slave-catching in the Indian Ocean*, pp. 7–8.
53 *Ibid.*, p. 8.

54 This sensation of separation perhaps accounts in part for the popular practice of producing a ship's newspaper on board the steamship, helping to assert a sense of contemporaneity and temporal continuity even while separated from the passage of time on land. See Roland Wenzlhuemer and Michael Offermann, 'Ship Newspapers and Passenger Life Aboard Transoceanic Steamships in the Late Nineteenth Century', *Transcultural Studies*, 1 (2012), 77–121.

55 William Westgarth, *Victoria and the Australian Gold Mines in 1857: With Notes on the Overland Route from Australia via Suez* (London: Smith, Elder & Co., 1857), p. 412.

56 *Ibid.*, p. 413.

57 Richardson, *The Anglo-Indian Passage*, p. 47.

58 Steinberg, *The Social Construction of the Ocean*, p. 208.

59 *Ibid.*

60 'En Route; Or, Notes of the Overland Journey to the East', p. 156.

61 Auerbach has suggested that the monotony of the imperial sailing ship voyage can be understood in the context of the modern emergence of the individual, and that shipboard boredom was characterised in part as an absence of the notion of individual happiness which was gaining traction at the time. Auerbach, *Imperial Boredom*, p. 42.

62 Pietsch, 'Bodies at Sea', p. 224.

63 *Ibid.*, p. 214.

64 *Ibid.*

65 *Grindlay and Co.'s Overland Circular, Hints for travellers to India, detailing the several routes* (London: Smith, Elder and Co., 1847), p. 46.

66 Richardson, *The Anglo-Indian Passage*, p. vii.

67 Max Weber, *The Protestant Ethic and the Spirit of Capitalism* (London: Allen & Unwin, 1976).

68 Zygmunt Bauman, *Liquid Modernity* (Cambridge: Polity Press, 2000), pp. 112–13.

69 'Communication with the East', p. 561.

70 *Ibid.*

71 Adas, *Machines as the Measure of Men*, p. 250.

72 Russell, *My Diary in India*, p. 44.

73 Miles Ogborn, *Spaces of Modernity: London's Geographies, 1680–1780* (London: Guilford Press, 1998), p. 3.

74 Warburton, *The Crescent and the Cross*, p. 6.

75 Pietsch, 'Bodies at Sea', p. 218.

76 Macleod, *Eastward*, p. 10.

77 This sense of simultaneity is at the core of Benedict Anderson's concept of 'imagined communities', the shared sense of community over vast areas produced by modern communication technologies. Anderson, *Imagined Communities*, p. 23.

78 Casey Blanton, *Travel Writing: The Self and the World* (London: Routledge, 1995), p. 20.

79 Smith, *To China and Back*, p. 11.

80 Ibid., p. 12.
81 Brumund, Schetsen eener Mail-Reize van Batavia naar Maastricht, p. 116.
82 Ibid., pp. 126–7.
83 Ibid., p. 127.
84 Ibid.
85 Hervey, The Ocean and the Desert, pp. 74, 45.
86 Albert Hervey, Ten Years in India: The Life of a Young Officer, Volume 1 (London: William Shoberl, 1850), pp. 1–19.
87 Thackeray, Notes of a Journey from Cornhill to Grand Cairo, p. xiii.
88 As described in Chapter 1.
89 Richardson, The Anglo-Indian Passage, p. 14.
90 Barak, On Time, pp. 27–35.
91 Stocqueler, The Hand-Book of India, pp. 164, 167.
92 Warburton, The Crescent and the Cross, p. 7.
93 Ibid., p. 24.
94 Ibid., pp. xi–xii.
95 Allen, A Visit to Queensland and Her Goldfields, p. 5.
96 Ibid., p. 4.
97 Ibid., p. 27.
98 Steven Adriaan Buddingh, Dagboek Mijner Overland-Mail-Reis van Batavia naar Nederland, via Triest, in 1857: Zijnde een Tegenhanger van het Dagboek Mijner Oveland-Mail-Reis van Rotterdam naar Java, vid Southampton, in 1852 (Arnhem: G. W. van der Wiel, 1857), pp. 10–11. This, and all subsequent translations of this source are my own.
99 Ibid., p. 10.
100 Ibid., p. 19.
101 Ibid., p. 6 (italics and capitalisation in original).
102 Schivelbusch, The Railway Journey, p. 193.
103 Robert Elwes, A Sketcher's Tour Round the World (London: Hurst and Blackett, 1854), pp. 355–6.
104 Harcourt, Flagships of Imperialism, pp. 86–113, p. 103.
105 Osterhammel, The Transformation of the World, pp. 731–2.
106 Train, An American Merchant in Europe, Asia and Australia, pp. 86–7.
107 Smith, To China and Back, p. 16.
108 'En Route; Or, Notes of the Overland Journey to the East', p. 217.
109 Macleod, Eastward, p. 10.
110 Carol E. Harrison, The Bourgeois Citizen in Nineteenth-Century France: Gender, Sociability, and the Uses of Emulation (Oxford: Oxford University Press, 1999), p. 88.
111 Gregory Votolato, Ship (London: Reaktion. 2011), p. 44.
112 The Popular Overland Guide, p. 25.
113 'Life in India', Fraser's Magazine for Town and Country, April 1870, pp. 469–70.
114 The Popular Overland Guide, p. 25.

4

'Not at home, yet so completely at home': Steamship domesticity

In 1858 the Dutch missionary Jan Brumund travelled from Point de Galle to Suez on board the *Bengal*. In his account of the voyage, Brumund described the ship in great detail, identifying in the vessel a peculiar kind of domesticity:

> But we turn to my cabin on the *Bengal* again. Yes, I am very pleasantly situated here. The cabin with its broad comfortable sofa is so spacious that I can easily imagine myself living within one small room. I spend a few hours there every day. I am, though not at home, yet so completely at home. And what is more agreeable when amongst strangers and surrounded by an uncaring, or at least not very attractive world, than to be at home.[1]

Brumund presents the steamship as an environment possessed of an unconventional and contradictory domesticity. In employing such terms to describe the P&O steamship, Brumund was not alone: narratives of overland route voyages are filled with allusions to the steamer as a homely, domestic space. The ubiquity of references to the steamship's domesticity indicates the development of new shipboard social, material and imaginative practices. This chapter considers this preoccupation with shipboard domesticity as a significant area of focus for engaging with colonial steamship mobilities.

Brumund's vivid description of the ship's cabin is instructive: like many accounts of the steamship's idiosyncratic domesticity, it characterises the homeliness of the interior with reference to the qualities of comfort and décor. This domesticity is defined against a hostile external world, articulating the inherent contradiction of dwelling in the flux and disruption of global transportation. As Brumund's observations suggest, steamship domesticity existed in a state of tension with the practicalities of this mobility – mobility and domesticity have long been seen as antithetical principals.[2] However, due to the length of time spent in transit during long-distance sea voyages, the ship has inevitably acted as a dwelling space for its occupants, in which passengers slept, ate and engaged in what other activities they could within the limitations of shipboard life. This chapter thus explores how the tension between these two conflicting principles played out in the novel and often unsettling experience of the steamship voyage. As will be seen, shipboard domesticity consisted largely in the recreation of familiar land-based practices, which operated particularly through the representational capacity of décor and the embodied experience of comfort.

Domesticity at sea: Normalising imperial mobilities

David Lester Richardson, discussing in 1845 the recent introduction of steamship travel to the East, was effusive regarding what he saw as the revolutionary transformations brought about by the steamship. A keen advocate of P&O's steamship service, Richardson described the overland route's development as 'an event of great importance, not in the history of England only, but in the history of the world'.[3] While he regarded the overland route as a momentous, global development, a decisive departure from what he considered the 'long and costly' voyage to India by sail, Richardson's description of the consequences of the global mobilities revolution was distinctly prosaic. 'The passage', he writes, 'is now a pleasure-trip.'[4] The revolution in global mobilities facilitated by steam was characterised by Richardson as ordinary, everyday, articulated specifically through its identification with the practices of leisure. This apparent contradiction was rooted in a shipboard domesticity which helped to normalise the steamship's emergent mobility. The discursive framing of the steamship as simultaneously a radical departure from sail and almost routinely quotidian was a persistent feature of accounts of travel aboard P&O steamers. It is reiterated in an 1861 article in *Blackwood's Magazine*:

> A voyage to China is a very different thing now to what it was seventy or even twenty years ago. The modern ambassador … takes a comfortable dinner, says good-by [*sic*] to his family, drives to London Bridge station, and in forty-eight hours he is smoking a cigar on the paddle-box of a Peninsular and Oriental Company's steamer.[5]

This blasé attitude toward the voyage presents the normalisation of a journey which had previously been conceived as an exotic departure from everyday life. The account presents a confident British imperial subject, at home in the midst of a global mobility. For many passengers, the steamship voyage presented a historical break with seafaring's past precisely in its banality. As has already been argued, this banality normalised and de-exoticised the imperial East, both for the passenger and for those who read these emphatic accounts of the ease and pleasure of global travel. Catherine Hall and Sonya Rose have explored this impact of the imperial imaginary on the British public. They note 'the emotional power of the connection between home, the domestic and the imperial metropole'.[6] Shipboard domestic practices allowed passengers to retain a sense of connection with such forms of British identity even in transit to the imperial East. They also produced a form of literature which emphasised the languid insouciance of imperial mobilities at sea.

The characterisation of the overland route voyage as the continuation of the everyday life of the modern, civilised European was a ubiquitous one. Yet it is in marked conflict with the widespread assertion in passenger accounts explored in Chapter 3, that the time spent in transit was experienced as an interruption, a departure from life's continuity. As Lambert and Merriman have written, mobility has long been seen as 'antithetical to notions of place'.[7] Life in transit is ostensibly incompatible with the permanence and familiarity which are at the heart of the close connections to localised geographies that typically characterise the domestic. This is consistent with the characterisation of 'being at home' in the imperial world explored by Hall and Rose, as a compromised and fraught endeavour. The domestic was perhaps in few cases so fraught as in the flux and disturbance of global travel. Yet it is clear from the ubiquitous references to the steamer's domestic idiosyncrasies that it was at the heart of passenger experiences and the cultural imaginary of the overland route.

It was precisely in the recreation of bourgeois domestic social practices that passengers were able to realise the performative expression of a leisured identity which, as suggested, operated as a corrective to the voyage's interruption of everyday life. In the traditional space of the sailing ship, where sailors' bodies moved in rhythms concurrent with the labour practices of sail, passenger comfort was generally considered of secondary importance.[8] Bringing with it a novel set of social relations and spatial practices – including the processes of order, hygiene, exclusion and hierarchy described in Chapter 2 – steam marked a departure from the improvisational spatial organisation of passenger quarters on the sailing ship.[9] Steamships saw the introduction to the voyage East of space dedicated solely to passenger use: permanent, furnished cabins, elaborately decorated saloons and dedicated bathrooms. It is instructive to compare this relative indulgence with the passenger space on board an East Indiaman. Cyril Northcote Parkinson has identified these shipboard spaces as of a more informal nature, whereby passengers were obliged to improvise dwelling within the interstices of the labour practices of sail. 'Cabins were not solid and permanent structures', writes Parkinson, 'they were made so as to allow of being struck in a few minutes when the ship cleared for action.' Accommodation allocated to the ship's officers was sold to passengers on an informal basis. This transaction afforded the passenger an empty space which they were obliged to furnish themselves. Furthermore, passenger accommodation on the East Indiaman was generally considered uncomfortable, unhygienic and damp, and was often overcrowded.[10]

The conditions encountered on the voyage by sail to India were thus seen as incompatible with the maintenance of domestic norms. William Hickey's account of a six-month voyage by sailing ship from India to England in 1808 makes this abundantly clear. Hickey describes his experience of embarkation as a transition 'from a house and establishment wherein not only every comfort but every luxury prevailed, to a little dirty hole of a cabin on board a ship'.[11] Hickey's description presents maritime mobility in the age of sail as antithetical to the domestic as an embodied, firmly terrestrial practice – and one expressive of class status. Conversely, the feeling of leisurely unconcern attributed to the traveller on the overland route frames the steamship voyage as a continuation of land-based domestic practices. Hickey's account is in stark contrast, for instance, to the homeliness ascribed by William Makepeace Thackeray to the *Lady Mary Wood*, on which he travelled from Southampton to Gibraltar at the outset of his 1844 Mediterranean excursion. Thackeray remarks that 'in the week we were on board – it seemed a year, by the way – we came to regard the ship quite as a home'.[12] Expressed – like so many other accounts of steamship travel – in the language of temporality, shipboard domesticity was for Thackeray experienced as simultaneously a temporal process and as an altered conception of time. However, he describes the voyage as a temporal extension not in its monotony, but one through which the steamship's familiarity, and thus homeliness, was established. The steamship's domesticity was an important aspect of the process by which its space came to be identified as British, normalising for passengers a confident imperial world view even in the flux of global mobility.

However, the various references to the steamship's homeliness found in passenger accounts delineate a myriad of meanings. They encompass articulations of domesticity which span the convolutions of social practice, embodied experience and – as this chapter explores in detail – the materialities of comfort and décor. 'For India Direct', an 1852 article from the weekly journal *Household Words* offers a particularly effusive and wide-ranging account of steamship domesticity. It affords a useful opportunity to establish a working understanding of the terminology's discursive complexity. Beginning by describing the bustle of the *Bentinck*'s departure from the Southampton docks, the article portrays this chaotic activity in stark contrast to the composed sense of normality attributed to the passengers on board. Referring to a young female passenger already mentioned in the article, its author describes the final loading of the *Bentinck*:

The bustle is intense. Everything, including boxes of specie, seems endowed with locomotive power; and I am the more struck with the calm unconcern of my ringletted friend. I espy her at her cabin window, behind a jar of beautiful flowers, reading, with the settled, unruffled air of having lived there for the last twelvemonth.[13]

The steamer is presented as a novel sphere of experience, where commodities appear to be animated by their own agency, but which the modern global traveller occupies with equanimity. The passenger's femininity emphasises the domestic nature of this imperturbability. As Nancy Pagh has argued, sea travel has typically been seen as antithetical to the feminine associations of domesticity.[14] However, while it was imperative that P&O cater for both the real and perceived needs of its wealthy female passengers, the persistent characterisation of the steamship as a home in transit was implicated more in the perpetuation of bourgeois class-based social practices than with specifically gendered ones. The *Household Words* article accentuates the image of this gendered domestic interior in its juxtaposition with the bustle of mobility and labour. While the ship's cargo was being stowed for the voyage, its human freight was already inert in the cabin, blithely at home amid the flux and activity of departure. The article again implicates the domestic in the production of the voyage not as a rupture in life's continuity, but its perpetuation. Further pursuing this concern, its author observes that even at the moment of the steamship's departure, 'nobody seems to do anything different here to what they do at home'. Again, the steamship's homeliness is characterised by a composed state of everyday familiarity, rooted in the perpetuation of domestic social practices. The article describes 'the composed calmness, the trusting unpreparedness of the outward bound. Why need travel disturb the lightest of their every-day habits?' The steamship passenger, about to embark upon a transnational voyage which little more than a decade before would have taken perhaps six months to complete, is depicted as manifesting a serene disregard for the magnitude of this global mobility. This blasé attitude is associated with the reproduction on board ship of familiar bourgeois domestic tropes. The article lauds 'the spacious luxuriousness of the saloon, the domestic snugness of the sleeping berths'.[15]

The journey to India, which would last more than a month, performed in the most advanced form of global transportation, was in this account embarked upon by the passenger as if they were not leaving the space of home. The writer attributes this feeling of normality to 'the calm completeness of the whole ship'. An ordered microcosm, the harmonious serenity of the bourgeois world was transposed into the space of the steam vessel by the methods of spatial discipline already documented in Chapter 2. Furthermore, the steamship's domesticity helped to establish a sense of place, a stable familiarity in which an impression of normality could be experienced despite the loss of spatial specificity and flux concomitant with global mobility. The article ascribes this familiarity not just to the passenger accommodations, but also to the general luxury and comfort met with on board ship. 'We, on board the Bentinck' it observes, 'need to bring nothing; we find every conceivable requirement that life in its highest state of pampered affluence can desire.'[16] The impression of continuity produced by the steamship's domesticity reflected the passengers' wealth and social status. In the first decades of P&O's overland service to the East, alcohol was included in the passage money, with champagne served twice a week; dinner menus were exultantly varied and ostentatious, every vessel carried a small library, and a band played in the evening while passengers danced on deck.[17] As suggested in Chapter 3, the voyage's interruption of the continuity of life could be alleviated through the shipboard reproduction of bourgeois leisure practices. 'The passengers, therefore,' surmises the article, 'are curiously unexcited.'[18] Domesticity played a significant role in the characterisation of the steamship voyage as a modern, effortless, and even natural form of mobility.

Mobility contra the domestic

Walter Benjamin was perceptive in his claim that modern life was not only typified by a bustling excess of sensory stimulation, but also by attempts to cushion against this excess. In *The Arcades Project*, Benjamin characterised the bourgeois domestic interior as a retreat both from the world of work and from the dynamic overstimulation of the modern city, a protective encasing which shielded against the shocks of modern life.[19] In an analogous sense, the identification of the steamship voyage as one of ease and pleasure was rooted in a domesticity which intervened between the passenger and the materiality of maritime mobility. As suggested, the steamship was ordered around strict disciplinary modes of spatial demarcation, separating the passenger from the bustle of labour practices aboard ship. Such a separation made possible the passenger's experience of the voyage as the perpetuation of everyday life rather than its interruption. This process helped mediate the relationship between the production and consumption of mobility on board the steamship. As Wolfgang Schivelbusch has argued in the context of the steam train, interior furnishings had a role to play in cushioning the Victorian passenger from the corporeal realities of industrial transport's production.[20] Schivelbusch frames this claim in the light of Karl Marx's insight that mobility is the one commodity that must necessarily be consumed in the location of its production.[21] Shipboard domesticity can thus be seen as part of a process of removing the passenger from the experience of production, a kind of cushioning against the shocks and disruption of shipboard labour. On board the steamer, this process occurred specifically within the conditions of the industrialisation of maritime mobility.

Domesticity was of course itself a deeply logistical concern – maintaining the standards of the bourgeois lifestyle aboard a large steamship many miles from the metropole was no simple matter, particularly given the logistical complexities explored in Chapter 3. In the case of the ships operating on Eastern routes this posed particular challenges, given the lack of contact with European ports. The steamship required coal, crew, provisions for the passengers and crew, and constant maintenance and repair work. Shipboard domesticity was both logistical, and based upon a certain repression of the logistical: coal, labour, maritime space, technology, bureaucratic precision – all of these elements were antithetical to the identification of the steamship as an environment of refined pleasure and relaxation.

Joachim Stocqueler, in his 1844 guidebook for the traveller to India, offers the reader an illustrative comparison of the journey East by sail and steam. Describing a representative voyage by the *Hindostan* from Suez to India, Stocqueler reassures the prospective passenger that 'the action of her machinery is almost inaudible – there is no tremulous motion perceptible when the paddles are at work'.[22] This echoes Albert Hervey's description (related in Chapter 1) of the steamship as a departure from the labour practices of sail: Hervey described how, cushioned against the industrial means of transportation, the passengers sensed the commotion of the engine as ever present but indistinct. His account records none of the constant fluctuation in sensory stimuli typical to narratives of industrial technology, but rather a steady, scarcely perceptible background noise and vibration. Significantly, Hervey went on to distinguish the steamship's relative tranquillity by noting that it allowed the bourgeois passengers to enjoy their leisure pursuits undisturbed, at a suitable remove from the voyage's industrial means of production. Due to the steamship's serenity, he observes, 'there was nothing to disturb our reading, writing, or drawing'.[23] The passengers' leisure activities could be enjoyed in consequence of the absence of the hallmarks of labour and production. This was in part due to steam's organisation of shipboard labour, the engine and boiler rooms' location in the lower decks of the ship, at a remove from the passenger spaces. As discussed in Chapter 3, the pursuit of bourgeois leisure practices offered passengers a means of engaging positively with their mobility, countering characterisations of the period spent in transit as unproductive, lost time.

Thus passenger claims regarding the voyage as both a departure from bourgeois normativity and its perpetuation aren't necessarily in contradiction – they both present distinctive responses to the separation from land and the absence of the demands of everyday bourgeois life and the world of work. Chapter 3 suggested that to identify the voyage as unremarkable, even pleasurable, rather than a tedious inconvenience, required a certain set of social, representational and embodied practices associated with bourgeois leisure and domesticity. The emergent social performances of the bourgeois class found new life on board: strolling, polite sociability, food and drink, dance, listening to music, reading, lounging, gambling, smoking, games – all these pastimes helped remake the experience of mobility. Moreover, this was a distinctly imperial performance, a show of the languid equanimity of a superior race whose identity was constructed through the refined sociality of shipboard life. Bourgeois leisure, no less than technological innovation, was at the heart of the steamship's modernity.

The *Household Words* account of the *Bentinck*'s departure narrates the passenger's removal from the often rough materiality of mobility's production. While the cargo was loaded with all the bustle of labour, the passenger was cushioned against this activity in part through the production of the ship as a familiar domestic space. It was only at a remove from the labour practices of mobility that the steamship could be experienced as a familiar, homely space. The extent to which this was borne out in passenger experiences is articulated particularly unequivocally in accounts of docking at the various points at which the steamer called to take on coal. When coaling, the passengers were encouraged to visit the shore, and the ship was carefully sealed in an attempt to prevent the coal spreading through the passenger space. David Lester Richardson, travelling on board the *Hindostan* from Calcutta to Suez in 1843, describes the experience of coaling at Madras. 'The operation of taking in coal is always disagreeable', writes Richardson, 'for the fine coal dust gets into every corner and cranny of the vessel.'[24] This contamination of passenger space by the materiality of mobility's production provides a graphic articulation of the incompatibility of the industrial and the domestic. It also emphasises the extent to which the shipboard separation of these two spheres was yet to be perfected in the early years of steamship travel. Passenger experience still bore the traces of the logistical. Inevitably, the steamer's subaltern crew were not able to enjoy even such a makeshift remove from the logistical. Steven Adriaan Buddingh's narrative of his 1852 voyage from Suez to Ceylon on board the *Oriental* features a rare account of the leisure practices of the ship's stokers, diversions not dissimilar to those of the bourgeois passengers. 'The Africans on board with us', he writes, 'are excessive card game enthusiasts. All day long they sit on deck to play with an extraordinary bustle and gaiety in their countenance and gestures.' However, Buddingh continues, these moments of respite from the labour of mobility's production were saturated with the traces of industrial shipboard labour: 'their English playing cards are as black as soot; their coal-covered hands have given the cards such a hue'.[25]

In transit, the steamship passenger could experience the voyage as a leisured, enjoyable journey only at a remove from the sphere of its production, particularly the engine and boiler rooms. The failure of this material separation, the uneasy association of the bourgeois passenger with the technology of steam, is vividly depicted in William Howard Russell's description of his cabin on board the *Nubia*, travelling from Suez to Calcutta in 1858. Russell had been obliged to relinquish his allotted cabin to some female passengers on a particularly crowded passage, and had been allocated one of the ship's officers' berths in its stead. Russell found much to complain about in his new accommodation, particularly regarding a proximity to the industrial sphere of production which no passenger cabin would exhibit:

> In the first place, it had a commanding view of the steam-engine, which worked pleasantly opposite the door, so that one could mark the details of the mechanism when in bed on the sofa. In the next place, there was an important portion of the steam-engine running down by the head of the bed in the shape of an immense waste-pipe, through which, at every throb of the engine, rushed and hissed a great column of water to the sea.[26]

This juxtaposition of two seemingly irreconcilable aspects of modernity – industrial technology and bourgeois domesticity – emphasises the necessity on board the steamship of spatial and material practices which played a disjunctive role between the two. As noted, the steamship, transitory in both its mobile placelessness and the brevity of its occupants' stay, was in many ways antithetical to the domestic. This tension is instantiated in a journal entry by Alfred Barton, a ship's surgeon in the employ of P&O, who maintained a record of his time working aboard the steamship *Cadiz* in the mid-1850s, travelling between Bombay and the Far East. The entry for 1 May 1855, the day he departed the ship at Bombay, opens with the following words: 'Give the "Cadiz" a long farewell look and then turn from the floating mass of iron and wood, my late home and conveyance for 20 months, having carried me upwards of 70,000 miles.'[27] Barton's description of the steamer as simultaneously unprecedentedly mobile, a long-term dwelling, and a vast technological assemblage suspended in the sea combines the seemingly contradictory facets of domesticity and technologies of global mobility.

Amy Richter has made a comparable intervention in the uneasy binary of domesticity and mobility, with regard to the American steam train of the nineteenth century. For early train passengers, claims Richter, 'a sense of newness – of modernity itself – inspired them to seek meaning and impose order'.[28] Richter places domestic practices at the core of this process. In an analogous sense, in the first decades of P&O's steamship service the nascent technology's novelty meant that it was subject to distinctive representational and discursive responses, as passengers came to terms with the new mode of mobility it facilitated. Shipboard domesticity was not merely a result of the steamship line's need to cater to an increasingly mobile class of colonial bourgeoisie, but represented a means for passengers to come to terms with the often disorienting and unsettling experiences of mobility at sea, through social rituals and imaginaries. Richter identifies in the domestic a set of material and social practices which were used to discipline, ameliorate and normalise spaces of nineteenth-century mobility whose unfamiliarity and newness could be a source of anxiety for passengers. This domesticity, she writes, was 'a shared fantasy that sought to bring order, comfort, and familiarity to sites of rapid social and cultural change'.[29] Richter equates this domesticity with a culture of conspicuous consumption, emphasising the passenger's identification with the domestic luxury of the mobile interior.[30] In contrast to the 'public domesticity' Richter attributes to the train, which 'attempted to bring the cultural associations and behaviors of home life to bear upon social interactions among strangers', steamship domesticity assuaged a different set of anxieties.[31] Although the steamship constituted a shipboard community with a shifting, nomadic population, this was on a more limited scale than the train, and the rules of entry and behaviour which governed the steamer's inhabitants were more stringent and easier to police. However, the experience of transnational mobility at sea could be overwhelming and uncomfortable, even terrifying; and, as Chapter 3 established, it could also be stultifyingly tedious. Domestic social practices therefore helped to assuage the discomforts, anxieties and monotony of shipboard life and the interruption of familiar land-based routine as the passenger was exposed to the new and challenging sensations of steamship mobility.

The rendering of transnational maritime mobility as normal, even pleasurable was achieved through the creation of an environment which facilitated the perpetuation of well-established spatial roles. The domesticity of the steamship played a significant part in this process, as a set of social, material and representational practices which intervened between the bourgeois consumer of mobility at sea and the material realities of its production. These facets of shipboard life were wide-ranging, including the noise, smoke and dirt of the ship's engines; the labour practices of industrial transportation; the inconveniences and sickness caused by rough seas, and even the boredom consequent on any protracted period of time spent at sea. An article from the periodical *Titan* in 1857 narrates the production of a luxurious shipboard domesticity which was able to act as at least a partial corrective to these tribulations:

From London to Hong Kong is a voyage of about seven weeks; that is, supposing we have been passengers by one of those gigantic ocean steamers which are owned by the Peninsular and Oriental Steam-ship Company. To say that this voyage, if the weather be fine, affords some degree of pleasure, is to speak very cautiously indeed. With every comfort, and even every luxury, we are as much at home as we possibly could be in the best appointed mansion of that comfort-loving country we have just left.[32]

This article elicits a familiar, if particularly voluptuous, image of the shipboard perpetuation of domestic life, particularly associating this quotidian luxury with the notion of comfort. Comfort is a concept which foregrounds the reproduction of the domestic as both an embodied and performative social practice. It also proved to be a contentious and mercurial site of struggle in the constitution of steamship domesticity.

Comfort: Frictionless imperial mobility

The dearth of opportunities to encounter 'authentic' experiences is a persistent trope of nineteenth-century travel accounts by Westerners.[33] An article in 1861 by the eminent and paradigmatically jaded Victorian writer George Augustus Sala laments just such an impossibility. Sala located the genesis of this concern in a world increasingly colonised by the culture of Western civilisation – a civilisation he identified with the logic of comfort and convenience. Instructively, Sala's satirical observations culminate in a pithily expressed rejoinder to complaints made against the standards of comfort met with on board the overland route steamship:

> People grumble against the admirable Peninsular and Oriental Company, because they are not quite comfortable in a voyage up the Red Sea. Ought they not to be thankful for getting to the Red Sea at all? The Red Sea was natural enough, when it swallowed up Pharaoh and his host, his chariots and his horses, and the riders thereof. At present it is merely a piece of water on whose shores we have coaling stations, and under whose waves (with indifferent success) we lay telegraph wires, and about whose coral reefs Mr. Tom Taylor writes comedies. This isn't Nature. I ask, is it natural that the highway to India should be strewn with soda-water corks?[34]

Sala places the notion of comfort at the centre of his conception of the overland route steamship's mobility. In his account, passenger expectations regarding comfort required an astonishing ignorance of the extensive infrastructure, complex logistical administration and radical technological innovations which had made the overland route – and indeed the comfort they enjoyed – possible. For Sala, the formerly 'natural' topography of Eastern space traversed by passengers on the overland route had been colonised by the technological complexes of British imperialism. In emphasising this point, Sala demonstrates the extent to which, scarcely two decades since its implementation, the steamship voyage to the East had become normalised. Highlighting the maritime detritus of bourgeois domesticity ('soda-water corks'), he insists that the normalisation of steamship travel, its characterisation as a fluid, frictionless form of mobility, was expressed through the material conditions of convenience and bodily ease. For Sala, comfort was a mode of embodied experience which contributed to the normalisation of the bourgeois steamship passenger's unprecedented mobility.

'From the moment the traveller embarks until he arrives at his destination, he will find that careful thought has been exercised with a view to minister to his comfort', proclaims *The Popular Overland Guide* of 1861.[35] Playing in to claims regarding the ease, pleasure and even banality of the steamship voyage, the notion of comfort emerges persistently as a shifting site of tension in the archive of the overland route: whether they bemoaned its absence, or paid tribute to its shipboard manifestations, comfort presented a striking preoccupation in the narrative of passenger life. It provides a conspicuous sign that the human body is a significant site for coming to terms with the history of global mobility at sea. As Tamson Pietsch has argued in the context of the voyage to Australia by sail in the mid-nineteenth century, embodied experiences of mobility gave voice to the global geographies of sea travel, and played a significant role in the construction of passenger subjectivities in transit.[36] In the case of the overland route, the discourse of bodily comfort has much to tell us, particularly regarding the shipboard construction of class and racial identity.

In one of the few non-Western accounts of the overland voyage, the Indian writer Lutfullah's record of a journey to England in 1844, the author comments on the standards of comfort on board the steamship *Bentinck* during its passage from Ceylon to Suez: 'All of us were made very comfortable on board the vessel, through the attention of the good captain and officers. I must say that all the passengers who go by the P. and O. Company's steamers are more comfortable than at home.'[37] As an Indian Muslim, Lutfullah's account of shipboard comfort appears to imply a universalised conception of domesticity, one that transcends national or racial cultural values and standards. However, upon boarding the *Great Liverpool* to begin the voyage from Alexandria to Southampton, he writes, 'we found ourselves more comfortable and more attended to than on board the *Bentinck*. The fact is that the more you proceed on towards England the more you find the English people endowed with politeness and civility.'[38] For Lutfullah, the domestic comfort encountered on the steamship was a manifestation of British identity and cultural norms, and one that shifted with the traveller's movement through global space. As John Crowley has argued, while the notion of comfort is rooted in the body's relationship with its environment, it is by no means a universal concept. Rather, he insists, the experience of comfort is socially and historically constructed, reflecting broader cultural values and assumptions which change over time and through space.[39] As such, it is a concept whose materiality is both elusive and unstable, but also one whose idiosyncrasies in accounts of steamship travel provides a useful means for engaging with historical attitudes to that mobility.

In an advertisement from 1837 published in the *Shetland Journal*, a newspaper belonging to P&O chairman Arthur Anderson, the fledgling company promoted their new steamship service to the Iberian peninsula as a form of maritime mobility that offered all the comforts of land:

> In the planning and layout of the accommodations, the comfort and convenience of passengers have been studiously kept in view. The saloons are very spacious and airy, and the sleeping cabins have been arranged so as to suit families or parties of friends, thus securing comfort, and also seclusion, when desirable. Each cabin is fitted with all the requisite conveniences for washing, dressing, &c., and from each cabin a bell communicates with the Steward's and Servants' rooms. The Ladies' cabins are tastefully fitted up, and contain every necessary for the toilet, and there are female attendants to wait on them.[40]

P&O's promotional material articulates the ship's domesticity around four distinct principles of comfort: décor, hygiene, order and service. With its abundant references to the ship's servants, it also hints at the extent to which social hierarchy was implicit within descriptions of the luxurious equanimity of shipboard life. No less than opulent interiors and comfortable surroundings, the servility of the ship's stewards contributed to the voyage's normalisation.[41] The Austrian travel writer Ida Pfeiffer, travelling second-class from Singapore to Point de Galle aboard the *Braganza* in 1847, experienced the absence of the carefully managed provision of comfort encountered constantly in the voyage accounts of more privileged passengers. As one of the few accounts of such a voyage by a woman, and the only one by a passenger from this period to travel second-class, Pfeiffer's book offers a counter-narrative of sorts to the prevalent accounts of the luxurious domesticity and comfort met with on board.[42] The second-class dining cabin, she writes, 'was certainly anything but comfortable. The furniture was of the most common description, the table was covered in stains and dirt, and the whole place was one scene of confusion.' She also complains that 'on reaching the vessel, I found no servant in the second places'.[43] For Pfeiffer, comfort was again manifested through the categories of décor, hygiene, order and service; or in the case of the second-class accommodations, by their absence.

Writing in the context of the domestic interior's history, Julia Prewitt Brown has identified comfort as an idiosyncratically bourgeois concern.[44] It is clear from Pfeiffer's account that on board the steamship, comfort was a privilege which only the wealthy were afforded access to. She bemoaned the absence of comfort experienced in the steamer's second-class accommodations: 'I should like to know what an Englishman, who has always got the words 'comfort' and 'comfortable' at the top of his tongue, would say, if he was treated in this manner on board a steamer belonging to any other nation?'[45] Pfeiffer characterises comfort as a distinctively English preoccupation, and one that operated as an exclusive domain which mediated shipboard social hierarchies. Like Pfeiffer, the French theorist Paul Virilio identified comfort as an idiosyncratically British concern. For Virilio, comfort emerged as a historical category of bodily experience specifically in response to the emergence of the British Empire as a global logistical system. 'It is from Britannic insularity that [the] demand came to us', he writes, 'of the *comfort of travelling*. This Anglo-Saxon ideology of "well being" is encountered in … what was first maritime mobility.'[46] Comfort is understood as a response to the bodily *dis*comforts of shipboard life. The constitution of bourgeois leisure practices in transit underpin the notion of mobility as a pleasurable experience.

Craig Martin has highlighted the extent to which the notion of the comfortable sea voyage is predicated upon the 'cushioning' of the privileged passenger's body from what he terms – after Virilio – the 'violence of speed'.[47] Martin defines this as a process of 'capsularisation', a 'separation' of the passenger from the violence which constitutes a central aspect of modern mobility. The corporeal experience of shipboard comfort was therefore a particularly important element in the separation of the production and consumption of mobility, extending the norms of bourgeois domesticity into a medium inherently antithetical to these norms, the inhospitable sea. Central to the violence ascribed by Virilio to speed is not just the inconvenience, discomfort and potential danger of increased mobility. It is also manifested in the separation undergone by the traveller from all that is familiar, from the sense of permanence and place provided by land-based routine and fixity. The violence which shipboard domesticity is intended to mitigate against is played out as much in the mundane dislocation of the passenger from their everyday life as in the corporeal discomfort and danger of the voyage.[48]

Sala's satirical critique of expectations regarding shipboard comfort makes passing reference to English dramatist Tom Taylor's play *The Overland Route* (1860). The play, a popular colonial farce set aboard a P&O steamship on the return voyage from India, illustrates the prominent place of the overland route in the British public imagination. In the play, one of its protagonists bemoans the discomforts of the voyage, complaining of the 'elevated coffin, which they call a berth'. The character attributes his shipboard discomforts to 'the shiver of the screw, and the gnawing of the timbers, and the clashing of the chains overhead; and the pitching and the tossing'.[49] The way in which the discomfort of the cabin is portrayed suggests an interior which had failed in its twofold protective function; against both the ship's industrial means of propulsion, and the sea's wildness. As the prevalent discourse (explored in Chapter 1) ran, steam propulsion had liberated mobility at sea from the forces of nature which constrained sailing vessels, playing in to the nineteenth-century ideology of the technological domination of – and liberation from – nature. This mastery of nature's power can be seen to have been manifested in part at the level of embodied experience, in the persistent preoccupation with maintaining standards of comfort at sea. Joachim Stocqueler, in his 1844 guide for the traveller to India, paints a typically understated picture of global steamship mobilities: 'The passage to India, *via* the Mediterranean and the Red Sea, has been rendered so facile of late years by the construction of magnificent steamers, the property of the Oriental and Peninsular Steam Navigation Company.'[50] The sense of effortlessness suggested by Stocqueler was produced in part through the production in transit of domestic familiarity, bodily comfort and bourgeois leisure. If steam had freed human agency from the limitations of nature, it followed that steam's mobilities revolution should be characterised by an embodied experience of ease and leisure. Expectations regarding comfort could thus be seen to imply the desire for a (white European, bourgeois) embodied experience of the new global mobilities of steam as frictionless.

As Julia Prewitt Brown has insisted, 'in bourgeois society, the pursuit of comfort is itself a sign of agitation and unrest'.[51] The sea's wildness, an inevitable cause of both seasickness and the disruption of passengers' everyday routine on board ship, was a persistent source of aggravation against which the experience of steamship comfort was constituted. Such a claim is substantiated by an observation made in *The Popular Overland Guide* to the steamship voyage:

> The usual civilizing influences of rapid communication with Europe have developed themselves on the journey ... and the refined Englishman, accustomed to the comforts and luxuries of life, can implicitly rely on his caterers, and will find, *malgré* [despite] the occasional *désagréments* [discomforts] inseparable from shipboard, every attention he could reasonably desire.[52]

Again, comfort on board the steamship was understood to have contributed to the perpetuation of English bourgeois social norms – norms equated in this account with (Western) civilisation. Echoing some of the themes of Sala's satire, this extension into global space of the normality of these social practices is staged specifically in the context of a comfort which is produced in opposition to the hardships inherent to mobility at sea. 'Everything which can be,' continues *The Popular Overland Guide*, 'is, done to alleviate and soften the unpleasantness of ship life'.[53] This notion of 'softening' evokes the image of an interior which was intended to cushion the passenger against the disrupting effects of maritime mobility.

Unsurprisingly, however, the sea's wildness often made such comfort impracticable. Albert Smith's account of his voyage aboard the *Norna* from Point de Galle to Singapore in 1868 was a litany of complaints regarding the tedium of life in transit. Smith narrates a particularly taxing encounter with the 'unpleasantness' of mobility at sea, describing a thwarted attempt to sleep during a storm:

> I never passed such a wretched night. The sea rose tremendously, and I was shaken from one side of my berth to the other, until I got actually sore; with a constant fear of falling off, and my sheet getting all into a ruck, and leaving only the horsehair for me to lie upon.

Smith's arduous experience of steamship mobility was a distinctly embodied one. 'It is astonishing', he goes on to note, 'how hard everything you sit on, on board ship, gradually becomes.'[54] Such experiences suggest a shipboard domesticity which had failed in its role as a cushion against the hardships of the steamship voyage. Shipboard comfort was in a continuous state of negotiation, a compromise with the material realities of global mobility at sea; and none more so than the shifts in temperature encountered on the overland route.

Heat: Imperial discomfort

Owing to the global scope of the ship's movements, the overland route passenger was exposed to environmental extremes which inevitably undermined the shipboard perpetuation of Western bourgeois domestic norms. The geographical locus of this discomfort was the Red Sea, where the temperature and humidity were frequently so high as to render Western standards of comfort completely inconceivable. As Sala's satire suggested, the very fact of the passage taking this route was a result of the logistical possibilities of steam propulsion, and even then posed a challenge in terms of provisioning and coaling the ships. Inevitably, this section of the voyage presents a persistent and traumatic preoccupation in overland route narratives. William Tyrone Power's account of his 1847 voyage up the Red Sea to Suez on board the *Haddington* provides a distinctive example of this recurrent trope. It emphasises the extent to which the mobilities of steam were viscerally encountered through the subtle – and not so subtle – textures of embodied, sensory experience. Power was travelling in November, a time of year at which the heat of the Red Sea was in stark contrast to the European autumn he was bound for. 'Steaming along rapidly,' he writes, 'but the heat is excessive. The thermometer 96° in the shade. We shall, in the course of another ten days, see it almost down to freezing point – a matter of some 60° difference, and rather trying to the nerves.'[55] For Power, the steamship's global mobility intervened in the natural rhythms of seasonal change. It was traced on the passenger's body and psyche.

As noted, comfort is not a static concept, but one given to shifts in its constitution which themselves often narrate wider social mores. Even in the passage of the steamer's voyage the conception of shipboard comfort was not fixed, but shifted with the ship's movement through global space. Two descriptions from the 1840s of the steamship *Hindostan*'s internal arrangements emphasise the extent to which mutable definitions of comfort were contested and negotiated through fluctuating conceptions of the ship's interior. An article from the *Morning Post* of 14 September 1842 praises the suitability of the newly launched *Hindostan* for travelling in the heat of the Red Sea:

> She is in every point adapted for a tropical climate, as light and air are the primary considerations in the arrangements for passengers; indeed, to such an extent are those essentials carried out that, when inspected by visitors in this autumnal quarter of *our* climate, there is, perhaps, too much of air to imply comfort.[56]

The *Hindostan*, viewed in Southampton harbour, was deemed to be appropriate to the environmental shifts of imperial mobility precisely in its departure from English standards of comfort. This claim is, however starkly contradicted by David Lester Richardson, recounting his 1843 voyage aboard the *Hindostan* from Calcutta to Suez. 'I have called the *Hindostan* a noble steamer, and she deserves the epithet', writes Richardson, emphasising an admiration which played into the notion of the steamship as a progressive technological wonder. 'She is large, and handsome, and swift – and yet she is far from being a comfortable dwelling in a sultry latitude.'[57] Richardson's exuberance at the vessel's speed, size and status as a visual spectacle is juxtaposed with the underwhelming reality of the embodied experience of a domesticity compromised by the voyage's departure from Western climactic norms.

The disparity between the two descriptions of the *Hindostan* narrates more than just a discrepancy between journalistic licence and lived experience. It illustrates the extent to which comfort can be seen as both fluid, shifting in response to environmental changes – and static, as an attempt to construct a normalised, stable environment in spite of such conditions. Richardson's preoccupation with the *Hindostan*'s shortcomings also feature in an article he had published in the *Hampshire Advertiser and Salisbury Guardian* the previous year:

There is no doubt that it will be found necessary to alter her accommodations. It is very odd that they should have been arranged by an old Indian, for such I was told is the fact, but he must assuredly have forgotten in his enjoyment of English cosiness, the luxury of air and space in a sultry climate.[58]

The antinomy of comfort is played out through the friction between the perpetuation of Western domestic norms ('English cosiness') and a climate in which such norms had become intolerable. The role of the steamship's luxurious domesticity as a means to perpetuate Western norms in transit was compromised at the moment its reassuring cosiness became oppressive in the heat of the tropics.

During the hottest sections of the voyage, the steamship's luxurious interior no longer offered the passenger a protective encasing. Instead, it presented a domestic sphere in which bourgeois, Western standards of comfort were impossible to maintain. In the heat of the tropics, where even wealthy passengers slept on the deck in order to escape the discomfort of their cabins, it was necessary that they be differentiated from the poorer passengers and the ship's subaltern workers, who always slept on the fore part of the deck. As has already been documented, in hot weather the space of the deck was arranged as much as possible to recreate the conditions of the bourgeois domestic interior. Arthur Lloyd Clay, of his voyage in the Red Sea on board the *Nubia* in 1862, writes that 'covered by double awnings, the deck resembles a huge tent, and forms a spacious and airy bed-room'.[59] Where the steamer's luxurious interior was antithetical to the norms of domestic comfort, its material culture and social practices were reproduced on deck. Norman Macleod, recounting his voyage down the Red Sea from Suez to Bombay aboard the *Rangoon* in 1867, provides a vivid description of this process. 'The scene each evening was particularly pleasing', he writes. 'The awning which covers the quarter-deck conceals the glorious stars. But as a substitute for these, lamps are hung from the awning roof, which serve to reveal indistinct groups, in the most favourable conditions for talking.'[60] Shipboard domesticity was reconstituted on deck, facilitated by the same environmental shifts which had compromised it. However, while the bourgeois passenger's equilibrium was strained by the Red Sea's heat, these extremes in temperature also reveal the extent to which this domesticity was predicated upon the sometimes-fatal hardships of subaltern bodies.

As the steamship travelled further away from the metropole it became increasingly difficult to sustain the norms of European bourgeois domesticity. Arthur Lloyd Clay, again narrating his steamship voyage to India through the heat of the Red Sea in 1862, details the shipboard labour practices employed in the vessel's saloon in order to create an environment more conducive to Western standards of comfort. Clay, whose diaries had also furnished one of the few descriptions of the ship's stokers, also describes the use of punkahs on the ship, large hand-operated fans which were suspended from the ceiling:

> The punkah-wallahs, little native boys in clean white frocks, caps of plaited grass with red pugrees twisted round and gaudy silk handkerchiefs tied round the waist – miniature Lascars – squat behind the seats and pull the ropes which pass over little brass wheels fixed above to the punkahs. Sometimes the ropes are carried through the upper deck and pulled from above. Punkah pulling in hot weather is drowsy work, and sometimes a little fellow begins to nod, the swing diminishing as the nods increase, till it stops altogether. Suddenly rousing he gives one or two vigorous pulls, but this does not last. Again the swing becomes less and less, and the punkah hangs quiescent till some irate passenger sings out: "*Punkah khaincho!*" (pull) when the sleeper is admonished by the nearest steward, or if he is on deck, a sudden tug at the rope reminds him of his duty.[61]

The employment of subaltern child labour for the comfort of the bourgeois Western passenger was inevitably detrimental to the labourer's own comfort. The use of the punkah, common in the colonial East, was for many steamship passengers an experience first learned and normalised in transit. Figure 4.1, from the American journalist Charles Carleton Coffin's account of his 1867–68 tour of the world, illustrates the use of the punkah in the saloon of the *Baroda*, during his voyage from Suez to Bombay. It illustrates the attempted reproduction of Western norms of comfort where they were difficult to sustain, foregrounding the production of shipboard social difference through the binary of bourgeois leisure and subaltern labour. 'Passengers must be prepared for hot weather', Coffin writes. 'The negro firemen have sometimes dropped dead by the furnaces in the months of June, July, and August.' However, he continues, 'the passage in the winter and spring months is delightful', highlighting the stark difference between the white consumer of mobility and its subaltern producer.[62]

As the steamer's fragile domesticity was threatened by the discomforts of the colonial climate and the hardships of maritime mobility, the relation between the body of the passenger and that of the subaltern worker who made such a domesticity possible was brought into focus. Such a perspective foregrounds the significance of a domesticity which, as Anne McClintock has insisted, 'denotes both a *space* (a geographic and architectural alignment) and a *social relation to power*'.[63] For McClintock, the Victorian cult of domesticity was deeply tied up with the imperial project. Coming to terms with steamship domesticity's imperial dimension involves not only interrogating the embodied mobilities of both passengers and crew, but also the relationships *between* these bodies which contribute to the production of experiences of mobility as a fundamentally social and political activity.

RATHER WARM.

4.1 'Rather Warm' (Charles Carleton Coffin, *Our New Way Round the World*, 1869)

A comparison of the passenger spaces with the accommodations of regular crew members is instructive in this regard. A 9 February 1867 letter from the Board of Trade Surveyor for the Port of Southampton, a Mr Murray, to the Board's Marine Department reported on the conditions of accommodation for seamen on merchant ships in the port. The contents of Murray's letter emphasise the disparity on board steamships, between the luxurious opulence of passenger social space, and the substandard, deleterious conditions of crew accommodations. It singles out for criticism two of P&O's ships. Murray reports that the forecastle (where the sailors, coal trimmers and firemen slept) of the *Ripon* was 'over-crowded': 'The quartermaster of the ship', he states, 'informs me he can scarcely find room for all the hammocks required.' On board the *Delta*, the cabin on the lower deck allotted to the stewards and other ship's servants was also found to be inadequate: 'the space allotted', Murray reports, 'falls below that required by the Act' (referring to the requirements of the Merchant Shipping Act 1854). In both vessels' crew areas, Murray continues, 'the ventilation is very contracted, being, I should say, not sufficient for the preservation of health'.[64] Inevitably, while many passengers considered the comforts of the steamship to fall well short of their expectations, the austere space occupied by the crew often failed to meet the lowest standards of bare existence at sea.

If domesticity was implicated in cushioning the consumer from the production of steamship mobility, this was nowhere more explicitly expressed than in the removal of the passenger from the experience of shipboard labour. This manifests a relation between white and subaltern bodies whose extremes articulate the violent brutality of empire. The corporeal ease with which privileged passengers experienced steamship mobility was predicated upon this violence. In his account of a voyage from Suez to India aboard the *Achilles* in 1853, Bayard Taylor describes the passage through the hottest part of Red Sea. 'The steamers at that time', he writes, 'almost invariably lose some of their stewards and firemen.' This passing reference to the corporeal violence of shipboard labour is complemented by Taylor's subsequent observation. 'The panting and sweltering passengers', he writes, 'drink claret and water and eat dry biscuits.'[65] The stark contrast between the experience of the subaltern worker (documented in Chapter 2) and the leisured passenger emphasises the extent to which the worker's body was the point at which the possibility of a 'comfortable' experience of mobility was constituted. As Taylor's remarks suggest, this was particularly true of those who shovelled coal in the ship's boilers – yet the passengers' separation from the productive processes of steamship mobility which facilitated the ship's production as a domestic space also meant that their experience of this labour was infrequent.

What passenger cognisance there was of the crew's circumstances could be rationalised through ideological claims regarding the corporeal naturalness of shipboard labour conditions. Robert Bowne Minturn travelled from Bombay to Suez on the *Ganges* in 1857. In the Red Sea, he writes, 'the weather is so intensely hot at certain seasons that many ladies faint from its effects'.[66] Conversely, the African stokers, he claims, were 'the only men who can bear to work in the intense heat of the engine rooms where the Scotch and English engineers sicken and often die'.[67] Yet again, it is worth noting that Coffin, Taylor and Minturn were all Americans. Accounts of racial difference and the subaltern labour conditions which underpinned British imperial mobilities are starkly absent from British narratives. This does not, however, mean that non-British writers were necessarily sympathetic. In Minturn's account, blackness is naturally associated with heat and labour. Through such racially charged fantasies, passengers could perceive their own leisure, and the deleterious labour conditions of the stoker as the natural order of things. The white body's putative inability to cope with the heat of the tropics, when compared to the subaltern labourer, was thus taken to be another sign of the implicit superiority of a more refined Western subject.

The image of the passenger beneath the punkah – sweltering in the heat of the Red Sea but attempting to maintain the normality of bourgeois social practices – and that of the stoker, stripped to the waist, shovelling coal in the ship's boiler room, are thus complementary. If the steamship's cabin was an interior in which the tropical heat of the voyage made bourgeois comfort impossible, the boiler room was an uninhabitable interior in which the body of the subaltern worker was violently negated. The ideology of frictionless mobility, of a comfortable body which registered none of the resistance of global movement, was a mythology which was produced through a moment of violence, inflicted on a body which was made to bear the full brunt of this friction. The domesticity which helped conceal this relation, the cushioning of the passenger from both the sea's wildness and the industrial labour practices which propelled the ship, also operated in the realm of representation and the imagination, normalised through the familiarity of décor.

Steamship décor

Accompanying the introduction of steam propulsion to passenger shipping, the interior decoration of ships became increasingly opulent and luxurious. The first few years of the transnational steamship's operation saw the extensive publication of journalistic descriptions of their interior spaces.[68] These accounts, which extol the steamer as a modern technological wonder, pay particular attention to the decorative embellishments which had been used to adorn the vessel's internal space. An 1842 article in the *Morning Post* describes the interior decorations of the newly built *Hindostan*, relating how its author entered the steamer with a sense of awe. 'We had a sight of the saloons of this splendid ship last night by candle light', the article relates, going on to eulogise the interior's ornamentation in minute detail. The steamship's interior, it concludes, 'surpasses anything of its kind ever yet done in this or any other country'.[69] While such descriptions are frequently guilty of what Douglas Burgess has referred to as the 'bloated hyperbole' employed to refer to steamship interiors at the time, they also bear witness to public interest in the ship not merely as a technological achievement, but also as a luxury environment.[70]

As previous chapters have explored, Albert Hervey's account of his 1843 overland route journey from India to England was particularly attentive to the novelty of the steamship, as both a means of transport and as a distinctive environment. Hervey provides an elaborate description of the rich decoration employed in the *Hindostan*'s saloon:

> The [walls] of this *salle a manger*, are decorated with gaudy *papier mache* colourings, descriptive of various subjects; the staunchions [*sic*] and rudder-head, as well as the mast, ... are all painted with flowers in the most beautifully arranged groups I ever saw, tastefully embellished with fountains and jettes d'eau, and other ornaments. The appearance of the whole was superb, when lighted of an evening, which it was with argaund [*sic*] lamps suspended from the ceiling; large mirrors at each end, and book-cases, neatly fitted up, containing useful and entertaining works. The furniture is entirely mahogany, and the fastenings, &c., of bronze.[71]

This florid description of the steamship's saloon, illuminated by the soft glow of the oil lamp, emphasises the extent to which the elaborate ornamentation of the ship's passenger spaces recreated exclusive, privileged land-based environments. 'Every one had access to it', Hervey continues, adding: 'that is to say, all first class passengers'.[72] The symbolic force of the saloon's ostentatious decoration lay in its ability to reproduce the material and visual culture of familiar land-based bourgeois interiors. The idiosyncratic domesticity of the steamship was achieved in part through decorative motifs which were utilised to transplant familiar bourgeois material culture into the space of the ship. The opulent décor was intended to create a shipboard environment suitable for the bourgeois passenger, overlaid on the vessel's functional interior.

While the commodity purchased by the steamship passenger was the vessel's mobility, there was a need for the construction of the ship as an environment which reflected their social status. This was achieved in part through the representational capacity of décor, which played a significant role in the production of the passenger's identity as the consumer of not just mobility, but of a privileged lifestyle. Thus the relation between the consumption and production of global mobility was mediated not only through the embodied experience of comfort, but also at the level of representation. As Amy Richter has observed in the context of the steam train, 'familiar domestic accents and furnishings inspired confidence by mimicking the secure environment of the home'.[73] The consumption of domestic spectacle contributed to the steamship passenger's constitution of the voyage as the continuation, rather than interruption, of their everyday life.

However, while the steamship constituted a radical departure from the traditions of maritime mobility, constructing a dynamic new relation with global space, the vessel's interior decoration appeared temporally retrograde. The form of interior decoration commonly utilised in early P&O steamships is detailed in a description of the *Oriental* from the *London*

Saturday Journal of 9 April 1842. The article observes that 'the saloon is a most splendid apartment, seventy feet in length by twenty-one feet in width. The style is Grecian: on each side and at the fore end, are Ionic columns, supporting the beams of the roof.'[74] The steamer's décor was possessed of an incongruous classicism – a popular decorative style of the early decades of the nineteenth century. It has been suggested that the pace of technological innovation in the nineteenth century was not matched by stylistic developments in the decorative arts. 'In every field', writes Sigfried Giedion, 'the nineteenth century cloaked each new invention with historicizing masks.'[75] The representational conservatism of steamship décor reflected a more widespread trend in the nineteenth century for obfuscatory facades of anachronistic design, divorced from the modern industrial forms which they were used to adorn. Witold Rybczynski comments on this anachronism: 'The Victorians, who were, after all, great engineers, and who were the first to glorify the idea of progress, never felt the need to develop what might be called an engineering aesthetic. The interiors of steamships, trains, and tramways – extraordinary inventions – always took comfortingly familiar forms.'[76] This failure of interior décor to reflect the radicality of modern technology contributed, claims Rybczynski, to the public acceptance of revolutionary innovation. 'Whatever new invention came along,' he writes, 'however innovative it might be, the Victorians felt comfortably at home with it.'[77]

The neoclassical facade was a particularly popular means of adorning the early railway station, softening the passenger's encounter with the most modern form of industrial mobility.[78] Something analogous could be said to be at play in the interior decoration of the steamship: the appeal of its dated, even staid character lay in part in its combination of extravagance and familiarity, which helped make the experience of global industrial mobility at sea easier to digest for the bourgeois passenger.

Yet the classical is not merely old – such design was used widely in the nineteenth century to communicate an ideology of order and dignity. As Alex Bremner has argued in the context of the British Empire, the classical was associated with modern civilisation. Its conservatism emphasised a kind of traditional, safe, particularly stolid Britishness. The classical, he writes, lent 'a degree of permanence to the oft-alluded correlation between the British empire and that of ancient Rome'.[79] The steamship's classical interior communicated a quality of enlightened empiricism – a soberness that its floridity and ornamentation sometimes exceeded. In some ways the interior design of early steamships seems to have been something of an afterthought, an arbitrary luxuriousness applied to a functional interior no longer appropriate to its discerning cargo. However, it is clear that such décor had to tread a fine line between a series of shipboard binaries which were identified in

Chapter 2: male and female; public and private; decorative and functional; tradition and modernity; luxury and protean; metropole and periphery.

Décor contra the maritime

While steamship interiors were often stylistically outmoded, the very presence of luxury environments in the maritime context was in itself a novel phenomenon. Passenger accounts persistently express a disorienting sense of awe on their first encounter with the steamship's luxurious interiors. Repeatedly, characterisations of luxurious décor tend to emphasise the steamship's departure from the culture of the maritime – accounts persistently express disbelief that such interiors could be found on board a ship. Franz Junghuhn's astonishment upon boarding the *Bentinck* at Point de Galle in 1848 has already been noted in Chapter 1. Junghuhn continued his awestruck description of the vessel, relating the profound impression his first sight of the steamer's opulent interior made upon him:

> The dining room was elegantly fitted up; therein were found three long tables, at which all passengers, namely those of the first class, could find a place; in this saloon, decorated with mirrors and paintings, when they saw themselves surrounded by such objects the guests sitting at the table entirely forgot that they are at sea, on board a ship.[80]

For Junghuhn, the almost fantastical luxury of the ship's saloon presented a marked departure from the material culture of mobility at sea. As shown, the passenger accommodation on board most sailing vessels was at that time improvised within the undecorated, functional space of the ship. Luxury interiors which echoed the culture of exclusive land-based spaces contributed to the sense of the steamship's 'newness'.

In Charles Henry Newmarch's effusive 1847 account of his voyage on board the *Hindostan* from Aden to Suez, he characterised the steam as marking a radical historical break with the culture of sail. Yet for Newmarch, this shift was not merely a logistical one: his description of the vessel's luxurious interiors again emphasises their status as a marked departure from the traditional visual and material culture of the maritime:

> It is much more natural to preserve the language to which we have been accustomed, and speak of 'up stairs,' and 'the left side of the deck,' than affect to be nautical and call them 'on deck,' and 'to port,' especially whilst on board a vessel of this description, where every thing bears the appearance of a floating hotel rather than a ship.[81]

For Newmarch, décor altered the passenger experience of the steamer. It appeared almost to mediate performative encounters with shipboard space, expressed through a departure from the linguistic culture of maritime tradition.

If the steamship's domesticity acted as a means of cushioning against both the sea's inhospitableness and the ship's industrial production of mobility, the luxurious décor which adorned – and disguised – the vessel's interior appears to have played a significant role in this process. As Albert Hervey's description of the *Hindostan* related, the visual signifiers of the saloon's identity as a shipboard space – the mast and rudder – were overlaid with delicate floral paintings. An article from the *Civil Engineer and Architect's Journal* of August 1843 documents similarly decorative embellishments found on board the *Bentinck*. It again describes the decoration as a façade overlaid on the interior space of the ship:

> The mizzen-mast is enclosed by a massive fluted Doric column, of wood painted in imitation of veined marble; and a similar but smaller column is placed to enclose an iron one in the centre of the entrance to the corridor. The corridor consists of a range of Ionic pilasters, painted in imitation of veined marble.[82]

The steamship's luxurious decorations created an interior which obscured the materiality of sea travel. A distinctive form of interior decoration came to prominence simultaneously with the rise of international steam navigation, which proved apt at lending itself to the adornment of steamship interiors. Papier mâché – light, resilient, durable, and capable of being moulded into a variety of shapes – proved to be a popular material for decorating early steamships. An article regarding the decoration of the *Oriental* in the *Literary World* of 5 September 1840 describes the material's advantages:

> The great cabin of the *Oriental* steam-ship is beautifully ornamented with panels of *papier-mâché*. There are forty-eight tablets on the doors and sides of the compartment, made of that material, by Messrs. Jennens and Bettridge, of Birmingham, prepared in a manner that renders them more durable than oak: they never can decay from dry rot, or become worm-eaten; nor are they combustible or capable of being broken.[83]

Papier mâché provided the ideal material for recreating the bourgeois interior on the ship – ornamental panels could literally be overlaid upon its bare functional interior. An 1855 advertisement for the products of Jennens and Bettridge, manufacturers of the papier mâché panels used on the *Oriental*, observes that the material 'possesses the great advantage of not being affected by climate, neither expanding by heat nor contracting by cold. It combines lightness and elegance with strength and durability'.[84] The resilience of papier mâché lent itself well to its use on board the steamship. It was also flexible, yielding to the inevitable warping of the ship's hull in rough seas.

In an analogous sense, the papier mâché panels which remade the steamship's internal space as a luxurious interior operated as a corrective to the flux, discomfort and anxieties of maritime mobility. The reproduction of everyday bourgeois leisure environments through recognisable design motifs played a role in countering the disruption of everyday life inherent in the transnational sea voyage. Allan Sekula has speculated that the relationship of steamships' interior design to the maritime landscape was not incidental. 'The opulent interior spaces', he writes regarding the nineteenth-century steamship, 'may well have been designed to compensate for [the] lack of external "tableaux" on the high seas.' Sekula suggests that the decorative opulence of the steamship's interior helped to counteract the blank inhospitableness of the open sea, a response to what he terms 'the monotony and malaise and occasional terror of pelagic space'.[85] As Gregory Votolato has suggested, the luxurious interior decoration of Victorian steamships was 'intended to promote a sense of security'. For the bourgeois passenger, he argues, 'the appearance of a ship's interiors could serve as a link with life on dry land even while wallowing over a choppy sea in mid-ocean'.[86] As Chapter 3 explored, the experience of the steamship voyage as a departure from the continuity of life on land was associated in part with the sea's characterisation as a wild void, antithetical to civilisation. The steamship's lavishly decorated interior afforded the reassertion of this continuity through representation. If the maritime landscape appeared chaotic, unpredictable and anti-modern, the ship's interior decoration provided the passenger with an environment which was fixed, familiar and comprehensible. The shipboard reproduction of the bourgeois interior allowed for the creation of a stable environment in the flux and disruption of maritime mobility. However, the very anxieties of sea travel which the familiarity of décor helped to mitigate against also contributed to concerns regarding the luxurious shipboard interior.

'Barren splendour': Décor contra comfort

An article from 1842 in the *London Saturday Journal*, dedicated to the newly launched steamship *Oriental*, describes the ship's interior design at great length:

> On looking generally at the *Oriental* and her accommodations, we are impressed with their completeness, although we search in vain for extrinsic embellishments. There is no gilding, no elaborate carving, no pictorial devices. All is plain, simple, and harmonious, but beautiful withal. Every thing is appropriate to the place and the occasion: comfort is combined with elegance.[87]

Notwithstanding the article's praise of the *Oriental*'s interior design, this description betrays a certain tension, between the opposing principles of practicality and opulence. It hints at an anxiety regarding the place of ostentatious décor in the traditionally functional space of the ship. Articulated in relation to the exigencies of comfort, it suggests that shipboard design trod a fine line between function and ornamentation. These tensions narrate wider shifts in the cultural meanings of mobility at sea. The opulent décor used to adorn steamship interiors helped to produce a familiar luxuriousness in the face of the various tribulations of transnational mobility at sea. It was also at times regarded as ill-suited to the gravity appropriate to that mobility.

The unrestrained approbation with which journalistic descriptions often praised the modern spectacle of the steamship was sometimes revealingly challenged by first-hand accounts of travel. An article from the *Illustrated London News* of 12 August 1843 provides a description of the *Bentinck*'s internal arrangements. The vessel's saloon, it notes, 'is upwards of 30 feet each way, having besides large stern windows, spacious ports on each side, thus giving abundance of light and air, and a full view of the sea in nearly every direction'.[88] The design of the steamer departed in this regard from that of the sailing ship, where windows were often small and scarce, and regarded as an extravagance given their lack of structural integrity in rough seas. The admission of natural light and fresh air became an important aspect of the new emphasis upon comfort aboard the steamer in Eastern seas. 'Light and ventilation, so desirable in tropical climates, have been abundantly provided', the article observes, 'and all manner of contrivances, are introduced to ensure a constant circulation of wholesome and refreshing drafts of air.' Conforming to the cultural norms of bourgeois domesticity marked a departure from the functionality of the sailing ship. Large windows also allowed the sea to be experienced by the passengers as landscape, facilitating its consumption as aesthetic experience.

However, a description from David Lester Richardson's account of his voyage from Calcutta to Suez in 1843 on board the *Hindostan* – the sister ship of the *Bentinck* – again manifests a discrepancy between journalistic accounts and the realities of travel. There is a tension in this passage which underscores the friction between the ship's luxurious interior and the risks associated with mobility at sea. The *Hindostan*, Richardson writes,

> is not fitted up appropriately for an Indian voyage … She has a superb saloon – perhaps too much money has been lavished on mere embellishments. All this finery makes the ship look as if she were meant rather for holiday pleasure trips on a smooth lake than to brave the dangers of the wide ocean. We scarcely ever sat down to dinner in the early part of our voyage that we did not wish one of the fine paintings had been a good port hole to admit a little air upon us.[89]

The disparity between journalistic exaggeration and first-hand experience again highlights the tension at play between décor and comfort. In the context of the hardships of mobility at sea, the painting – epitomising the functionless decorative object – is perceived as superfluous, a hubristic excess not appropriate to the gravity of maritime travel. As we have already seen, in his 1847 account of a voyage from Aden to Suez on board the *Hindostan*, Charles Henry Newmarch had identified the steamship's interior design as a decisive departure from the cultural traditions of mobility at sea. He again articulates the apparent incompatibility, between the sea's violence and the niceties of bourgeois interior design, describing the 'magnificence of the saloon, which in its decorations resembled the drawing room of a house on shore, rather than part of a ship which was to be exposed to the fury of the open sea'.[90] Again, the reproduction of bourgeois domestic norms on land, responsible for a marked impression of the departure from the culture of maritime travel, is considered to be in direct tension with the wildness of nature.

Function and form, utility and decoration were seen as antagonistic principles on the steamship. This is again manifested in an article written in response to Richardson's criticisms of the *Hindostan* which appeared the following year in *Chamber's Edinburgh Journal*. The article observes that

> finery in steamboats, the proprietors of such vessels should be made to understand, is generally thrown away. What the public want is comfort, as respects accommodation, attention, and fresh air, not barren splendour. How many a passenger would prefer a roomy to an elegant berth! How few care for looking at themselves in mirrors, when agonised with sea-sickness![91]

The identification of the luxurious shipboard interior as inappropriate to the practicality of maritime mobility is articulated specifically as a critique of the ship's decorative embellishments, particularly fixing upon the mirror as a symbol of superfluous vanity. The notion of comfort is again mobilised to criticise the steamship's decorative interior, identifying the latter as a superficial surface manifestation which was antithetical to the passenger's basic needs.

This tension between décor and comfort, fundamental but often antagonistic facets of shipboard domesticity, is raised again by Jan Brumund. In the account of his 1858 voyage from Point de Galle to Suez on board the *Bengal*, Brumund recounts his experience of first boarding the ship. Like his countryman Franz Junghuhn, Brumund's description of his stupefied response characterises the opulent interior as a marked departure from the cultural representation of maritime tradition:

> When you have climbed the gangway and are within, especially on board one of the ships between Calcutta and Suez – like our *Bengal* more than three hundred feet long – then there is a moment when, struck and astonished, you look around. What a space of enormous dimensions you are in the midst of! A look at the beautiful and long saloon, with its tables, benches, mirrors, carved

and richly gilt; a stroll along the cabins on either side of the whole length of the ship, and you forget you are on board a vessel; you believe yourself to be in rather I do not know what wonderful and strange building.[92]

For Brumund, the steamship's interior was a fantastical one whose luxurious décor contributed to an impression which was antithetical to the saloon's identity as a shipboard space. However, Brumund continues, the spectacle of the saloon's opulent decoration was in fact a façade beneath which the material realities of sea travel were thus perceived as doubly traumatic:

> But because upon entering your cabin it occurs to you that two, three, sometimes four passengers are to reside together in the low and narrow space of a few square feet, you suddenly tumble down from the pinnacle of your fantasies into the depths of a very tragic reality.[93]

The shock of Brumund's movement from the saloon to the cabin is a revealing one, a transition, he suggests, from illusion to reality. If the elaborately decorated social space of the steamer's saloon exhibited an extravagant opulence, the private space of the cabin emerged as an inhospitable interior. Brumund's description suggests that the steamship's luxurious domesticity was an illusory one. According to Amy Richter, the domesticity encountered aboard the nineteenth-century steam train was both 'a shared fantasy' and enacted through 'new social and spatial arrangements'.[94] Domesticity in transit simultaneously operated at the level of the imagination and was characterised by very real delineations of space, material and social attributes which themselves contributed to the nature of that domesticity. The demarcations between semi-public opulence and private discomfort on board articulate the performative nature of steamship domesticity. This was not the private domesticity of the bourgeois home, but a form of social display, a set of social and embodied leisure practices which were perhaps less important in themselves than the fact of their being witnessed by the fellow occupants of the ship.

The identification of the steamship cabin as an inhospitable interior was again expressed by Albert Hervey. The Indian army officer's descriptions of the *Hindostan* were representatively hyperbolic, heaping praise on the new ship as a masterful example of modern engineering. 'There is not a vessel in the world, her superior', he writes. Yet if, like Brumund, Hervey's description of the *Hindostan*'s saloon was filled with admiration for its elegant ornamentation, his portrayal of the ship's cabins was far less complimentary:

> Her accommodations for passengers are poor, cramped, and badly ventilated, built with the intentions, evidently, of cramming as many living souls into as small a space as possible. The number of people between decks, to say nothing of the fires in the engine room, render the heat insufferable … The cabins are

so small, that there is scarcely room for one individual, far less for two; and it is so dark down below, that you can scarcely see.[95]

There was a stark contrast between the voluptuous excess of the richly ornamented saloon and the impoverished functionality of the cabin. Beneath the surface manifestations of the steamship's luxurious décor, the passenger's private space is again depicted as a site of discomfort. In William Makepeace Thackeray's account of his 1844 voyage from Southampton to Gibraltar on board the *Lady Mary Wood*, Thackeray refers to 'the indescribable moans and noises which had been issuing from behind the fine painted doors on each side of the cabin'.[96] Maintaining the standards of bourgeois domesticity within the flux and disruption of transnational maritime mobility was ultimately a problematic and compromised aim. The steamship's decorative interior embellishments acted as a façade which was not always adequate to the task of obscuring this fragility.

Domesticity and social relations

The passenger's experience of steamship domesticity operated on two levels: the exclusive social space of the saloon (and, in fine weather, the deck) where bourgeois social relations were perpetuated; and the cabin, where the austerity of a domesticity able to offer the passenger little comfort against the vicissitudes of shipboard life was laid bare. This contradiction at the heart of steamship domesticity was analogous to the social relations encountered on board, which were characterised by the principles of display, artifice and exclusion: it is this sense that shipboard domesticity could be said to be performative. The steamship's interior can be seen as both implicated in and a material manifestation of these social relations. To reinvoke Jacob van Heerdt's description of his experience aboard the *Hindostan* in 1846 from Chapter 2, the character of life on board the steamer was a collective form of social display, articulated in his likening of the ship to 'a full club, or a crowded city coffeehouse', from which there was neither respite nor escape.[97] The opulent space of the saloon was a social one, reproducing the formulaic semblance of a communal domesticity, rather than the private space of the bourgeois home.

For Jan Brumund, the public space of the *Bengal*'s saloon which he found so entrancing and fantastical was characterised by social relations which exhibited a cold inhospitableness behind an outward spectacle of benevolence. To the Dutchman the mainly English passengers who populated the steamer were

often well-endowed with a spirit of haughtiness, reservation and constraint toward the stranger; ... so that when this stranger is for example aboard an

Indian mail vessel and surrounded by England's sons of liberty and friends of philanthropy, he feels often either as a waif or as a prisoner, and is never at home or completely at ease.[98]

Brumund's account describes social relations antithetical to the domestic equanimity for which the steamer was often lauded. For an outsider, the exclusion from the bourgeois social milieu of the passengers recalls the austerity of the cabin, a space to which, it will be recalled, Brumund retreated from the 'uncaring' world in which he found himself. This contradiction goes right to the heart of the steamship's idiosyncratic domesticity, a space in which Brumund claimed to be 'not at home, yet so completely at home'.

This inhospitable, impersonal aspect of shipboard life can be seen as part of a more general shift in Victorian social relations, reflecting the increased social atomisation and rationalised impersonality of modern society. This shift was played out in microcosm in the move from sail to steam in shipping, reflecting the anonymity which characterises modern forms of mobility. Aboard sailing vessels, the apportioning of passenger space had generally been performed by the captain, governed by an informal system of socially mediated exchange. Traveller numbers were low enough that the captain would personally enter into negotiations with prospective passengers.[99] The transition to the passenger steamship was to a state of anonymity, to a purely financial transaction. Access to mobility at sea was thus mediated no longer by a process of social exchange, but solely by the money spent on the passage. In his 1872 account of life in India, in which he frames the overland route as a radical departure from the sailing voyage, Edward Braddon characterises this departure specifically as a shift in social relations:

> Being on board an overland steamer the passenger finds none of that formality which distinguishes the sailing vessel. He is one of a large party occupying an hotel, and, whether count or cobbler, receives such accommodation as he pays for ... To the purser he is a number, like a convict at Portland. To the stewards also he is a number: and to the captain he is nobody.[100]

What this description exhibits is a fundamentally modern set of social relations, related to the anonymity produced by the increase in the number of passengers and the fungibility of purchasing the space and time of passage aboard the steamship as a commodity. This socially alienating aspect of shipboard life was a manifestation of the bureaucratic rigour with which steam navigation was administered, as regularity and precision came to dominate global networks of transport and communication. In this context, the steamship's domesticity can be understood as part of wider rationalisation of modern life, marked by increasingly bureaucratic interventions in social relations. As James Vernon has written, modernity was characterised by the rise of anonymity and atomisation whereby traditional social relations 'were slowly displaced by increasingly abstract and bureaucratic ways of making economic, social, and political relations between distant strangers possible'.[101]

The steamship's formulaic domesticity can thus be seen as a means to cushion not only against the hardships of maritime mobility, but also the anonymous and impersonal character of shipboard life. Two rare accounts of personal expression in the austere interiors of the steamship's cabins are instructive in this regard. Albert Smith, travelling from Suez to Point de Galle aboard the *Bentinck* in 1858, describes the junior officers' attempts to create a domesticity inevitably lacking in the lives of these occupationally itinerant individuals, for whom the ship constituted a long-term home. Smith observes that 'the cabins were fitted up according to their tastes. One officer had daguerreotypes of all his family, and his little country home in Devonshire.'[102] These images register the crew member's desire for a domesticity which was inevitably denied in transit. The second account, by Scottish travel writer Constance F. Gordon-Cumming, recounts her voyage from Suez to Calcutta aboard the *Candia* in 1868. She describes her 'little cabin half full of corals and green love-birds', objects purchased during the steamer's stop at Ceylon.[103] The decoration of the ship's cabin with exotic curios illustrates the extent to which passengers' global mobility could be expressed through practices of consumption. These two very different examples are complementary, holding together the contradictions of the steamship interior, caught between domestic and imperial space, metropole and periphery.

Shipwreck: Domesticity as hubris

Beneath the spectacle of the ship's luxurious décor, life aboard the steamship was at times cheerless, inhospitable and uncomfortable – it could also be dangerous. As we have already seen, the steamship's opulent interior was viewed by many as antithetical to the culture of the sea as a sometimes violent force of nature. At sea, the failure to overcome the excesses of nature's inhospitality finds its most extreme articulation in the shipwreck, and despite the hubristic veneration of the steamship's technological domination of nature it was of course not immune to such catastrophes.[104] The history of P&O in fact begins with such a disaster, with the steamer *Don Juan* shipwrecked in dense fog on 15 September 1837 while returning from its first voyage in fulfilment of the fledgling company's new mail contract to Gibraltar.[105] While its cargo and passengers were saved, the ship sank off the southern coast of Spain near Tarifa. Arthur Anderson, co-founder and chairman of P&O lamented the loss of the ship in the *Shetland Journal* of 31 October 1837: 'The *Don Juan* was the largest steam vessel and had the most powerful engines yet constructed in the kingdom. She was fitted up in such a style of elegance as to resemble in her interior a floating palace rather than a ship.'[106] In expressing his admiration for the lost ship, Anderson stressed the steamer's technological supremacy – its size and power as a symbol of modern progress even at the moment of its failure – in parallel with the splendour of its interior. This was an interior which produced the illusion of a security which was negated in the moment of shipwreck. The steamship interior's decorative opulence is again depicted as antithetical to its identity as a ship. Anderson's alignment of technology and décor as distinct spheres emphasises their alienation as irreconcilable facets of the steamship's modernity.

Nathaniel Cheever, a passenger travelling on board a sailing vessel off the south coast of Spain in 1837, just seventeen days after the wreck of the *Don Juan*, relates his sighting of the submerged ship:

> We could see very plainly, close under the point, the wreck of the magnificent steam-ship 'Don Juan.' … She was a perfectly new and splendidly finished steamship of 800 tons … All her splendid finishing, her rich adornments, are the mockery of the waves in the stables of sea-monsters.[107]

The shipwreck is articulated as an archaic, anti-modern moment, a return into myth – represented by the anthropomorphised sea and the leviathans of the deep – precisely at the moment of nature's overcoming of the technology designed to dominate it. The reliance of modernity's mythology upon the symbolic overthrow of nature as a sovereign force was spontaneously inverted at the moment of the failure of this domination. Cheever, like Anderson, framed the shipwreck of the *Don Juan* specifically in relation to the steamer's lavish decoration. The ship's decorative features are characterised almost as a symbol of hubris; that the creation of such a decadent interior in the midst of the sea's violence and unpredictability marked a failure to appreciate the gravity of transnational maritime mobility. Cheever's choice of words is also perhaps an allusion to some lines from Milton's *Paradise Lost* which describe the biblical deluge: 'Sea without shore; and in their palaces | Where luxury late reigned, sea-monsters whelped | And stabled.'[108] Much like the descriptions of subaltern labour, this reference mobilises a kind of pre-modern gothic, deepening the sense of shipwreck as a departure from the temporality of the modern. The wreck was not merely an anti-modern moment, but a reversion into a state outside of history.

Paul Virilio's familiar assertion that 'to invent the sailing ship or steamer is to invent the shipwreck' posits the accident as the founding principle of logistics; the shipwreck is imminent within the materiality of maritime logistics, the ultimate failure to protect against the 'violence of speed'.[109]

Understood in this way, as the sudden and unexpected breakdown of the social, spatial and representational façade of domesticity which played a decisive role in cushioning the bourgeois passenger against this violence, it is unsurprising that accounts of P&O steamship wrecks exhibit a striking preoccupation with the ship's idiosyncratic domesticity. Such accounts are often marked by a sudden lurch from the illusory normality of leisured bourgeois mobility to an experience of terrifying elemental danger, as the passenger John Underwood Champain's account of the wreck of the *Carnatic* in the 16 October 1869 edition of the *Illustrated London News* discloses. Southbound in the Red Sea, the *Carnatic* was wrecked on a reef at the mouth of the Gulf of Suez, with the loss of twenty-six lives. Champain's narrative opens with a fairly archetypal description which combines the pleasures of the overland route voyage with the steamship's technological prowess:

> At ten o'clock on the morning of Sunday, Sept. 12, the steamship Carnatic, a magnificent vessel of 1,700 tons, commanded by Captain Jones, left Suez on her way to Bombay. There were on board, altogether, some 230 souls and a valuable cargo. The weather was lovely and, with a fair breeze, we went at ten or twelve knots an hour.

With the vessel's grounding on a reef, however, the narrative lurches into a description of the ship's luxurious passenger space, whose genteel repose and ordered domesticity is shattered by the irruption of nature's violence into bourgeois equanimity:

> The saloon was full of water, which poured in with amazing violence through the shattered skylights, every advancing wave threatening to carry away the whole after part of the ship. Tables, chairs, and benches were careering about, washed hither and thither by the swirling water.[110]

The sea's violence is exaggerated by its juxtaposition with the steamship interior's idiosyncratic modernity, revealing the fragility of a domesticity which had been carefully maintained in the midst of an implacable sea. The shipwreck has long held a privileged place in the cultural imagination. In the age of steam, it was lent even greater significance by the excessive investment in the steamer's modernity as both a technological wonder and a luxury domestic environment. If the steamship was seen as a material manifestation of the dynamic driving force of Western progress, its sudden immersion in the natural space of the sea (which it was lauded for overcoming) was loaded with an overdetermined symbolism. Even in the age of steam, the shipwreck remained a sudden and violent reminder of the vulnerable materiality of mobility at sea.

An account of the 1862 wreck of the *Colombo* from the *London Journal* again reproduces a familiar set of tropes concerning steamship travel: the technophilic lauding of the steamship's mechanical prowess and the characterisation of the passengers as presenting a microcosm of the wider world:

> The Colombo, one of the great ocean steamers of the present day – a miracle of naval architecture, a prodigy of size, strength, and speed, that, at the time the elements proved too powerful for her, was carrying an assemblage that might have been taken for a body of citizens, going out with all the attributes of the nation, to found a colony, there being gentlemen and ladies, officers and civilians, wives and daughters, mothers and children.[111]

This hubristic veneration of the steamer, rooted in an imperialistic characterisation of its passengers as representatives of the British state on the world stage, is fraught by an elemental struggle between the ship and the elements in which the former's failure to overcome the latter is portrayed as a violently catastrophic inversion of the steamer's modernity. Again, this account of the shipwreck evinces a curious preoccupation with the steamer's equanimous domesticity, even at the moment of its negation:

> A few minutes sufficed to make a small colony of English people homeless, houseless, and destitute of almost every necessary. Not half an hour elapsed between the time when they had been as comfortably lodged, and as merrily entertained, as they would have been at home, and when, in the darkness of a November morning, they were shivering on a dreary island.[112]

The shipwreck is presented as the spontaneous inversion of the steamship's domestic cushioning of the passenger from the hardships of mobility at sea. It represents the violent negation of the steamer's modernity as both the technological overcoming of nature and an embodied experience of domestic comfort. Despite this anti-modern sentiment, the article was still able to characterise the wreck in relation to a discourse of a regimented, quotidian, modern form of maritime mobility, going on to note 'the gaiety, the *abandonment*, the evident thorough enjoyment which attends a P&O shipwreck'.[113] This lackadaisical attitude was perhaps due to the fortuitous lack of casualties arising from the wreck of the *Colombo*, a circumstance which many P&O shipwrecks were unable to avoid. At such a moment of crisis, when the façade of bourgeois domesticity was suddenly torn away, the contradiction at the heart of the colonial steamship's mobile domesticity was laid bare, as is articulated by the 1846 wreck of the *Great Liverpool*, off Cape Finisterre. Three people drowned in the wreck, a white female passenger, her infant child and the Indian ayah who was employed to care for the child. An account of the wreck from the *London Daily News* of 21 March 1846 presents an exemplary image of empire: 'Mrs Archer, the passenger who was drowned,' it relates, 'sunk with ninety sovereigns round her neck; and the ancles [*sic*] and wrists of the native servant, who was also drowned, were loaded with silver ornaments.'[114]

Passenger experiences of the steamship's mobility were expressed through their embodied subjectivity. The overland route steamship was a globally mobile environment in which the bourgeois passenger's everyday social practices were inevitably disrupted, but where nevertheless the domestic was persistently encountered as a material practice. While incomplete and compromised, this domesticity offered passengers a means to establish familiar material, social and spatial practices while in transit. It helped identify the steamer as a fixed, unchanging world of safety, certainty and regularity in the midst of spatio-temporal flux and fragmentation. The steamship's domesticity was established both in spite of, and as a panacea to, a range of disruptive elements of mobility at sea, including the sea's wildness and the steamer's industrial technologies and labour forms. Shipboard domesticity helped to normalise imperial steamship mobilities through the separation of the bourgeois consumer of mobility from its production, a process of cushioning against the hardships of travel at sea. This separation was poised uneasily between the corporeality of comfort and the representational function of décor. The domestic as a social, spatial and material practice, situated in the complex interstitial relations between these elements, was a contested notion in constant renegotiation.

The widespread descriptions of the overland route steamship's domesticity chart a shift in subjectivity, an altered perception of life at the cutting edge of imperial mobilities. Travelling at an unprecedented rate across the thresholds of imperial space, experiencing climactic changes which strained at the limits of endurance, steamship passengers were the pioneers of a mobility which was elucidated both through imaginative practices and at the level of the body. An account of the colonial steamship's domesticity must be attentive not just to the opulent saloon in which the bourgeois passenger sipped claret under the breeze of the punkah. It must also be mindful of the boiler rooms in which anonymous African labourers shovelled the coal which propelled the ship, workers to whom even the most basic domesticity was denied. The steamship's décor, a representational reproduction of familiar bourgeois space, helped to normalise the vessel's reliance upon exploitative subaltern labour practices. Ultimately, the steamship's domesticity offered a familiarity, a stable centre from which the contingency of imperial mobility at sea could be experienced as coherent and natural. For many passengers, this domesticity helped them maintain a relatively stable sense of their identity in their journey through a world of sometimes threatening difference. The following chapter explores how this imperial performativity was played out in the field of vision, remaking the steamship as a privileged site from which to consume and come to terms with the imperial landscape.

Notes

1 Brumund, *Schetsen eener Mail-Reize van Batavia naar Maastricht*, p. 118.
2 Susan Roberson, *Antebellum American Women Writers and the Road: American Mobilities*. (New York: Routledge, 2012), p. 4.
3 Richardson, *The Anglo-Indian Passage*, p. vi.
4 *Ibid.*, p. vii.
5 'English Embassies in China', *Blackwood's Magazine*, January 1861, p. 46.
6 Catherine Hall and Sonya Rose, 'Introduction: Being at Home with the Empire', in *At Home with the Empire: Metropolitan Culture and the Imperial World*, ed by Catherine Hall and Sonya Rose (Cambridge: Cambridge University Press, 2006), pp. 1–31, p. 24.
7 Lambert and Merriman, 'Empire and Mobility', p. 10. See also Marc Augé's influential conception of the non-place, the space of transit resistant to the practices of social and cultural life. Marc Augé, *Non-Places: Introduction to an Anthropology of Supermodernity*, trans. by John Howe (London: Verso, 1995).
8 For an extensive account of the improvisatory mode of dwelling engaged with on the East-Indiamen, the large sailing vessels which carried cargo and passengers round the Cape of Good Hope, see Parkinson, *Trade in the Eastern Seas*, pp. 264–85.
9 As Chapter 2 also explored, P&O's steamships were conceptualised as an extension into global space of British imperial territory, a process in which these domestic practices also played a significant role.
10 Parkinson, *Trade in the Eastern Seas*, pp. 264, 270, 274–5. See also Stocqueler, *The Hand-Book of India*, pp. 157–8.
11 William Hickey, *Memoirs, Volume IV (1790–1809)* (London: A. A. Knopf, 1925), p. 366.
12 Thackeray, *Notes of a Journey from Cornhill to Grand Cairo*, p. 40.
13 'For India Direct', p. 145.
14 Nancy Pagh, *At Home Afloat: Women on the Waters of the Pacific Northwest* (Calgary: University of Calgary Press, 2001), pp. xiii–xvii.
15 'For India Direct', pp. 142, 145.
16 *Ibid.*, pp. 145, 147.
17 Joachim Stocqueler, in *The Hand-Book of India*, an 1844 guide for the colonial traveller which included an extensive account of the overland route voyage, gives a representative description of the rich variety of food served on board P&O's steamships: 'Mock turtle soup and bouilli – boiled legs of mutton – roast ditto – jugged hare – roast capons – corned pork – pigeon pies – roast geese – stewed breast of mutton and green peas – boiled and roast turkeys – ham – roast shoulder of mutton and onion sauce – harricot [*sic*] – boiled capons and tongues – stewed ducks and green peas – roast beef – curried mutton and chickens – rice – potatoes, boiled and baked – pickles and sauces of every description – jam puddings – gooseberry, plum, currant, and cherry tarts – stewed pippins – macaroni and cheese – rice puddings. A dessert of

almonds, raisins, brandy – fruits and preserves, oranges, plaintains, biscuits. At dinner, sherry, claret, champagne, ale, and porter. At dessert, port, madeira, and sherry. – The wine well iced.' Stocqueler, *The Hand-Book of India*, p. 184.

18 'For India Direct', p. 142.

19 Benjamin, *The Arcades Project*, p. 220.

20 Schivelbusch, *The Railway Journey*, pp. 120–2.

21 Karl Marx, 'Capital, Volume II' (1885), *Marx Engels Collected Works, Volume 36*, trans. by I. Lasker (Moscow: Progress Publishers, 1998), p. 62.

22 Stocqueler, *The Hand-Book of India*, p. 185.

23 Hervey, *The Ocean and the Desert*, p. 15.

24 Richardson, *The Anglo-Indian Passage*, pp. 48–9.

25 Buddingh, *Dagboek Mijner Overland-Mail-Reis van Rotterdam naar Java, via Southampton in 1852*, p. 52.

26 Russell, *My Diary in India*, p. 48.

27 Barton, *Journal of further voyages for the P.&O. Company* (1 May 1855), p. 138.

28 Amy G. Richter, *Home on the Rails: Women, the Railroad, and the Rise of Public Domesticity* (Chapel Hill: University of North Carolina Press, 2005), p. 5.

29 *Ibid.*, p. 60.

30 *Ibid.*, pp. 78–87.

31 *Ibid.*, p. 60.

32 'Our Tea Table', p. 244.

33 Mitchell, *Colonising Egypt*, pp. 29–30.

34 George Augustus Sala, 'The Streets of the World: Their Ins and Outs, their Lights and Shadows, their Houses and their Inhabitants', *The Welcome Guest* (London: Houlston and Wright, 1861), p. 183. Sala's reference to Tom Taylor is to the playwright who wrote the 1860 play *The Overland Route*.

35 *The Popular Overland Guide*, p. 2.

36 Pietsch, 'Bodies at Sea'.

37 Lutfullah, *Autobiography of Lutfullah*, p. 359.

38 *Ibid.*, p. 376.

39 John Crowley, *The Invention of Comfort: Sensibilities and Design in Early Modern Britain and Early America* (Baltimore: Johns Hopkins University Press, 2001), pp. ix–x.

40 *Shetland Journal*, 1 May 1837, unpaginated.

41 An archival document dated 10 July 1848 records that of the 177 crew of the *Bentinck*, 31 were stewards and servants. The ship was carrying 102 passengers and 50 passengers' servants. Often overlooked shipboard labour practices played an essential role in maintaining bourgeois domestic standards during the voyage. London, National Maritime Museum Archive, P&O Company Records: 'Individual Ships: Bentinck, miscellaneous material', 1848, P&O/65/67.

42 As already noted, there was no formal second-class accommodation provided in the first decades of P&O's service. Those who chose to pay a lower fare were obliged to lodge in the same part of the vessel as the crew.

43 Pfeiffer, *A Woman's Journey Round the World*, p. 116.

44 Julia Prewitt Brown, *The Bourgeois Interior: How the Middle Class Imagines Itself in Literature and Film* (Charlottesville: University of Virginia Press, 2008), pp. xi–xii.

45 Pfeiffer, *A Woman's Journey Round the World*, p. 118.

46 Paul Virilio, *Negative Horizon: An Essay in Dromoscopy*, trans. by Michael Degener (London: Bloomsbury Publishing, 2006), p. 54.

47 Craig Martin, 'Desperate Passage: Violent Mobilities and the Politics of Discomfort', *Journal of Transport Geography*, 19(5) (2011), 1046–52, p. 1048.

48 Virilio, *Negative Horizon*, p. 42.

49 Tom Taylor, *The Overland Route: A Comedy in Three Acts* (New York: Robert M. De Witt, 1866), pp. 18–19.

50 Stocqueler, *The Hand-Book of India*, p. 167.

51 Brown, *The Bourgeois Interior*, p. xii.

52 *The Popular Overland Guide*, p. 2.

53 *Ibid.*, p. 2.

54 Smith, *To China and Back*, pp. 10–11, 13.

55 Power, *Sketches in New Zealand*, p. 257.

56 'The Hindostan Steam-Ship', *Morning Post*, 14 September 1842, unpaginated.

57 Richardson, *The Anglo-Indian Passage*, p. 43.

58 David Lester Richardson, 'Travels', *Hampshire Advertiser and Salisbury Guardian*, 6 January 1844, p. 7. It should be noted that Richardson's reference to an 'Indian' would most likely have been to an English former resident of India.

59 Clay, *Leaves from a Diary in Lower Bengal*, p. 15.

60 Macleod, *Peeps at the Far East*, p. 9.

61 Clay, *Leaves from a Diary in Lower Bengal*, p. 14.

62 Charles Carleton Coffin, *Our New Way Round the World* (Cambridge, MA: Fields, Osgood, & Co., 1869), p. 77.

63 McClintock, *Imperial Leather*, p. 34.

64 *Accounts and Papers of the House of Commons*, 'Shipping (United Kingdom)', Session 5 February–21 August 1867, vol. 63 (1867), p. 26.

65 Taylor, *A Visit to India, China, and Japan*, p. 23.

66 Minturn, *From New York to Delhi*, p. 406.

67 *Ibid.*, p. 403.

68 After this early period of novelty such articles were more often reserved only for iconic vessels, vast in size or technologically innovative.

69 'The Hindostan Steam-Ship', *Morning Post*, 14 September 1842, unpaginated.

70 Burgess, *Engines of Empire*, p. 8.

71 Hervey, *The Ocean and the Desert*, pp. 11–12. The stanchions were the numerous pillars which supported the deck above. 'Arguand' is presumably a reference to the then ubiquitous oil lamp invented in 1780 by Aimé Argand.

72 *Ibid.*, p. 12.

73 Richter, *Home on the Rails*, p. 71.

74 'The "Oriental" Steam-Ship', pp. 170–1.

75 Sigfried Giedion, *Building in France* (Santa Monica, CA: The Getty Centre for the History of Art and the Humanities, 1995), p. 85.

76 Witold Rybczynski, *Home: A Short History of an Idea* (New York: Viking, 1986), p. 174.

77 *Ibid.*, p. 175.

78 As Wolfgang Schivelbusch has suggested, the neoclassical façade of the Victorian railway station served the function of integrating the railway into the city – making the logistical easier to digest. Schivelbusch, *The Railway Journey*, pp. 174–5. Although, as Laura Bear has explored, Indian railway stations tended to be plain brick buildings in their first decades, in the years after the rebellion of 1857 they began to take on a new symbolic role, possessing elaborate architectural facades with an ideological function: 'What was important was not that these facades cushioned a transition into the industrial space of the platform, but that they announced the fusion of European technology and a generic force of civilization.' Laura Bear, *Lines of the Nation: Indian Railway Workers, Bureaucracy, and the Intimate Historical Self* (New York: Columbia University Press, 2007), p. 40.

79 Alex G. Bremner, 'Nation and Empire in the Government Architecture of mid-Victorian London: The Foreign Office and India Office Reconsidered', *Historical Journal*, 48 (2005), 703–42, p. 710.

80 Junghuhn, *Terugreis van Java naar Europa*, p. 41.

81 Newmarch, *Five Years in the East*, pp. 166–7.

82 'The Bentinck Steam-Ship', *Civil Engineer and Architect's Journal*, August 1843, p. 287.

83 'Oriental Steam-Ship', *Literary World: A Journal of Popular Information and Entertainment*, 5 September 1840, p. 386.

84 *Paris Universal Exhibition, 1855: Catalogue of the Works Exhibited in the British Section of the Exhibition, in French and English; together with Exhibitors Prospectuses, Prices Current, &c.* (London: Chapman & Hall, 1855), unpaginated.

85 Sekula, *Fish Story*, p. 45.

86 Votolato, *Ship*, p. 45.

87 'The "Oriental" Steam-Ship', p. 171.

88 'The Bentinck', *Illustrated London News*, 12 August 1843, p. 107.

89 Richardson, 'Travels', p. 7. It is worth recalling that the following year Richardson would refer to the voyage as a 'pleasure trip' in a more complimentary vein. As I have suggested, such antinomies often narrate broader tensions in steamship mobility's discursive constitution.

90 Newmarch, *Five Years in the East*, p. 166.

91 'A Hint to Steamboat Proprietors', *Chambers Edinburgh Journal*, 20 January 1844, p. 48.

92 Brumund, *Schetsen eener Mail-Reize van Batavia naar Maastricht*, p. 107.

93 *Ibid.* This passage may seem contradictory, given that Brumund had been so effusive about the homeliness of his cabin. However, Brumund had been fortunate, travelling on a very quiet passage which meant he had a spacious cabin to himself.

94 Richter, *Home on the Rails*, pp. 60, 88.

95   Hervey, *The Ocean and the Desert*, pp. 6–7.

96   Thackeray, *Notes of a Journey from Cornhill to Grand Cairo*, p. 1.

97   Van Heerdt, *Mijne Reis met de Landmail van Batavia over Singapore*, pp. 29–30.

98   Brumund, *Schetsen eener Mail-Reize van Batavia naar Maastricht*, p. 104.

99   Gilchrist, *The General East India Guide and Vade Mecum*, p. 21.

100   Braddon, *Life in India*, p. 308.

101   Vernon, *Distant Strangers*, p. xi.

102   Smith, *To China and Back*, p. 8.

103   Constance Frederica Gordon-Cumming, *Two Happy Years in Ceylon* (London: Chatto & Windus, 1893), p. 24.

104   In the period covered by this book alone, the following P&O vessels were wrecked: *Don Juan* (1837); *Great Liverpool* (1846); *Ava* (1858); *Alma* (1859); *Malabar* (1860); *Colombo* (1862); *Hindostan* (1864); *Jeddo* (1866); *Singapore* (1867); *Benares* (1868); *Carnatic* (1869); *Rangoon* (1871).

105   This event occurred before the company had been awarded the mail contract to Egypt and its incorporation by Royal Charter, when it was known as simply the Peninsular Steam Navigation Company.

106   *Shetland Journal*, 18 September 1837, unpaginated.

107   Henry T. Cheever, *Memorials of the Life and Trials of a Youthful Christian in Pursuit of Health: as Developed in the Biography of Nathaniel Cheever, M.D.* (New York: Charles Scribner, 1851), pp. 234–5.

108   John Milton, *Paradise Lost* (London: Routledge, 2013), p. 638.

109   Paul Virilio, *The Original Accident*, trans. by Julie Rose (Cambridge: Polity, 2007), p. 10.

110   'The Wreck of the Carnatic', *Illustrated London News*, 16 October 1869, p. 390.

111   'The Loss of the Mail Steamer Colombo', *London Journal: And Weekly Record of Literature, Science, and Art*, 7 February 1863, p. 93.

112   *Ibid.*

113   *Ibid.*

114   'Suicide of Captain McLeod', *London Daily News*, 21 March 1846, p. 5. As the article's title indicates, McLeod, captain of the *Great Liverpool*, committed suicide shortly after the wreck.

5

'Dissolving views in the panorama of travel': Producing the maritime landscape

In 1847 William Tyrone Power travelled from Calcutta to Suez on board the *Haddington*. In his account of the voyage, he mobilises a familiar characterisation of the steamship as a sphere of Western comfort and bourgeois normativity, in the midst of its global mobility:

> These large steamers are the heights of sea-going luxury, and we have all the comforts of light winds, smooth water, a large deck to promenade on, with library, chess, &c. for amusement, and the almost positive certainty of being each day some two hundred miles nearer our destination.[1]

Power's description engages a familiar set of concerns, encompassing the combined pleasures of the steamship's opulence, favourable weather conditions, embodied leisure, elite forms of recreation and global mobility. In the following passage, his narrative switches focus from the vessel itself to the landscape viewed from the ship. 'We have to-day', he writes, 'been running along the coast of Ceylon in view of a perfect chaos of picturesque hills and mountains of all shapes and sizes.'[2] If the steamship was familiar, ordered and Western, the landscape was anything but. Yet in its very reproduction of the norms of Western life, the steamship provided a privileged vantage point from which to view the Eastern world. 'It is rather a pretty place as seen from the sea', Power writes of Point de Galle, the ship's calling point at Ceylon. However, he goes on to conclude, 'there is not much to be seen on landing'.[3] The distance facilitated by the steamship allowed travellers to encounter the East as landscape, which with a surprising frequency in overland route narratives is considered preferable to actually visiting the locations seen from the vessel.

As Chapter 4 explored, the steamer's identification as a safe, familiar space relied in part upon its contrast to an often incomprehensible, threatening, fundamentally 'other' space outside. The steamship's traversing of both heterogeneous geographical locations and temporalities of development, and the 'wild void' of the open sea meant that its modernity was posited against a fluctuating 'constitutive outside'. This final chapter before the conclusion focuses on responses to this maritime landscape. This involves a turn away from the book's close focus on the ship itself, to gaze at the world outside. Looking at the view from the ship offers the opportunity to explore how the steamer became a significant discursive site for comprehending the British imperial world, an outlook shaped and mediated by the imaginative geographies of steamship travel. This focus clarifies the extent to which there was extensive interplay between the conception of the overland route in the popular imagination, and in the passenger experience. It foregrounds the importance of the overland route steamship in the production of the British imperial world view. This is achieved by engaging with a trope encountered with striking frequency in passenger descriptions of the view from the ship: as a means of framing and articulating their perception of the Eastern landscape, passengers repeatedly compared the view to the popular Victorian entertainment form of the panorama.

Imperial panorama

Power's juxtaposition, of the comforts of shipboard life with the chaotic Eastern landscape, can again be seen in Franz Junghuhn's account of travelling along the southern coast of the Arabian peninsula on board the *Bentinck* in 1848. As seen in Chapter 4, Junghuhn had been effusive about the steamship's opulent interiors and congenial atmosphere, in particular, characterising them as a departure from the traditions and culture of travel at sea. Taking this theme further, Junghuhn suggests that the equanimity of shipboard life was such that the ship appeared not to be in motion at all:

> Since nothing was heard or felt of the pounding of the engine or the roaring of the paddle wheels, the ship – by virtue of its size – glided so evenly through the waves from Ceylon to Suez that one could not detect the slightest movement on deck, and one had to look outside of the ship to convince himself that it was not standing still.[4]

For Junghuhn, the experience of the production of steamship mobility was so subdued that the sensation of movement could only be encountered through the field of vision, by gazing at the shifting landscape seen from the ship. The steamer appeared almost to stand still as the landscape moved around it. Junghuhn's subsequent account is filled with detailed descriptions of the Eastern coastline, representative of a general preoccupation in overland route narratives with the various coastal landscapes viewed from the ship during the voyage. In one such description, of the mountainous coastline in the vicinity of Aden, he refers to the landscape's 'inhospitable, anxiety and fear-inspiring appearance'.[5]

Junghuhn's description plays into widespread nineteenth-century discourses regarding landscape, particularly evoking the kind of characterisations which were commonly associated with the sublimity of mountainous regions. He was no stranger to the Eastern landscape, and the cultural associations it inspired. Junghuhn was a prominent and influential author, dubbed the 'Humboldt of Java' due to the extensive drawings, maps and writings he had produced on the geography, flora and fauna of Java, where he had lived for over a decade as a Dutch colonial employee.[6] His books were possessed of a great sensitivity to landscape, describing, measuring and making the East legible for a Western audience. As his moniker suggests, his was not merely a scientific gaze, but one which viewed the natural world as a great repository of meaning, emotion and cultural value. As such, it is clear that Junghuhn would have been well aware of the Romantic tradition of the sublime landscape, versed in applying Western conceptions of landscape to his extensive encounters with Eastern geographies.

Although steam was considered to have brought the East and West closer together, the normative domesticity of the vessel itself could be seen to emphasise their difference. Viewed from the orderly microcosm of the ship, the Eastern landscape's alterity was exaggerated. It was perceived as dangerous, incomprehensible and undisciplined. The kind of density of meaning which characterised Junghuhn's descriptions of landscape was distinctly lacking from his engagement with the coastline in the vicinity of Aden. His description continues, rendering the unfamiliar view as a surreal landscape: 'If one did not see that friendly little house in the quiet curve of the deep valley, if the eye did not perceive the blue, smiling sky stretched out above this chaos of mountains, one could fancy that one was on a strange, desolate planet.'[7] Junghuhn's description of the Eastern coastline is of a hostile, barren landscape, only saved from its characterisation as a threatening and alien world by the presence of minor reassuring signs of domestic normativity. As one whose discussions of landscape were generally informed by extensive knowledge of the geology, botany and culture of the place, Aden presented to Junghuhn an alien landscape indeed.

Passenger attempts to articulate their impressions of the various unfamiliar landscapes they encountered on the overland route often exhibit distinctive techniques of discursive production. Constance Gordon-Cumming travelled from Aden to Ceylon aboard the *Candia* in 1868. Her description of this section of the voyage provides a characteristic, if particularly vivid example of passenger engagements with the landscape:

> It would be difficult to imagine a contrast more complete, as opposite types of Creation, than the scenes thus successively revealed, like dissolving views in the panorama of travel – Aden and Ceylon – the former like a vision of some ruined world, the latter the very ideal of Eden.[8]

Gordon-Cumming's utilisation of two scopic technologies of popular nineteenth-century bourgeois entertainment forms as a means to discursively articulate the view from the steamship is striking. Her reference to 'dissolving views' is to a nineteenth-century magic lantern entertainment which exhibited the gradual transition from one projected image to another. The vision she suggests, of a pair of panoramic images which dissolve one into the other, elides the more than two thousand miles of the Indian Ocean covered between these locations, the longest sustained section of open sea on the overland route, which took more than ten days to traverse.

Gordon-Cumming's description reflects a common trope found in overland route narratives – the conception of the open sea as an absence. As Chapter 3 explored, this characterisation of pelagic space was perhaps amplified by the privileging of terrestrial space which had been made possible by the logistical geographies of steam propulsion. With its regular calling points, and frequent travel within sight of land, the overland route voyage tended to exaggerate the monotony of the open sea. This can be seen in *The Overland Guide-Book* of 1845, describing the view from the steamship in the Red Sea: 'The shores are dreary and barren, and are only agreeable to the eye of the landsman, because they present a somewhat less monotonous scene than the expanse of "blue above and blue below," which distinguishes the ocean in parts remote from land.'[9] On the protracted voyage by sailing ship from Europe to India, the vessels followed a route south which took them far from the land due to the contrary wind and currents in the vicinity of Africa's western coast. This journey was thus characterised for the passenger by an experience of sensory detachment, surrounded by the open sea for weeks on end, immersed in pelagic space.

In contrast, only a relatively short portion of the overland route passed through the open ocean, the steamer instead travelling mainly in the vicinity of land. Due to their means of propulsion, steamships were also able to travel closer to the coast than sailing vessels, and were compelled to land to make periodical stops for coaling. Thus the open sea was secondary in the overland steamship passenger's experience of the maritime landscape to the points of contact with land and the view of the coast which the technology of steam facilitated. The introduction of steam navigation to the journey East was marked therefore by a transition from the pelagic monotony of the open sea to a linear narrative of discrete coastal views. The coastline became a new focal point for steamship passengers' visual experience of the journey, a geography which the traveller, in the monotony of shipboard life, consumed as landscape. William Tyrone Power, whose 1847 descriptions of the Ceylon coastline opened this chapter, had travelled from Gibraltar to China on the overland route five years earlier. In his account of the Mediterranean section of the journey, he reported that the steamer had been taken closer to the North African coast specifically so that the passengers could enjoy the view.[10]

It is thus perhaps unsurprising that in Gordon-Cumming's account the pelagic space of the ocean was written as a blank. Such a characterisation reflects the topological absence which Philip Steinberg has suggested provided an increasingly prevalent conceptualisation of the open sea in the nineteenth century, simultaneous with the privileging of terrestrial space. The imaginative annihilation of ocean space which underpins Gordon-Cumming's distinctive means of narrating steamship mobility was also manifested in Cadwalladar Cummerbund's account of his 1858 overland route journey from England to Calcutta. Cummerbund again mobilises the visual apparatus of the dissolving view as a means to conceptualise the voyage's scopic logic:

> Travellers in the secure clutch of the P. and O. Company, become of necessity 'fast fellows.' Scarcely have their eyes taken in one novelty, and their minds begun to analyse it, ere some few revolutions of a certain magical screw deposit them in a locality totally different to the last, breeding a confusion of ideas similar to that confusion of sight experienced when gazing on a dissolving picture in process of transformation. 'Heigh presto!' as conjurors say, and Malta vanishes in thin air, giving place to an Egyptian prospect, the port and city of Alexandria.[11]

Even by steamship, the over 800 miles of sea between Malta and Alexandria would have taken around five days to traverse. The imaginative geographies of steam, which effaced distance through the omission of the open sea were articulated by Cummerbund as a revolution in the mental and visual experience of mobility, rooted in steamship technology, the 'magical screw'. Cummerbund's playful description is just one of many examples of the discursive creativity which overland route travellers employed in their attempt to account for the novel experiences of steamship mobility. However, it would be Gordon-Cumming's use of the panorama form as the mode for describing these experiences which provided the more prevalent means for articulating and framing the visual experience of the overland route. This preoccupation with panoramic vision provides the lens through which passenger visualisations of the Eastern landscape were rendered comprehensible.

The overland mail panorama

The panorama was a popular nineteenth century entertainment form, comprised of vast painted canvases realistically depicting notable landscapes. P&O's steamship service to the East was represented in one of the most successful spectacles of this type, *The Route of the Overland Mail to India*. This panorama entertainment was exhibited in 1850 at the Gallery of

Illustration on Regent Street, London. The panorama form's popularity experienced a resurgence in England during the mid-century, after a relative lull in interest following its initial popularity in the early 1800s.[12] The *Overland Mail* panorama was one of the most popular, enjoying over 250,000 visitors from 1850 to 1852.[13] This upsurge of interest in the panorama was partly attributed to a specifically peripatetic iteration of the entertainment form dedicated to the depiction of a journey – of which the *Overland Mail* was an example – which capitalised upon the privileged place in the popular imagination of the space then being opened up by an increasingly global revolution in mobility.[14] Contemporaneous with the Great Exhibition, the *Overland Mail* panorama appeared at a time of high public interest in Britain's imperial world, with Egypt and India occupying prime positions in the British geographical imagination.

The popularity of this panorama was testament to the overland route's place in the Victorian popular imagination, particularly situating the steamship line in relation to Britain's global empire. A contemporary review of the spectacle emphasises this relationship: 'At the Gallery of Illustration, we can accompany the Overland Mail to India, as it proceeds from Southampton in its rapid course across ocean and desert. Who would remain unacquainted with a route that has hitherto no precedent in the world's history?'[15] The *Overland Mail* portrayed a sequence of seventeen views of notable sights seen during the journey made by a passenger travelling from Southampton to India on board a P&O steamship on the overland route. Among them were the various stops made for coaling on the voyage, depictions of various coastlines as viewed from the steamer, and a section portraying the journey made overland through Egypt.

The *Overland Mail* panorama presented a mode of engaging with the geographies of global space that had been made possible by P&O's introduction of steam to colonial shipping scarcely a decade before, and in fact the company had some involvement in the panorama's production: a number of the preparatory sketches for the paintings had been made on board their steamers, and the company was reported to have provided 'Eastern' costumes for the panorama's presentation.[16] It was thus fitting that the viewers of the *Overland Mail* panorama beheld global space as it was seen from the deck of the P&O steamer, privileging the ideal vantage point of the steamship passenger. Such a vision emphasises the influence of the overland route on the British imperial world view. Furthermore, no less than the panorama, the many textual responses to the overland route encouraged those in the metropole to view imperial space through the eyes of the steamship passenger. The steamship provided a discursive vantage point for comprehending global space, shaping perceptions in Britain of the British Empire. It offered a coherent, linear means for doing so, based on the organising principle of the steamship voyage. Analogously, the panorama inflected passenger engagements with their own experiences of imperial mobility, emphasising the considerable cultural interplay between metropole and mobility.

With the *Overland Mail* panorama's rendering of the maritime landscape, the viewer was presented with the sea voyage as a series of tableaux which depicted notable points seen along the route, a fragmentary mode of representation which reproduced the steamship passenger's experience. Britain's imperial geography was rendered as a series of discrete landscapes, Gibraltar, Malta, Aden, the ship's coaling points, isolated sites of British imperial territory in global space. The discontinuity of the panorama's various views presented the geographical constitution of global mobility produced through the technology of steam, naturalising the geography of imperial logistics through representation. The panorama presented an exemplary representation of the linear space of the voyage produced by the steamship, the predictable narrative reproducibility of the overland route's geographical constitution. Such a mode of engaging with the journey East had only been made possible by P&O's introduction of steam into the voyage: steam facilitated travelling in a straight line; travelling parallel to the coastline; passing through spaces such as the Red Sea, where the coastline was often visible from the ship; and it also necessitated the frequent stops for coaling which brought the ship into contact with the land.

The voyage was thus narrated as a series of punctuations interrupting the continuity of the route, which, like Gordon-Cumming's panoramic description repressed the monotony of the open sea in favour of a succession of stimulating vignettes which revealed themselves in succession. This representational mode reproduced the elision of the Indian Ocean narrated by Gordon-Cumming, as the panorama passed from a depiction of Aden to one of Ceylon, evoking Philip Steinberg's description of the ocean as an absence, whilst privileging the terrestrial landscape. 'Pelagic space', writes Allan Sekula, 'resisted conversion into the "rich diet of changing tableaux"' through which panoramic space was constituted.[17] The *Overland Mail* panorama presented a maritime landscape specifically ordered and disciplined by British colonial power. Such a claim is exemplified in the rise to prominence of Aden, a location whose geopolitical significance rested upon its use as a coaling station to fuel P&O steamers on the Eastern side of the Gulf of Suez.[18]

The *Overland Mail* panorama was subject to two notable instances of journalistic satire. Both play in to the popular nineteenth-century figure of the 'armchair traveller', the (bourgeois) individual who travelled virtually through the increasingly prevalent media forms allowing for vicarious experience of global travel, a notion which emphasised the destabilising of the relationship between actual travel and its representation. In an article entitled 'Putting a Panorama Round the Earth', the magazine *Punch* satirised the relationship between the space–time compression achieved by P&O steamers and the experience of the metropolitan viewer of the panorama. 'Travelling', it announces, 'is now-a-days so cheap, that it is brought within the means of the meanest pocket. A miser, starting from Burlington Arcade, could easily travel round the world for five shillings.' The simulation of travel achieved by the panorama form was employed as a metaphorical exaggeration of the extent to which steam had opened up global space. 'Paintings', the article states, 'now move with the rapidity of steam.'[19]

The second article, by Charles Dickens in his publication *Household Words*, employs a similar theme, describing a character named Mr Booley, who travels the world without ever departing from the comfort of the metropolis. His excursions included a visit to the *Overland Mail* panorama, which, the article claims, Booley finds to be both '"a beautiful piece of scenery" and "a perfect picture"'. 'In all the immense journies [*sic*] he has since performed,' quips Dickens, 'he has never laid aside the English dress, nor departed in the slightest degree from English customs. Neither does he speak a word of any language but his own.'[20] Dickens' satire articulates not just the nineteenth-century vogue for technologically mediated imaginary travel, but also the logic of steamship travel which this book has identified in shipboard domesticity; that of a global mobility characterised by the normativity of home. Passenger narratives attest to a steamship mobility which was increasingly coming to resemble the imaginative mobilities encountered by the metropolitan viewer of the phantasmagorical spectacle of the panorama.

Complete with accompanying commentary and musical embellishment, the *Overland Mail* panorama organised and structured the world of colonial transport and communication into a comprehensible, rational narrative. As On Barak has suggested, the panorama was just one of several such means – including guidebooks, timetables and maps – which helped to present the novelty and contingency of the overland route voyage as a linear, ordered and comprehensible totality.[21] For passengers, the panorama provided a useful discursive and representational means for organising their experience of the landscape viewed from the ship. The particularity of the way that this experience is described and negotiated in travel narratives can be seen to reflect their textual constitution through the discursive processes of global travel: steam made possible new geographical imaginaries. Yet the novel ways of conceiving of and writing about the maritime landscape were not the result of a simplistic technological determinism, but reflect the various cultural narratives invested in steam power. In this regard, it is significant that the motif of the panorama was employed by P&O steamship passengers as a means of conceptualising and framing the experience of travel on the overland route with a striking frequency.

This repeated mobilisation of the panorama as a discursive tool provided a means for passengers to come to terms with the multiplicity of geographical locations they encountered during the voyage. Frederick Walter Simms, recounting his journey through the Red Sea from Suez to Calcutta on board the *Hindostan* in 1845, writes that 'we now sailed along the African coast, and for several days enjoyed the sight of a fine moving panorama, with this difference, that it was ourselves, and not the scene that was in motion'.[22] Simms's distinctive description of the Red Sea coast suggests a passive consumer of the imperial landscape, a figure who, like the metropolitan viewer of the panorama, experienced this landscape as a leisured spectacle. Allan Sekula has suggested a shift in the aesthetic production of the maritime landscape in the mid-nineteenth century, in which, he writes, the 'mobile spectator had been transformed into a figure of passive consumption'.[23] Associated with the emergence of steam power and the factory system, Sekula suggests, the panoramic representation of the sea was mechanised and standardised. While the *Overland Mail Panorama* presented an aesthetic mode of engaging with the geographies of global space that had been made possible by P&O's introduction of steam to colonial shipping scarcely a decade before, it also fed back in to passengers' experiences of the steamship voyage itself. The mechanical form of vision facilitated by the panorama not only offered passengers a means of representing their experience of steamship travel, but presented a Western mode of viewing the Eastern landscape in which representation came to precede reality – travellers reported that the Eastern landscape viewed from the steamer resembled the panorama, rather than the other way round.

In his account of his 1845 steamship tour of the Mediterranean, William Makepeace Thackeray recalls his arrival at Constantinople aboard the *Lady Mary Wood*, describing his first impressions of the city from the vantage point of the ship. Thackeray frames this description in reference to the work of Clarkson Frederick Stanfield, a popular nineteenth-century painter of vast maritime panoramas, including an example from 1829 entitled *A Grand View of Constantinople*. 'Stanfield's panorama', observes Thackeray, 'used to be the realisation of the most intense youthful fancy. I puzzle my brains and find no better likeness for the place. The view of Constantinople resembles the *ne plus ultra* of a Stanfield diorama.'[24] Thackeray found himself unable to articulate a description of the Eastern landscape without reference to the motif of the panorama's hyper-realism. In an inversion between signifier and signified, the landscape of the East viewed from the steamship came to resemble the constructed, the illusory. Experience of reality was preceded by representation.

Florence Nightingale, in a letter relating the progress of her journey to tend the sick and wounded from the Crimean War, describes her first view of Constantinople upon arrival aboard the *Vectis* in 1854. 'We made Constantinople this morning at 9 in a thick and heavy rain,' she writes, 'through which Santa Sophia, Suleiman, the seven Towers, the Walls and the Golden Horn looked like a bad daguerreotype washed out.'[25] Nightingale's description relies upon what was certainly a different scopic technology from Thackeray's panoramic articulation of the city. Yet it again iterates the perception of the Eastern landscape from the vantage point of the steamship as one in which representation preceded reality: modern technologies of vision acted as a means for European travellers to frame, order and articulate the Eastern landscape.

Making explicit reference to the *Overland Mail* panorama, Henry Stedman Polehampton's 1858 account of his overland route journey from Southampton to Calcutta provides a typical example of this motif. 'The diorama of the overland route', he writes, 'is a most faithful representation of all that takes place.'[26] The topos of the panorama subsumed the landscape seen on the overland route under a schema of representation which preceded experience, delimiting the possible modes of perceiving the Eastern landscape.[27] On Barak has written that it was common for nineteenth-century European travellers to compare their view of the real East to the experience of viewing a panoramic representation of the landscape without having left their own country. 'In such disorientations', he writes, 'reality and its representations switched parts.'[28] Barak suggests that this aesthetic motif was linked to the mechanistic experience of viewing the Egyptian landscape from the train window. In much the same way, the steamship provided passengers with a powerful discourse of mechanised mobility with which to frame their encounters with the landscape.

Like the steamship, the panorama offered a discursive means for taming the Eastern landscape, for rendering comprehensible what Western travellers often found resistant to more conventional forms of representation. Timothy Mitchell has suggested that European visitors to the East attempted to experience the world they encountered there as if it was a picture – enframed, comprehensible, ordered. The aim of these travellers, writes Mitchell, was 'to separate oneself from the world and thus constitute it as a panorama'.[29] The overland route steamship offered the perfect means by which to achieve such a separation, an ideal vantage point from which to constitute the 'world as picture'. For Mitchell, Europeans occupied an image world which meant that their experience of the East was always mediated by prior representation. It thus came to be encountered as 'real' only to the extent that it could be represented by the Western viewer: 'The Orient was something one only ever rediscovered. To be grasped representationally, as the picture of something, it was inevitably to be grasped as the reoccurrence of a picture one had seen before, as a map one already carried in one's head, as the reiteration of an earlier description.'[30]

David Lester Richardson travelled from Calcutta to Suez in 1843 on board the *Hindostan*. In his description of Aden, he registers his disappointment at the Eastern landscape. 'It is one of the dreariest places imaginable', he writes. However, this disappointment did not prevent him from engaging in practices intended to remake this landscape as representation: 'I made a sketch of it. The outlines of the heights being really fine, it looks far better in a drawing than in the reality.'[31] In Richardson's reckoning, his quickly rendered drawing of the Aden coastline was superior to the view itself. Western representations of the landscape were seen to be more comprehensible than the reality of the East. The Western remaking of the world was achieved not only through such material forces as the logistics of steam, but also through representational practices. Such practices, both visual and textual, were intended to render the Eastern landscape legible, readable and comprehensible, to tame a landscape which itself fell short of Western expectations.

The passenger's favoured textual response to the coastline invoked the mechanical form of the panorama to express the unfolding, linear character of the view, echoing the steamship's technological production of a linear, panoramic mobility. This representational trope was particularly employed to describe the coastline of Arabia, especially in the vicinity of Aden. The use of the vocabulary of the panorama to describe the view from the steamer was perhaps related to a difficulty in articulating an Eastern landscape which passengers considered unfamiliar and alien. Albert Hervey, travelling on board the *Hindostan* in 1843, filled his account of the journey with detailed descriptions of the new experiences and sensations of the overland route. Yet he struggles in his attempt to describe the southern coastline of Arabia. Lacking the means to do so, he employs the panorama form to stand in for an adequate vocabulary of representation:

> Steaming along very pleasantly, we approached the land in the neighbourhood of Aden; there was something grand and sublime in the scenery of this part of our voyage, which I cannot, I am afraid, describe. I never beheld anything so magnificent. Something new, and more calculated to draw forth exclamations of wonder than that last seen, appeared in panoramic succession, as we followed up the bendings of the coast; promontory, and headland, frowning precipice, and shelving beach; all presented themselves, one after the other, like magic.[32]

Hervey, faced with the challenge of constructing a coherent description adequate to the apparently ineffable Eastern landscape, utilised the form of the panorama to structure and rationalise the unfolding view – a view which appeared to be mechanically produced. Hervey's designation of the landscape as sublime can be seen as an example of what has been described in Chapter 1 as the technicised sublime: the steamer's means of propulsion appeared to play a role in the aestheticisation of the landscape, the production as a linear, narrative view of a landscape apparently resistant to textual description. The mobilisation of the panorama as a means to order and articulate the landscape suggests a mode of viewing maritime space which was mediated and tamed by a mechanised form of seeing.

Passenger accounts projected Western forms of ocular consumption onto the landscape, as a mode of knowing and narrating the East. The landscape was consumed as spectacle, folded into the experiences of bourgeois leisure practices. In the panoramic mode of viewing, conceptions of the subjective appreciation of landscape (epitomised in the sublime, romantic response) met a sort of mass-produced commodification of the world. This can be seen as a reflection of the more general sense in which bourgeois tourism commodified the experience of global travel, of encounters with the exotic. The travel writer and entertainer Joachim Stocqueler provided live commentary for the public exhibition of the *Overland Mail* panorama, and the text which accompanied the 1850 book of prints which reproduced the images from the show. In *The Hand-Book of India* he provides a description of Aden:

> Aden presents us with one of those phenomena which the giant 'steam' is everyday and everywhere achieving. Barren rocks, and a few yards of sandy shore, once tenanted only by the sea-gull and the crab, are now covered by cheerful domiciles, and animated by a small but busy and contented population, who live by unloading the fuel-ships, storing and protecting the coal, and embarking it upon the steamers.[33]

As David Arnold has explored, nineteenth-century descriptions of the Eastern landscape were shot through with the logic of the imperial project.[34] Stocqueler's vivid description suggests that the arrival of the steamship marked Aden's emergence out of nature, into history. The colonial mobilities of steam had not only a significant geopolitical impact in the Middle East – they were seen to have played a role in the production of the Eastern landscape itself.[35]

The imperial sea voyage in the age of its technological reproducibility

In *Imperial Eyes*, Mary Louise Pratt offers a distinctive perspective on the way in which descriptions of landscapes found in Victorian travel narratives often narrated broader issues regarding imperial power structures, social relations, and the production of global subjectivity and knowledge. Pratt highlights the discursive processes of imperial discovery through the textual production of landscape. She employs the orientalist Richard Burton's strikingly prolix description of his 'discovery' of Lake Tanganyika during an African expedition in 1858 as a particularly discursive example of the use by European explorers – who claimed to have 'discovered' places which had long been occupied and cultivated – of their subsequent descriptions of landscape to emphasise the value of their accomplishments. This was achieved, Pratt writes, through three key discursive methods: a process of aestheticisation, often by comparing the scene to a painting; the production of a 'density of meaning', a verbosity which attested to the landscape's wealth of material significance; and through privileging the vantage point of the European viewer, the 'monarch of all I survey', a figure uniquely positioned to communicate the aesthetic pleasure and meaning of the landscape.[36] All of these scopic mechanisms contributed to the production of imperial space as a landscape which was produced and ordered through the logic of Western vision. Compared to this elaborate representational practice, Burton's treatment (mentioned in Chapter 1) of the maritime landscape viewed from the steamship *Bengal* during his 1853 voyage from Southampton to Alexandria is striking for its brevity and indifference. His description of Gibraltar is similarly perfunctory, stressing the banality of the view. 'Gibraltar, is', he writes, 'probably, better known to you, by Gautier and Warburton, than the regions about Cornhill.'[37] While this passage presents a distinctly unremarkable example of the increasingly ubiquitous nineteenth-century descriptions of sites of travel in which representation precedes the real, Burton's description bears witness to a world which the steamship had made not just more accessible – and thus familiar – but also legible.

Descriptions of the view seen from the vantage point of the steamship can be said to both reproduce and invert the logic of Pratt's account of the visual discourse of imperial landscapes, relying not upon the painting as a means of foregrounding the landscape's aesthetic production, but on a mechanically produced entertainment form; and through suggesting not density of meaning but its lack, through an emphasis upon the landscape's arbitrariness and fungibility. The 'masterly' production of meaning Pratt attributes to the explorer is also absent, with the production of the view attributed not to an individual, authoritative Western subject, but to the technology of steam itself. The panoramic mode of articulating the view from the steamship thus could be seen to reflect a crisis of representation related to the perceived otherness of Eastern space, a landscape often described in voyage narratives as dangerous, incomprehensible and undisciplined. In what has proved to be perhaps the most influential approach to thinking about the processes by which the East has been conceptualised by the West, Edward Said suggests that the East threatens what he terms the European 'rationality of time, space, and personal identity'.[38] The steamship marked the emergence of a space in which these values could be maintained in rigid adherence to Western norms, even in the midst of such a threat. Western travellers remade the Eastern landscape through the imaginative geographies of steam, projecting a mechanised mode of vision onto the landscape viewed from a mechanised mode of transport.

Just as Burton's description of Gibraltar rendered the foreign landscape familiar and banal, passengers employed the same discursive methods to engage with the Eastern landscape. In a prominent example of this reductive engagement with the new geographies of steam, Aden was commonly known as the 'Gibraltar of the East' – both of these ports of call on the overland route had been occupied by Britain due to their geopolitical, strategic significance.[39] This discursive trope rendered Aden familiar – it could be seen to obey a recognisable, Western logic, and could be ascribed with the same familiarity as Burton attributed to Gibraltar. Another instance in which the Eastern landscape was tamed and rendered legible through the projection of a simplistic, Western narrative is illustrated by American journalist Bayard Taylor in his account of an 1853 voyage from Suez to India. If, as we saw in Chapter 2, Taylor had enjoyed identifying the typology of racial difference which characterised the crew of the *Achilles*, an analogous principle was at play in his description of the view of the coastline seen in the Red Sea: 'The shores had a grand continental significance. Here was Africa, there Asia. Like the Bosphorus which parts Europe and Asia, or the straits of Gibraltar, where Africa confronts Europe, this part of the Red Sea possesses a grandeur beyond that which Nature gives it.'[40] Taylor communicates a knowing mastery of a world he is aware that his readers will have little knowledge of themselves, presenting himself as a seasoned traveller well able to adapt to the unfamiliar landscapes of global travel. His engagement with the coastal view was one mediated by discursive processes which emphasised classification and difference. This geo-historical gaze disciplined the view, projecting an ordering principle on to the landscape. Taylor does not merely identify the coastlines as separate continents, but ascribes their very aesthetic appeal to this status. The landscape in itself lacked a visual 'density of meaning', but gained in stature through the Western subject's identification of its geographical significance. The kind of imaginative geography of global space exhibited by Taylor was of course not limited to the steamship passenger. However, the steamer provided a space in which the rational European values Said identifies as threatened by the alterity of otherness could be maintained, offering a useful vantage point for a subject who could imbue what they saw with meaning.

The discursive mode of panoramic vision served a similar function. It provided a convenient representational trope, an imaginative geography which steamship passengers employed as a means of framing and disciplining the landscape into a familiar, comprehensible, Western mode of seeing. This allowed passengers to rationalise imperial geographies, identifying them as orderly, linear and tangible. The panoramic view was facilitated by the steamship voyage, characterised – like the panorama itself – as both mechanically produced and repeatable. On board the steamship, as the landscape took on the character of the panorama, the sensation of mobility gave way almost to an experience of stasis. For many passengers, it almost seemed that they had not left the metropole, but rather that the views which unfolded before them were themselves in motion. Although as this book has attested to, labour remained relatively marginal to passenger accounts of the overland route, labour – or rather its absence – is at the centre of the experience of the production of global space and landscape delineated in the panoramic mode of vision. As with the spectacular rendering of the sublime struggle between technology and nature encountered in Chapter 1, the phantasmagoric unfolding of the panoramic vista as if by magic relied upon the visual repression of racialised labour forms in the depths of the ship and the consequent forgetting of their role in the steamship's mobility.[41] The machine-perception of panoramic vision was facilitated in part by the illusory autonomy of the steamship, itself contingent on the disappearance of maritime labour from the realm of perceptibility.

Imperial geographies were mediated by the field of vision. On board the steamship, separated by the open sea from a coastline which played an increasingly significant role in the visual narrative of their voyage, passengers were able to project their own preconceptions onto the landscape. The complexity of colonial encounters was thus reconstituted by the orderly linear space of the panoramic view seen from the deck of the ship. However, as William Makepeace Thackeray observed in narrating his 1844 steamship tour of the Mediterranean, this imaginary was disturbed by the steamer's reconnection with land at its various calling points. For Thackeray, steamship travel offered a compromised and incomplete experience of the East:

> Wherever the steamboat touches the shore adventure retreats into the interior, and what is called romance vanishes. It won't bear the vulgar gaze; or rather the light of common day puts it out, and it is only in the dark that it shines at all ... The paddle wheel is the great conqueror. Wherever the captain cries 'Stop her,' Civilisation stops, and lands in the ship's boat and makes a permanent acquaintance with the savages on shore.[42]

In stepping ashore, the distance which sustained the ground of panoramic vision was negated, troubling the neat binary of ship and shore, sea and land, West and East, civilised and savage, modernity and its constitutive other. Thackeray's 1846 account of his tour, *Notes of a Journey from Cornhill to Grand Cairo*, is a compendium of similarly thwarted attempts on the author's part to enjoy an unmediated, 'authentic' experience of the East. While this was a familiar and persistent trope in accounts of Western travellers in the East, Thackeray's description is significant for the way in which it is staged specifically from the perspective of the steamship.[43] As a familiar, ordered space, a discrete fragment of what Thackeray terms 'civilisation', the steamship precluded the possibility of an encounter with the trappings of adventure, the unfamiliarity of otherness. For Thackeray, upon landing, the civilisation which the steamship was the bearer of extended the sphere of domesticity from the confines of the ship out into imperial space, taming and normalising everything with which the passenger came into contact, delimiting the frame through which the East could be encountered. Thackeray's characteristically jaded commentary performs a kind of satire of Western tourism, the encounter with an East that had already been reproduced ad infinitum – in a sense the steamship appeared to do in reality what the media had done in the imagination. This was a comment on a world which the steamship had brought closer, but made more banal.

This presents the simultaneous inversion and realisation of the panoramic mode of experiencing the world lampooned by Dickens, of the virtual traveller who never left the comfort and safety of home. Like this figure, the steamship passenger could experience global travel from a space of relative comfort and familiarity – yet this comfort and familiarity was seen to limit the possibility of unmediated experience. As such it is fitting that Thackeray's claims operate around the logic of vision, the gaze from which the otherness of the East retreated into its own 'interior', those inland spaces the steamship passenger was unable to encounter. Like Thackeray, passenger descriptions of the landscape seen from the ship often compare favourably with their accounts of disembarking and encountering the locations in person, an experience which was often met with disappointment. This claim, that with increased mobility, the possibility of encounter with the new experiences of travel to unfamiliar locations was diminished, appears paradoxical. Yet the various accounts which have provided the raw material of this book's account of the lived history of the overland route, and which present attempts to textually render the diverse experiences of steamship mobility, articulate like Thackeray a limit. The persistent bathos exhibited by Thackeray's account communicates more than a world-weary knowingness. It can be seen as part of an emergent literary form which has also been seen in the writings of numerous other commentators on the overland route, particularly that of George Augustus Sala, Albert Smith, William Howard Russell and George Colomb. These writers are in marked contrast to the earliest accounts of the overland route by authors such as David Lester Richardson and Albert Hervey, which exhibit an almost wide-eyed amazement at the steamship's innovation of global mobility. Repeatedly accounts of the overland route have attested – in the experience of boredom and homogeneous time, no less than with that of domestic leisure and comfort – to the challenges of narrating a voyage which had become standardised, reproducible. For Thackeray, as for many other steamship passengers, the logic of modern mobility mediated his possible experiences of the East.

An instructive illustration of this mediation is provided by a prominent example of colonial encounter which took place on board the steamer. Frequently, narratives refer to the practice of local young men at Aden diving in the sea for coins thrown from the ship's deck.[44] The English social reformer Mary Carpenter travelled to Bombay on the overland route in 1866. She records a typical encounter with the divers at Aden:

> The strangest human figures, in boats equally strange, soon surrounded our ship, some bringing various articles for sale, others wishing to exhibit their skill in diving for a piece of money. Many passengers threw a coin into the water, and the dexterity was wonderful with which these boys caught it before it reached the bottom.[45]

In this practice can be witnessed an encounter with difference mediated by the logic of colonial mobility. Passenger descriptions of the divers tend to compare them with animals. One writes that 'they swim just as naturally as fishes'; another, that they 'are extremely agile in the water, where they appear to be quite as much at home as diving ducks; and being, with a slight exception, in nature's costume, they looked very like gigantic black frogs'.[46] Like passengers' shipboard interactions with the subaltern crew, this encounter was staged in a structure of inequality which was both representational and spatial: the passenger, on the one hand, from the ship's deck able to retain a sense of superiority, modernity, power; the diver, on the other, immersed in the natural space of the sea, corporeal, animalistic, reduced to the status of spectacle. The divers' very presence was in part due to the logistics of steam – they were generally East African migrant workers who performed the coaling of the steamers which called at Aden. Money provided the nexus which governed this encounter with the Other. Through such performative instances of colonial exchange, the heterogeneity of racial difference was subsumed under the universality of the money form. As the repeated references to this practice suggest, such experiences were standardised, normalised encounters, so predictable that they appeared in guidebooks to the route.

As Jeffrey Auerbach has suggested, the long-distance sea voyage in the nineteenth century presented an increasingly normalised experience of travel.

The repetition and predictability which characterised the establishment of regularised global communication, trade and transportation networks meant that such voyages lost the excitement of adventure and novel experiences:

> Distance voyages during the sixteenth and seventeenth centuries were harrowing and perilous. They could also be thrilling, as sailors encountered people and places, as well as birds and fish, which had never been seen before. But as ships grew in size and safety, navigation improved, and the routes to India and Australia became more frequently traversed during the first half of the nineteenth century, ocean travel became normalized.[47]

Although Auerbach's observations refer to voyages by sail, the temporal regimentation of the steamship voyage, and the minimal variation in the geographical course of its passage meant that the overland route journey was even more predictable. Persistently, in the textures and rhythms of shipboard experience, the imaginative geographies of maritime mobility, the material practices of steamship space and the visual culture of the voyage, we have seen the persistence of recognisable discursive tropes. Just as the fledgling steamship served passengers as a symbolic technological means for overcoming the messy contingency of the intractable sea, this book has shown the extent to which the voyage was employed as a discursive means to tame the heterogeneity of global space. The reproducibility of the steamship journey, made possible by the technology of steam facilitating temporal and spatial predictability, meant that imperial mobility at sea in the nineteenth century was increasingly seen as not a voyage of discovery into the unknown, but of the world conforming to an idea.

Yet, simultaneously as this limiting of experience took place, the steamship was characterised as a privileged site for encountering the East – but at a distance, in the form of landscape. In contrast to his repeated disappointments with his experience of the East on land, Thackeray was effusive regarding his first view of Smyrna, on the western coast of Turkey. This was an encounter which was made from the vantage point of the deck of the *Tagus*, through the lens of a telescope:

> There lay the town with minarets and cypresses, domes and castles; great guns were firing off, and the blood-red flag of the Sultan flaring over the fort ever since sunrise; woods and mountains came down to the gulf's edge, and as you looked at them with the telescope, there peeped out of the general mass a score of pleasant episodes of Eastern life.[48]

From the deck of the steamship, a number of oriental 'vignettes' unfolded for Thackeray. Only there was the author able to encounter the romance of the East, in tableau form. Through the telescope, the Orient could be viewed by an observer who could not in turn be observed, who was removed from the scene, which thus did not retreat from the onlooker's 'vulgar gaze'. Like the panorama, which provided for Thackeray a representational means for enframing and making legible the Eastern landscape as an object of the Western gaze, the steamship allowed the Eastern landscape to be made to conform to the passenger's existing conceptions. The view from the steamship provided the double function of removing the viewer from the scene and facilitating the conditions required for viewing the East as landscape, as a pictorial representation. As Timothy Mitchell has written, 'the representation of the Orient, in its attempt to be detached and objective, would seek to eliminate from the picture the presence of the European observer'.[49] Mitchell emphasises the extent to which, in order to represent the East, it was essential for the European visitor to separate themselves from the landscape which they surveyed.

The steamship thus could be seen as a privileged vantage point for conceptualising, enframing and ordering the apparently chaotic world of the East. Just as the identity of the steamship as a stable, familiar environment was produced in contrast to its 'constitutive other', so it tamed and made legible that which was external in the form of landscape. This perspective is pithily expressed in an article by George Augustus Sala in 1852, again in *Household Words*. Here he narrates the familiar orientalist trope of disappointment felt by the Western traveller at the failure of their first encounter with the East to conform to the ideal image they had formed beforehand. For Sala, the epitome of this imagined orient could be found in 'the expectant tourist on board Peninsular and Oriental Company's steamer, who … opens wide his eyes with wonder, admiration and delight, when he first surveys the City of the Sultan from the Golden Horn'. Upon disembarking from the vessel and exploring Constantinople itself, however, Sala's traveller was met with a disappointing reality: 'Ask for Stamboul the romantic, the beautiful, the glorious', he writes, 'and you shall be told that this dirty, swarming, break-neck city is it.' Sala, conscious of the weight of representation which bore upon the Western traveller's perceptions of the Eastern city, suggests that a more satisfactory impression of the orient might in fact be obtained by returning to the deck of the ship. He thus advises the reader: 'Go on board the Peninsular and Oriental Company's steamer again as fast as you can; from whose deck you may again survey the enchanting and superb prospect of the city, and solace yourself with engravings after Messrs. Allom and Lewis.'[50] The steamer's deck is conceived of as a privileged vantage point, a space from which the imagination could play freely on the constructed fantasy of the East. The panoramic vista and the steamship are thus complementary: they both provided a significant discursive device for the production of the imperial world view, for the emergence of a touristic mode of consuming the world. It was precisely in its idiosyncratic modernity that the steamship became a superlative vantage point for framing, explicating and ordering the imperial landscape.

Notes

1 Power, *Sketches in New Zealand*, p. 254.
2 *Ibid.*
3 *Ibid.*, pp. 254–5.
4 Junghuhn, *Terugreis van Java naar Europa*, pp. 41–2.
5 *Ibid.*, p. 53.
6 Andrew Goss, *The Floracrats: State-Sponsored Science and the Failure of the Enlightenment in Indonesia* (Madison: University of Wisconsin Press, 2011), p. 18.
7 Junghuhn, *Terugreis van Java naar Europa*, p. 53. For an example of the tone and language which Junghuhn employs elsewhere in his inexhaustible descriptions of the coastal landscape seen from the steamer, he describes the nocturnal coastline in the vicinity of Penang (also compared to 'an uninhabited, distant planet') thus: 'All nature slept and was covered with the veil of such rare, beautiful, such sublime [verhevene] tranquillity, that I can no more express in words the spell it breathed than the profane could describe the harmonic sound of beautiful music.' *Ibid.*, pp. 24–5.
8 Gordon-Cumming, *Two Happy Years in Ceylon*, p. 12.
9 Barber, *The Overland Guide-Book*, p. 33.
10 William Tyrone Power, *Recollections of a Three Years' Residence in China; Including Peregrinations in Spain, Morocco, Egypt, India, Australia; and New Zealand* (London: Richard Bentley, 1853), p. 69.
11 Cadwalladar Cummerbund, *From Southampton to Calcutta* (London: Saunders, Otley and Co., 1860), p. 39.
12 I have chosen here to dispense with the distinction made by some scholars between the overlapping forms of the panorama, diorama and similar spectacles, which was in practice quite fluid, with nineteenth-century observers generally using such terms interchangeably.
13 Erkki Huhtamo, *Illusions in Motion: Media Archaeology of the Moving Panorama and Related Spectacles* (Cambridge, MA: MIT Press, 2013), pp. 169, 194–6; Richard D. Altick, *The Shows of London: A Panoramic History of Exhibitions, 1600–1862* (Cambridge, MA: The Belknap Press, 1978), p. 207.
14 Barak, *On Time*, p. 33.
15 'Gallery of Illustration, etc.', *Parlour Magazine of the Literature of all Nations*, 3 May 1851, p. 46.
16 Joachim Stocqueler, *The Route of the Overland Mail to India, from Southampton to Calcutta* (London: Gallery of Illustration, 1850), p. 1. The panorama was accompanied with a lecture by Stocqueler.

17 Sekula, *Fish Story*, p. 45. The text in double quotation marks is from Dolf Sternberger, *Panorama of the Nineteenth Century*, trans. by Joachim Neugroschel (New York: Urizen, 1977), p. 39.

18 Robert Blyth has described the 1839 seizure of Aden by the British East India Company for the purposes of establishing a coaling station which was able to serve steamships travelling between Suez and India. Blyth, 'Aden, British India and the development of steam power in the Red Sea'.

19 'Putting a Panorama Round the Earth', *Punch, or the London Charivari, Volume 17*, July–December 1849, p. 208.

20 Charles Dickens, 'Some Account of an Extraordinary Traveller', *Household Words*, 20 April 1850, pp. 73–6.

21 Barak, *On Time*, pp. 31–2.

22 Simms, *England to Calcutta by the Overland Route in 1845*, p. 41.

23 Sekula, *Fish Story*, p. 44.

24 Thackeray, *Notes of a Journey from Cornhill to Grand Cairo*, p. 68. Thackeray's book documents a Mediterranean leisure voyage taken aboard three P&O steamers in 1844, hence his deviation from the overland route. Constantinople was at this time served by a branch line. It is notable that Thackeray employs the Latin 'ne plus ultra' (nothing more beyond) in his description of the panoramic view from the steamer. This term can be seen to possess a dual meaning, not only signifying the pinnacle of painterly realism, the 'nothing more beyond' the surface appearance of representation, but also the phrase's legendary inscription on the Pillars of Hercules, the promontories flanking the entrance to the Strait of Gibraltar which marked the limits of the ancient Greek maritime world. In this latter context, nothing more beyond denoted the vast, inhospitable openness of the Atlantic Ocean. The ordered panoramic mode of vision, rooted in the coastal view, was haunted by the threat of pelagic space, the wild absence of a maritime landscape not reduceable to the comprehensible schema of the panorama.

25 Florence Nightingale, *The Crimean War: Collected Works of Florence Nightingale, Volume 14*, ed. by Lynn McDonald (Waterloo, Ontario: Wilfrid Laurier University Press, 2010), p. 58.

26 Henry Stedman Polehampton, *A Memoir, Letters, and Diary* (London: Richard Bentley, 1858), pp. 64–5.

27 The problematic of a representation of the East which precedes and limits possible encounters with the actual East is a key trope of Edward Said's theory of Orientalism. Said's description of the French writer Gérard de Nerval's disappointment in his 1843 tour of the Near East articulates a similar problematic to that reported by many steamship passengers: that the 'real' East was always compared unfavourably to a pre-imagined Orient rooted in Western representations. Said, *Orientalism*, pp. 100–101.

28 Barak, *On Time*, p. 37.

29 Mitchell, *Colonising Egypt*, p. 24.

30 *Ibid.*, p. 30.

31 Richardson, *The Anglo-Indian Passage, Homeward and Outward*, p. 52.

32 Hervey, *The Ocean and the Desert*, p. 53.

33 Stocqueler, *The Hand-Book of India*, p. 185.

34 David Arnold, *The Tropics and the Traveling Gaze: India, Landscape, and Science, 1800–1856* (Seattle: University of Washington Press, 2006).

35 As passenger Mary Carpenter points out, at the aptly named 'Steamer Point' where the vessels refuelled at Aden, passengers enjoyed the view of 'the not very picturesque but useful ridges of coal'. Mary Carpenter, *Six Months in India: Volume 1* (London: Longmans, Green & Co., 1868), p. 12.

36 Pratt, *Imperial Eyes*, pp. 197–204.

37 Burton, *Personal Narrative of a Pilgrimage to Al Medinah and Meccah*, p. 7. The reference to Gautier and Warburton is presumably to the popular accounts of Gibraltar found in Théophile Gautier, *Wanderings in Spain* (London: Ingram, Cooke & Co., 1853) and Warburton, *The Crescent and the Cross*. Warburton's account includes extensive descriptions of travel aboard P&O steamers, and features in Chapter 2. Cornhill, in the City of London, was historically the financial centre of the city.

38 Said, *Orientalism*, p. 167.

39 Both were significant coaling stations on the overland route, Aden having been seized in 1839 largely for this reason.

40 Taylor, *A Visit to India, China, and Japan*, p. 22.

41 Instructive here is Michael Taussig's insistence that we comprehend Marx's concept of commodity fetishism as characterised by the simultaneous displacement of the materiality of production, and its re-emergence as spectacle, as imagination, as a reconfigured conception of time and space. Michael Taussig, 'The Beach (A Fantasy)', *Critical Inquiry*, 26 (2000), 249–77, p. 250.

42 Thackeray, *Notes of a Journey from Cornhill to Grand Cairo*, p. 93.

43 See, for instance, Mitchell, *Colonising Egypt*, pp. 29–30.

44 See, for example, *The Popular Overland Guide*, p. 61. The practice was also recorded at Singapore.

45 Carpenter, *Six Months in India*, p. 11.

46 Mrs Charles Thomson, *Twelve Years in Canterbury, New Zealand: With Visits to the Other Provinces, and Reminiscences of the Route Home Through Australia, etc. (From a Lady's Journal)* (London: S. Low, Son and Marston, 1867), p. 176; George Waters, *Indian Gleanings and Thoughts of the Past* (Chatham: G.H. Windeyer, 1864), p. 80.

47 Auerbach, *Imperial Boredom*, p. 12.

48 Thackeray, *Notes of a Journey from Cornhill to Grand Cairo*, p. 82.

49 Mitchell, *Colonising Egypt*, p. 26. Mitchell even makes note of the ship as a particularly apt means for viewing the coastal city from the detached perspective of the Western observer, pp. 56–7.

50 George Augustus Sala, 'Cities in Plain Clothes', *Household Words*, 17 July 1852, p. 420. Sala refers to Thomas Allom and John Frederick Lewis, two popular contemporary orientalist artists who had produced extensive depictions of Constantinople, including views of the city from the sea.

Conclusion

An article in *The Times* from 1858 speculates on the commercial opportunities presented by the island group comprising what is today known as Maritime Southeast Asia. Reflecting on the potential of what it terms the region's 'great political and financial importance in the hands of civilised possessors', the article is notable for its staging of this geopolitical conjecture from the vantage point of a ship:

> The microcosm of a Peninsular and Oriental steamer listens with a half-credulity to stories of flying monkeys, and prodigious serpents, and a population of cannibals, while the vessel dashes through an archipelago of islands thickly clad with tropical foliage and canopied with lofty palms. The passengers are looking towards their point of destination, and spare few thoughts to the untamed regions that lie upon their path. Yet they are skirting the precincts of a future empire which must at some not very distant day take part in the world's history.[1]

This passage exemplifies a number of the discursive tropes which have featured prominently in this book's exploration of the overland route and its place in nineteenth-century imaginative geographies of empire. The steamship is presented as a microcosm, a familiar (and highly selective) reproduction in miniature of the wider world, in contrast to which the geography of the East, a region 'bordering', the article notes, 'on the highway of commerce', is portrayed as strange, savage, untouched by modern civilisation.[2]

That in narrating the commercial potential of this 'untouched' global territory the article's author poses this imperialist speculation from the space of a steamship is thus significant. The steamship operates as an apt vantage point for this perspective precisely in the extent that it provides the juxtaposition of a space which functions as other to this untamed region. The characterisation of the territory as one for which 'history', by which this account appears to mean modern capitalism, was yet to begin – a location external to the culture of the 'civilised' world – is performed from a space which was able to act as a mobile bearer of the spirit of civilisation, of the Western present. In this capacity, the steamship is presented by the article as an apt vantage point for engaging with the Eastern world – it was precisely due to its idiosyncratic modernity, temporally and spatially distinct from its surroundings, that the steamer was able to perform in this capacity.

This book set out to investigate what *The Times* article intimates, albeit in a different spirit: that a productive understanding of the making of the modern world might be gained from the vantage point of the P&O steamship. As I have suggested, the safe, familiar microcosm of the ship emphasised the alterity of the unfamiliar locations encountered in transit, while simultaneously allowing them to be rendered comprehensible, narratable, consumable. The steamship's modernity can be seen as a framing device, a perspective employed both by passengers – and those in the metropole – for coming to terms with and narrating the global, and their place in it. This book has traced the history of this modernity, gathering together the subjective material of the overland route to produce a composite picture of life in transit. This approach has been rooted in the contention that historical encounters with steamship mobilities, and their textual expressions, have much to tell us about the constitution of imperial experience and knowledge during this significant period of the expansion and consolidation of the British Empire. It insists that the stories told about networks, mobilities and technologies have as significant a role to play in this process as those imperial structures in themselves.

Lives in transit offer distinctive perspectives on the history of British imperialism, particularly shedding new light on the complex affective investments in the relationship between metropole and periphery. One of the core contributions of the 'new' imperial history has been to highlight that the imperial periphery shaped the metropole as much as the metropole shaped the periphery, through cultural exchange and imaginative valences. This book has illustrated that in the 'space between' of the ship, in the processes of transit itself, empire was also made and remade. The subsequent narrative passage, from reality to representation, from experience to text, brought empire to life in the metropole, acting as a potent symbol of Britain's place in the world. It communicated a convincing sense of a confident, superior, pioneering nation on the world stage, evidencing 'British pluck', to refer back to one of the many quotations which this book has drawn upon.

As John Mackenzie has suggested, Victorian literary representations of the imperial world often projected normative British perspectives onto the locations they claimed to document, rooted in a familiar narrative of Western progress and modernity.[3] Analogously, accounts of the overland route produced a perspective on global space which was tamed and normalised through its integration as part of British imperial networks. 'Colonialism', Nicholas Dirks has written, 'was a moment when new encounters within the world facilitated the formation of categories of metropole and periphery.'

The overland route helped shape shifting characterisations of empire, normalising distant, exotic locations in its apparent compression of global space. Simultaneously, however, it emphasised difference: the steamship's mobility was the property of the Western, modern subject. As we have seen, this association was employed to portray other races as primitive, inferior. The steamship's modernity provided a convincing narrative frame to conceive of colonialism as, in Dirks's terms, 'a process that began in the European Metropole and expanded outward'.[4]

Steamships were implicated in what might be termed the 'globing' of the world, the nineteenth-century conceptualisation of the earth (and imperial territory) as a finite, comprehensible totality. The rise of steam at sea could be said to have marked a shift in what Mary Louise Pratt has referred to as the European 'planetary consciousness', the means of conceptualising global space which lay at the heart of the imperial project.[5] This was characterised by the Western imaginative geography of the world as an object of knowledge to be comprehended as a coherent totality, but also as a site of European expansion, exploitation and colonisation, historically constituted in part through global mobilities. As the lines of steamship routes integrated global space into a complete system, they helped construct a conception of the world as truly global – integrated in a fundamentally Western, capitalist global economy.[6]

The opening of the Suez Canal in 1869 was the event which marked the end of the overland route's history. An epoch-defining, world-historical moment, appropriately enough it was one narrated from the deck of a P&O steamship. The *Delta* was the second vessel to enter the canal at its opening ceremony, close behind the French royal yacht *Aigle*, which was carrying the Empress Eugenie. On board the *Delta* were the journalists who documented (and visually represented) this momentous occasion for those in the British metropole.[7] However, one must be wary of the persistent historical narrative which maintains that the canal's opening marked a revolution in global mobility through radically shortening the sea voyage between Britain and India.[8] As this book has explored, the canal's completion was preceded by almost three decades of steamship travel to the East via Egypt; a history of mobilities which not only saw mail, cargo and thousands of imperial travellers carried between East and West, but also provided a rich cultural reserve for the narrative of Britain's place in its imperial world.

Nevertheless, the canal's opening brought to a close the period covered by this book. If it was not quite the radical logistical departure that many claim, as a powerful symbol of Western progress in the East, the canal was possessed of its own distinctive modernity.[9] Its opening also inevitably marked a significant moment in P&O's history. Not only did it render redundant the 'overland' section which had given their route its name, the canal helped to open up the voyage East to competitors, challenging P&O's long-held dominance on the route.[10] The canal's completion also occurred at a time that technological advances in shipbuilding were beginning to transform steamship mobilities.[11] Vessels became ever larger, faster, voyages more reliable, predictable and comfortable. Most importantly, they began to embody more convincingly the hubristic claims about the steamship which this book has documented – the modernity which was often disappointed by the reality of the steamship in the years covered in this book really seemed to come into being. The Suez Canal provided a powerful symbol of Western global dominance, marking the beginning of the 'heroic' era of the British Empire, marked by a culture of affirmative confidence. The period covered by this book was much more of an uncertain time in the history of the British Empire in the East. The accounts which I have drawn upon could be seen to evince this uncertainty precisely in their ambivalent swinging between heroic techno-utopias and bathetic mundanity, discomfort and boredom. That this bravado and hubris might have helped obscure a lack of certainty and confidence does not detract from the extent to which these literary productions of imperialism in transit helped to build and shape the myth of empire.

The apotheosis of the confident, unfazed, above all modern steamship passenger to the East was Phileas Fogg, the protagonist of Jules Verne's 1872 novel *Around the World in Eighty Days*. Fogg's fictional circumnavigation of the globe included extensive travel aboard P&O's vessels.[12] His instrumentalised, blasé attitude toward steamship mobility seems almost a parody of the experiences of travel found in the archive of the overland route. Fogg is portrayed as a supremely indifferent traveller – he shows little interest in the geographical space he traverses, but is rather concerned with his mobility as a means to an end. Throughout his journey, which is overwhelmingly preoccupied with the question of time and temporality, Fogg maintains a powerful sense of his own identity, rarely departing from a calm state of British equanimity and normativity. The P&O steamship had become by the end of the overland route's history something of a shorthand for forms of bourgeois imperial sociality and leisure. Contemporary with Verne's fiction, Thomas Cook, the travel entrepreneur seen as the father of modern tourism, organised an around-the-world tour in 1872, which inevitably relied heavily upon P&O's steamships.[13] As the overland route's history drew to a close, the imperial travel it had pioneered was increasingly associated with a form of touristic jouissance rooted in the kinds of affective investments, experiences and textual valences which passenger narratives had given voice to.

As *Imperial Steam* has explored, a distinctive cultural perspective on the lived world of empire grew out of the voluminous travel literature of the overland route – centred on the hyper-mobile yet disinterested, masterful yet supine figure of the bourgeois passenger. The panoramic mode of encountering the Eastern landscape was merely the most emphatic articulation of a more general trend, in which the imperial world was characterised as a commodity to be consumed by a mobile bourgeois subject from an equanimous position of leisured insouciance. In the blasé attitude to global mobility found in these texts – in the bathos, the world-weary disappointment expressed by passengers, in their characterisation of overland route travel as banal, boring, uncomfortable, disappointing, they are commenting on this commodification of the global, on an imperial world made more accessible, and more mundane. The identification of the passenger with the gratifications and disappointments of bourgeois leisure was rooted in a certain repression of the logistical complexes of steamship mobilities – accounts are filled with references to the steamship's apparent obfuscation of the labour which drove it, of the maritime space it traversed, of its noisy and dirty technologies, of the bureaucratic precision which made its mobility possible. Yet, far from being completely absent from passenger narratives, all of these elements recur as spectacle in the form of bourgeois leisure practices: in the pleasures of their ethnographic encounters with the ship's crew; in consuming the imperial landscape; in tracing their progress on maps; in gambling on the temporality of the steamer's mobility, passengers articulated a powerful vision of their place in the imperial world.

The overland route steamship provided a vantage point – both literal and literary – from which to view the imperial world. As this book has explored, the steamship was significant not just as a functional means to reach the East, but as a site for engaging with and encountering the world specifically as a British imperial world. The steamship's modernity instilled in its passengers not only a hubristic sense of identification with the British Empire. The overland route also had significant corollaries for the perceptions of empire for those in the metropole. In addition to the apparent bringing closer together of Britain and India, transforming the relationship between imperial metropole and periphery in the Victorian public imagination, the much-vaunted reliability and regularity of the steamship normalised travel to a location which had previously been seen as an exotic departure from the Western world. Furthermore, the steamship's modernity also emphasised difference. It was at the centre of a discourse of Western superiority over those who peopled Britain's global empire. Overland route narratives offered a unified, linear means for coming to terms with and imagining this empire, helping to repress difference and diversity, to conceive of it as a coherent totality. The steamship provided a simple organising discourse, emphasising a familiar Britishness rooted in technological prowess, punctuality, comfort and safety.

Notes

1 'In the Way Towards That Eastern Coast of China', *The Times*, 5 October 1858, p. 6.
2 *Ibid.*
3 John Mackenzie, 'Empires of Travel: British Guide Books and Cultural Imperialism in the 19th and 20th Centuries', in *Histories of Tourism: Representation, Identity and Conflict*, ed. by John Walton (Clevedon, UK: Channel View Publications, 2005), pp. 19–38, pp. 24–6.
4 Nicholas Dirks, 'Introduction: Colonialism and Culture', in *Colonialism and Culture*, ed. by Nicholas Dirks (Ann Arbor: The University of Michigan Press, 1992), pp. 1–26, p. 6.
5 Pratt, *Imperial Eyes*, pp. 11, 29–30.
6 As Karl Marx suggested in 1850, 'one can really say that the earth has only begun to become round since this world-wide ocean steam navigation has become necessary'. Karl Marx and Frederick Engels 'Review (May to October 1850)', in *Marx Engels Collected Works, Volume 10*, trans. by Christopher Upward (Moscow: Progress Publishers, 1978), pp. 490–532, p. 506.
7 'Opening of the Suez Canal', *Illustrated London News*, 11 December 1869, p. 598.
8 See, for example, *Archives of Empire Volume I: From the East India Company to the Suez Canal*, ed. by Barbara Harlow and Mia Carter (Durham, NC: Duke University Press, 2003), p. xxi. Yrjö Kaukiainen has argued that the canal did not in fact, reduce passage times until some time after its initial opening, due to the fact that ships had to travel slowly through the relatively narrow canal, and could not travel at night. Kaukiainen, 'Shrinking the World', p. 16.
9 Huber, *Channelling Mobilities*, p. 3.
10 Although Arthur Anderson, one of the company's chairmen, had explored the feasibility of a canal across the Isthmus of Suez in 1842, and produced a pamphlet advocating for its construction, given the extent of the company's investment in the overland section of the route, and the competitive advantage they accrued from it, by the time of the canal's completion they were far less enthusiastic about the project.
11 Compound marine steam engines saw great developments in the 1870s, vastly improving steamships' fuel efficiency. Increases in boiler pressure, innovations in hull design, and the use of refrigeration and electric lights all contributed to improvements in the passenger experience.
12 Fogg travelled from Brindisi to Bombay via the Suez Canal aboard the *Mongolia*, Calcutta to Hong Kong on the *Rangoon*, and had intended to travel from Hong Kong to Yokohama aboard the *Carnatic*, but missed the steamer's departure (his servant Passepartout was on board). All three of these ship's names refer

to actual P&O vessels which had been in service in the East during the decade before the book's publication. (Although the latter two had been wrecked in 1871 and 1869, respectively. Fogg's journey was set in late 1872.) Jules Verne, *Around the World in Eighty Days*, trans. by George Towle (Philadelphia: Porter & Coates, 1873).

13 Thomas Cook, *Letters from the Sea & from Foreign Lands, Descriptive of a Tour Around the World* (London and New York: Thomas Cook & Son, 1873).

Bibliography

Accounts and Papers of the House of Commons, 'Shipping (United Kingdom)', Session 5 February–21 August 1867, vol. 63 (1867).

Adamson, William, 'P&O Company Records: "Diary kept by William Adamson (later a Director of P&O) on a voyage to Singapore in the Himalaya and Oriental, in the form of letters to his father, plus a typescript copy"', January–March 1854, P&O/92/1, London, National Maritime Museum Archive.

Adas, Michael, *Machines as the Measure of Men: Science, Technology, and Ideologies of Western Dominance* (Ithaca, NY: Cornell University Press, 1990).

Adorno, Theodor, *Minima Moralia: Reflections on a Damaged Life*, trans. by E.F.N. Jephcott (London: Verso, 2005).

Aguiar, Marian, *Tracking Modernity: India's Railway and the Culture of Mobility* (Minneapolis: University of Minnesota Press, 2011).

Ahuja, Ravi, 'Capital at Sea, Shaitan Below Decks? A Note on Global Narratives, Narrow Spaces, and the Limits of Experience', *History of the Present*, 2 (2012), 78–85.

Aiton, John, *The Lands of the Messiah, Mahomet, and the Pope: As Visited in 1851* (London: A. Fullarton & Co., 1854).

Allen, Charles Harris, *A Visit to Queensland and Her Goldfields* (London: Chapman & Hall, 1870).

Altick, Richard D., *The Shows of London: A Panoramic History of Exhibitions, 1600–1862* (Cambridge, MA: The Belknap Press, 1978).

Anderson, Arthur, *Communications with India, China, &c.: Observations on the practicability and utility of opening a communication between the Red Sea and the Mediterranean, by a ship-canal through the Isthmus of Suez* (London: Smith, Elder & Co., 1843).

Anderson, Benedict, *Imagined Communities: Reflections on the Origin and Spread of Nationalism* (London: Verso, 1991).

Anim-Addo, Anyaa, '"A Wretched and Slave-like Mode of Labor": Slavery, Emancipation, and the Royal Mail Steam Packet Company's Coaling Stations', *Historical Geography*, 39 (2011), 65–84.

Anim-Addo, Anyaa, '"The Great Event of the Fortnight": Steamship Rhythms and Colonial Communication', *Mobilities*, 9 (2014), 369–83.

Anim-Addo, Anyaa, '"Thence to the River Plate": Steamship Mobilities in the South Atlantic, 1842–1869', *Atlantic Studies*, 13 (2016), 6–24.

Anim-Addo, Anyaa, William Hasty, and Kimberley Peters, 'The Mobilities of Ships and Shipped Mobilities', *Mobilities*, 9 (2014), 337–49.

Appadurai, Arjun, *Modernity at Large: Cultural Dimensions of Globalization* (Minneapolis, MN: University of Minnesota Press, 1996).

Armstrong, John, and David Williams, 'The Steamship as an Agent of Modernisation, 1812–1840', *International Journal of Maritime History*, 19 (2007), 145–60.

Arnold, David, *Science, Technology and Medicine in Colonial India* (Cambridge: Cambridge University Press, 2000).

Arnold, David, *The Tropics and the Traveling Gaze: India, Landscape, and Science, 1800–1856* (Seattle: University of Washington Press, 2006).

Auerbach, Jeffrey, *Imperial Boredom: Monotony and the British Empire* (Oxford: Oxford University Press, 2018).

Augé, Marc, *Non-Places: Introduction to an Anthropology of Supermodernity*, trans. by John Howe (London: Verso, 1995).

Baker, Samuel W., *Eight Years' Wanderings in Ceylon* (London: Longman, Brown, Green, and Longmans, 1855).

Balachandran, Gopalan, 'Cultures of Protest in Transnational Contexts: Indian Seamen Abroad, 1886–1945', *Transforming Cultures eJournal*, 3 (2008), 45–75.

Balachandran, Gopalan, 'Indefinite Transits: Mobility and Confinement in the Age of Steam', *Journal of Global History*, 11 (2016), 187–208.

Ballantyne, Tony, *Orientalism and Race: Aryanism in the British Empire* (Basingstoke: Palgrave, 2002).

Ballantyne, Tony, and Antoinette Burton, eds., *Moving Subjects: Gender, Mobility, and Intimacy in an Age of Global Empire* (Urbana: University of Illinois Press, 2009).

Barak, On, *On Time: Technology and Temporality in Modern Egypt* (Berkeley: University of California Press, 2013).

Baranowski, Shelley, and Ellen Furlough (eds), *Being Elsewhere: Tourism, Consumer Culture, and Identity in Modern Europe and North America* (Ann Arbor: University of Michigan Press, 2001).

Barber, Captain James, *The Court of Directors of the East India Company, Versus Her Majesty's Ministers, the Resolutions of the House of Commons, and the Public of India and England, as Regards a Complete Plan of Steam Communication Between the Two Empires* (London: Smith, Elder & Co., 1839).

Barber, Captain James, *The Overland Guide-Book: A Complete Vademecum for the Overland Traveller, to India via Egypt* (London: W.H. Allen & Co., 1845) .

Barton, Alfred, *Journal of further voyages for the P.&O. Company between Bombay, Singapore and Hong Kong, and on a return voyage to England, August 1854–June 1855*, MS.5959, London, Wellcome Archives.

Bashford, Alison, 'Terraqueous Histories', *The Historical Journal*, 60 (2017), 253–72.

Baudelaire, Charles, *The Painter of Modern Life and Other Essays*, trans. and ed. by Jonathan Mayne (New York: Da Capo Press, 1986).

Bauman, Zygmunt, *Liquid Modernity* (Cambridge: Polity Press, 2000).

Bear, Laura, *Lines of the Nation: Indian Railway Workers, Bureaucracy, and the Intimate Historical Self* (New York: Columbia University Press, 2007).

Benjamin, Walter, *The Arcades Project*, trans. by Howard Eiland and Kevin McLaughlin (Cambridge, MA: Harvard University Press, 1999).

Benjamin, Walter, 'On Some Motifs in Baudelaire' (1939), in *Selected Writings: Volume 4, 1938–1940*, trans. by Edmund Jephcott and others, ed. by Howard Eiland and Michael W. Jennings (Cambridge, MA: Harvard University Press, 2003), pp. 313–55.

Bennett, Tony, *The Birth of the Museum: History, Theory, Politics* (London: Routledge, 1995).

Bentinck, Lord William, 'Letter from the Governor General to G. Norton Esq., April 11, 1834', in Captain James Barber, *A Letter to the Right Hon. Sir John Cam Hobhouse, Bart. M.P., President of the India Board, etc. etc. etc: On Steam-Navigation with India, and Suggesting the Best Mode of Carrying it into Effect via the Red Sea* (London: Pelham Richardson, 1837).

Berman, Marshall, *All That Is Solid Melts into Air: The Experience of Modernity* (London: Verso, 1993).

Black, Archibald Pollok, *A Hundred Days in the East: A Diary of a Journey to Egypt, Palestine, Turkey in Europe, Greece, the Isles of the Archipelago, and Italy* (London: J.F. Shaw & Co., 1865).

Blanton, Casey, *Travel Writing: The Self and the World* (London: Routledge, 1995).

Blyth, Robert, 'Aden, British India and the Development of Steam Power in the Red Sea, 1825–1839', in *Maritime Empires: British Imperial Maritime Trade in the Nineteenth Century*, ed. by David Killingray, Margarette Lincoln and Nigel Rigby (Woodbridge: Boydell Press, 2004), pp. 68–83.

Boyce, Gordon, *Information, Mediation, and Institutional Development: The Rise of Large-scale Enterprise in British Shipping, 1870–1919* (Manchester: Manchester University Press, 1995).

Braddon, Edward, *Life in India: A Series of Sketches Showing Something of the Anglo-Indian, the Land He Lives In, and the People Among Whom He Lives* (London, Longmans, Green & Co., 1872).

Bremner, Alex G., 'Nation and Empire in the Government Architecture of Mid-Victorian London: The Foreign Office and India Office Reconsidered', *Historical Journal*, 48 (2005), 703–42.

The British Almanac – Containing Astronomical, Official and Other Information Relating to the British Isles, the Dominions (London: Charles Knight, 1851).

Brown, Julia Prewitt, *The Bourgeois Interior: How the Middle Class Imagines Itself in Literature and Film* (Charlottesville: University of Virginia Press, 2008).

Brumund, Jan Frederik Gerrit, *Schetsen eener Mail-Reize van Batavia naar Maastricht op Reis en Thuis* (Amsterdam: 1862).

Buck-Morss, Susan, *The Dialectics of Seeing: Walter Benjamin and the Arcades Project* (Cambridge, MA: MIT Press, 1989).

Buddingh, Steven Adriaan, *Dagboek Mijner Overland-Mail-Reis van Rotterdam naar Java, via Southampton in 1852* (Batavia: Lange & Co., 1852).

Buddingh, Steven Adriaan, *Dagboek Mijner Overland-Mail-Reis van Batavia naar Nederland, via Triest, in 1857: Zijnde een Tegenhanger van het Dagboek Mijner Oveland-Mail-Reis van Rotterdam naar Java, via Southampton, in 1852* (Arnhem: G.W. van der Wiel, 1857).

Burgess, Douglas, *Engines of Empire: Steamships and the Victorian Imagination* (Stanford, CA: Stanford University Press, 2016).

Burton, Antoinette, 'When Was Britain? Nostalgia for the Nation at the End of the "American Century"', *Journal of Modern History*, 75 (2003), 359–74.

Burton, Sir Richard Francis, *Personal Narrative of a Pilgrimage to Al Medinah and Meccah, Volume 1* (London: Longman, Brown, Green, Longmans and Roberts, 1857).

Carpenter, Mary, *Six Months in India: Volume 1* (London: Longmans, Green & Co., 1868).

Carter, Mia, and Barbara Harlow (eds), *Archives of Empire Volume I: From the East India Company to the Suez Canal* (Durham, NC: Duke University Press, 2003).

Chakrabarty, Dipesh, 'The Muddle of Modernity', *American Historical Review*, 116 (2011), 663–75.

Chase-Levenson, Alex, *The Yellow Flag: Quarantine and the British Mediterranean World, 1780–1860* (Cambridge: Cambridge University Press, 2020).

Cheever, Henry T., *Memorials of the Life and Trials of a Youthful Christian in Pursuit of Health: as Developed in the Biography of Nathaniel Cheever, M.D.* (New York: Charles Scribner, 1851).

Clay, Arthur Lloyd, *Leaves from a Diary in Lower Bengal* (London: Macmillan, 1896).

Coffin, Charles Carleton, *Our New Way Round the World* (Cambridge, MA: Fields, Osgood, & Co., 1869).

Colomb, Philip Howard, *Slave-Catching in the Indian Ocean: A Record of Naval Experiences* (London: Longmans & Co., 1873) .

Cook, Thomas, *Letters from the Sea & from Foreign Lands, Descriptive of a Tour Around the World* (London and New York: Thomas Cook & Son, 1873).

Coopland, Ruth M., *A Lady's Escape from Gwalior, and Life in the Fort of Agra during the Mutinies of 1857* (London: Smith, Elder, & Co., 1859).

Cresswell, Tim, *On the Move: Mobility in the Modern Western World* (London: Routledge, 2006).

Cresswell, Tim, 'Towards a Politics of Mobility', *Environment and Planning D: Society and Space*, 2 (2010), 17–31.

Crowley, John, *The Invention of Comfort: Sensibilities and Design in Early Modern Britain and Early America* (Baltimore: Johns Hopkins University Press, 2001).

The Crystal Palace Penny Guide: By Authority of the Directors (London: Robert K. Burt, 1864).

Cummerbund, Cadwalladar, *From Southampton to Calcutta* (London: Saunders, Otley and Co., 1860).

Curless, Gareth, Stacey Hynd, Temilola Alanamu, and Katherine Roscoe, 'Editors' Introduction: Networks in Imperial History', *Journal of World History*, 26 (2015), 705–32.

de Courcy, Anne, *The Fishing Fleet: Husband-Hunting in the Raj* (London: Weidenfeld & Nicolson, 2012).

Darwin, John, *Unlocking the World: Port Cities and Globalisation in the Age of Steam 1830–1930* (London: Penguin, 2020).

Dening, Greg, *Mr Bligh's Bad Language: Passion, Power and Theatre on the Bounty* (Cambridge: Cambridge University Press, 1992).

Denison, Lord Albert, *Wanderings in Search of Health* (London: Printed for private circulation, 1849).

Deynoot, Gevers, *Herinneringen eener Reis naar Nederlandsch-Indië in 1862* (The Hague: Martinus Nijhoff, 1864).

Dickens, Charles, *Letters of Charles Dickens: 1833–1870*, ed. by Georgina Hogarth and Mary Dickens (Cambridge: Cambridge University Press, 2011).

Dirks, Nicholas (ed.), *Colonialism and Culture* (Ann Arbor: The University of Michigan Press, 1992).

Douglas, Mary, *Purity and Danger: An Analysis of Concepts of Pollution and Taboo* (London: Routledge, 2013).

Driver, Felix, and Luciana Martins (eds), *Tropical Visions in an Age of Empire* (Chicago: University of Chicago Press, 2005).

Duncan, James, and Derek Gregory, 'Introduction', in *Writes of Passage: Reading Travel Writing*, ed. by James Duncan and Derek Gregory (London and New York: Routledge, 1999), pp. 1–13.

Dusinberre, Martin, and Roland Wenzlhuemer, 'Being in Transit: Ships and Global Incompatibilities', *Journal of Global History*, 11 (2016), 155–62.

Eastwick, Edward B., *A Handbook for India: Being an Account of the Three Presidencies, and of the Overland Route; Intended as A Guide for Travellers, Officers, and Civilians, Part I. – Madras* (London: John Murray, 1859).

Elwes, Robert, *A Sketcher's Tour Round the World* (London: Hurst and Blackett, 1854).

Ewald, Janet J. 'Crossers of the Sea: Slaves, Freedmen, and Other Migrants in the Northwestern Indian Ocean, C. 1750–1914', *American Historical Review*, 105 (2005), 69–91.

Featherstone, Mike, Scott Lash, and Roland Robertson (eds), *Global Modernities* (London: Sage, 1995).

Freeman, Michael J., and Derek Aldcroft (eds), *Transport in Victorian Britain* (Manchester: Manchester University Press, 1988).

Garvey, Michael Angelo, *The Silent Revolution, or, The Future Effects of Steam and Electricity Upon the Condition of Mankind* (London: William and Frederick G. Cash, 1852).

Gautier, Théophile, *Wanderings in Spain* (London: Ingram, Cooke & Co., 1853).

Giddens, Anthony, *The Consequences of Modernity* (Cambridge: Polity, 1990).

Giedion, Sigfried, *Building in France* (Santa Monica, CA: The Getty Centre for the History of Art and the Humanities, 1995).

Gilchrist, John Borthwick, *The General East India Guide and Vade Mecum: For the Public Functionary, Government Officer, Private Agent, Trader Or Foreign Sojourner, in British India, and the Adjacent Parts of Asia Immediately Connected with the Honourable the East India Company* (London: Kingsbury, Parbury, & Allen, 1825).

Gilroy, Paul, *The Black Atlantic: Modernity and Double Consciousness* (London: Verso, 1993).

Goedde, Lawrence Otto, 'Convention, Realism, and the Interpretation of Dutch and Flemish Tempest Painting', *Simiolus*, 16 (1986), 139–49.

Gordon-Cumming, Constance Frederica, *Two Happy Years in Ceylon* (London: Chatto & Windus, 1893).

Goss, Andrew, *The Floracrats: State-Sponsored Science and the Failure of the Enlightenment in Indonesia* (Madison: University of Wisconsin Press, 2011).

Gregory, Derek, 'Between the Book and the Lamp: Imaginative Geographies of Egypt, 1849–50', *Transactions of the Institute of British Geographers*, 20 (1995), 29–57.

Gregory, Derek, 'Imaginative Geographies', *Progress in Human Geography*, 19 (1995), 447–485.

Grindlay and Co.'s Overland Circular, Hints for travellers to India, detailing the several routes (London: Smith, Elder and Co., 1847).

Guy, Richard, 'Calamitous Voyages: The Social Space of Shipwreck and Mutiny Narratives in the Dutch East India Company', *Itinerario*, 39 (2015), 117–40.

Hall, Catherine, and Sonya Rose (eds), *At Home with the Empire: Metropolitan Culture and the Imperial World* (Cambridge: Cambridge University Press, 2006).

Hand Book of Information for Passengers and Shippers by the Peninsular & Oriental Steam Navigation Company's Steamers (London: Peninsular and Oriental Steam Navigation Company, 1849).

Harcourt, Freda, *Flagships of Imperialism: The P&O Company and the Politics of Empire from Its Origins to 1867* (Manchester: Manchester University Press, 2006).

Harrison, Carol E., *The Bourgeois Citizen in Nineteenth-Century France: Gender, Sociability, and the Uses of Emulation* (Oxford: Oxford University Press, 1999).

Harvey, David, *The Condition of Postmodernity: An Enquiry into the Origins of Cultural Change* (Oxford: Blackwell, 1989).

Headrick, Daniel R., *The Tentacles of Progress: Technology Transfer in the Age of Imperialism, 1850–1940* (Oxford: Oxford University Press, 1988)

Hervey, Albert, *The Ocean and the Desert, by a Madras Officer* (London: T.C. Newby, 1846).

Hervey, Albert, *Ten Years in India: The Life of a Young Officer, Volume 1* (London: William Shoberl, 1850).

Hickey, William, *Memoirs, Volume IV (1790–1809)* (London: A. A. Knopf, 1925).

Huber, Valeska, *Channelling Mobilities: Migration and Globalisation in the Suez Canal Region and Beyond, 1869–1914* (Cambridge: Cambridge University Press, 2013).

Huhtamo, Erkki, *Illusions in Motion: Media Archaeology of the Moving Panorama and Related Spectacles* (Cambridge, MA: MIT Press, 2013).

Hyslop, Jonathan, 'Steamship Empire: Asian, African and British Sailors in the Merchant Marine c.1880–1945', *Journal of Asian and African Studies*, 44 (2009), 49–67.

Jackson, Gordon, and David M. Williams (eds), *Shipping, Technology and Imperialism* (Glasgow: Scolar, 1993).

Johnson, Walter, *River of Dark Dreams: Slavery and Empire in the Cotton Kingdom* (Cambridge, MA: Harvard University Press, 2013).

Junghuhn, Franz Wilhelm, *Terugreis van Java naar Europa: Met de Zoogenaamde Engelsche Overlandpost, in de Maanden September en October 1848* (Zaltbommel: J. Noman, 1851).

Kaukiainen, Yrjö, 'Shrinking the World: Improvements in the Speed of Information Transmission, c.1820–1870', *European Review of Economic History*, 5 (2001), 1–28.

Kay, James Phillips, *The Moral and Physical Condition of the Working Classes Employed in the Cotton Manufacture in Manchester* (London: James Ridgway, 1832).

Kendall, Franklin R., *Letters* (P&O: 1968) (Typescript copies of letters from Franklin Richardson Kendall (1839–1907), employed by the Peninsular and Oriental Steam Navigation Company, to his mother in England. Held in the Caird Library at the National Maritime Museum, London, reference: 347.792P&O).

Kern, Stephen, *The Culture of Time and Space, 1880–1918* (Cambridge, MA: Harvard University Press, 2003).

Khan, Syed Ahmed, *A Voyage to Modernism*, trans. and ed. by Mushirul Hasan and Nishat Zaidi (Delhi: Primus Books, 2011).

Kuehn, Julia, and Paul Smethurst (eds), *Travel Writing, Form and Empire: The Poetic and Politics of Mobility* (New York: Routledge, 2009).

Lambert, David, 'Reflections on the Concept of Imperial Biographies: The British Case', *Geschichte und Gesellschaft*, 40 (2014), 22–41.

Lambert, David and Alan Lester (eds), *Colonial Lives Across the British Empire: Imperial Careering in the Long Nineteenth Century* (Cambridge: Cambridge University Press, 2006).

Lambert, David, and Peter Merriman (eds), *Empire and Mobility in the Long Nineteenth Century* (Manchester: Manchester University Press, 2020).

Lambert, David, Luciana Martins and Miles Ogborn, 'Currents, Visions and Voyages: Historical Geographies of the Sea', *Journal of Historical Geography*, 32 (2006), 479–93.

Latour, Bruno, *We Have Never Been Modern*, trans. by Catherine Porter (Cambridge: Harvard University Press, 1993).

Law, John, 'On the Methods of Long-Distance Control: Vessels, Navigation and the Portuguese Route to India', *The Sociological Review*, 32 (1984), 234–63.

Lepsius, Richard, *Discoveries in Egypt, Ethiopia, and the Peninsula of Sinai, in the Years 1842–1845, During the Mission Sent Out by His Majesty Frederick William IV of Prussia*, trans. and ed. by K.R.H. Mackenzie (London: Richard Bentley, 1852).

Lester, Alan, *Imperial Networks: Creating Identities in Nineteenth-Century South Africa and Britain* (London: Routledge, 2001).

Lester, Alan, 'Imperial Circuits and Networks: Geographies of the British Empire', *History Compass*, 4 (2006), 124–41.

Lester, Alan, Kate Boehme, and Peter Mitchell, *Ruling the World: Freedom, Civilisation and Liberalism in the Nineteenth-Century British Empire* (Cambridge: Cambridge University Press, 2020).

Lewis, Sir George Cornewall, *On Foreign Jurisdiction and the Extradition of Criminals* (London: John W. Parker and Son, 1859).

Lutfullah, *Autobiography of Lutfullah, a Mohamedan Gentleman and His Transactions with His Fellow-Creatures: Interspersed with Remarks on the Habits, Customs, and Character of the People with Whom He Had to Deal* (London: Smith, Elder, & Co., 1858).

Mackenzie, John, *Propaganda and Empire: The Manipulation of British Public Opinion 1880–1960* (Manchester: Manchester University Press, 1984).

Macleod, Norman, *Eastward: Travels in Egypt, Palestine and Syria* (London: Strahan & Co., 1869).

Macleod, Norman, *Peeps at the Far East: A Familiar Account of a Visit to India* (London: Strahan & Co., 1871).

Magee, Gary, and Andrew Thompson, *Empire and Globalisation: Networks of People, Goods and Capital in the British World, c.1850–1914* (Cambridge: Cambridge University Press, 2010).

Marsden, Ben, and Crosbie Smith, *Engineering Empires: A Cultural History of Technology in Nineteenth-Century Britain* (Basingstoke: Palgrave Macmillan, 2007).

Marsh, Matthew Henry, *Overland from Southampton to Queensland* (London: Edward Stanford, 1867).

Martin, Craig, 'Desperate Passage: Violent Mobilities and the Politics of Discomfort', *Journal of Transport Geography*, 19 (2011), 1046–52.

Marx, Karl, *Grundrisse: Foundations of the Critique of Political Economy*, trans. by Martin Nicolaus (London: Penguin, 1973).

Marx, Karl, 'The Future Results of British Rule in India', in *Marx Engels Collected Works, Volume 12* (Moscow: Progress Publishers, 1979), 217–22.

Marx, Karl, 'Capital, Volume I', *Marx Engels Collected Works, Volume 35*, trans. by Samuel Moore and Edward Aveling (Moscow: Progress Publishers, 1996).

Marx, Karl, 'Capital, Volume II' (1885), *Marx Engels Collected Works, Volume 36*, trans. by I. Lasker (Moscow: Progress Publishers, 1998).

Marx, Karl, 'Capital, Volume III', *Marx Engels Collected Works, Volume 37*, trans. by Ernest Untermann and others (Moscow: Progress Publishers, 1998).

Marx, Karl, and Frederick Engels 'Review (May to October 1850)', in *Marx Engels Collected Works, Volume 10*, trans. by Christopher Upward (Moscow: Progress Publishers, 1978), 490–532.

Marx, Leo, *The Machine in the Garden: Technology and the Pastoral Ideal in America* (New York: Oxford University Press, 2000).

Mathieson, Charlotte (ed.), *Sea Narratives: Cultural Responses to the Sea, 1600–Present* (Basingstoke: Palgrave Macmillan, 2016), 1–21.

McClintock, Anne, *Imperial Leather: Race, Gender and Sexuality in the Colonial Contest* (New York and London: Routledge, 1995).

McKeown, Adam, 'Periodizing Globalization', *History Workshop Journal*, 63 (2007), 218–30.

Mentz, Steve, *At the Bottom of Shakespeare's Ocean* (London: Continuum, 2009).

Mills, Sara, *Gender and Colonial Space* (Manchester: Manchester University Press, 2005).

Minturn, Robert B., *From New York to Delhi by way of Rio de Janeiro, Australia and China* (London: Longman, Brown, Green, Longmans and Roberts, 1858).

Mitchell, Timothy, *Colonising Egypt* (Cambridge: Cambridge University Press, 1988).

Mitchell, Timothy (ed.), *Questions of Modernity* (Minneapolis, MN: University of Minnesota Press, 2000).

Moser, Ludwig, *The Caucasus and its People; With a Brief History of their Wars, and a Sketch of the Achievements of the Renowned Chief Schamyl* (London: David Nutt, 1856).

Nanni, Giordano, *The Colonisation of Time: Ritual, Routine and Resistance in the British Empire* (Manchester: Manchester University Press, 2012).

Newmarch, Charles Henry, *Five Years in the East, Volume 2* (London: Longman, Brown, Green & Longmans, 1847).

Nightingale, Florence, *The Crimean War: Collected Works of Florence Nightingale, Volume 14*, ed. by Lynn McDonald (Waterloo, Ontario: Wilfrid Laurier University Press, 2010).

Nye, David, *American Technological Sublime* (Cambridge, MA: MIT Press, 1994).

Offermann, Michael, and Roland Wenzlhuemer, 'Ship Newspapers and Passenger Life Aboard Transoceanic Steamships in the Late Nineteenth Century', *Transcultural Studies*, 1 (2012), 77–121.

Ogborn, Miles, *Spaces of Modernity: London's Geographies, 1680–1780* (London: Guilford Press, 1998).

Oppenheim, Janet, *'Shattered Nerves': Doctors, Patients, and Depression in Victorian England* (Oxford: Oxford University Press, 1991).

Osborne, Peter, *The Politics of Time: Modernity and the Avant-Garde* (London: Verso, 1995).

Osterhammel, Jürgen, *The Transformation of the World: A Global History of the Nineteenth Century* (Princeton: Princeton University Press, 2014).

Overland Route to India and China (London: T. Nelson and Sons, 1858).

'P&O Company Records: Book of "Instructions for Chief Engineers"', 1867, P&O/9/1, London, National Maritime Museum Archive.

'P&O Company Records: "Individual Ships: Bentinck, Miscellaneous Material"', 1848, P&O/65/67, London, National Maritime Museum Archive.

Pagh, Nancy, *At Home Afloat: Women on the Waters of the Pacific Northwest* (Calgary: University of Calgary Press, 2001).

Paris Universal Exhibition, 1855: Catalogue of the Works Exhibited in the British Section of the Exhibition, in French and English; together with Exhibitors Prospectuses, Prices Current, &c. (London: Chapman & Hall, 1855).

Parkinson, Cyril Northcote, *Trade in the Eastern Seas, 1793–1813* (Cambridge: Cambridge University Press, 1937).

Pfeiffer, Ida, *A Woman's Journey Round the World: From Vienna to Brazil, Chili, Tahiti, China, Hindostan, Persia, and Asia Minor* (London: Ingram, Cooke & Co., 1852).

Pietsch, Tamson, 'A British Sea: Making Sense of Global Space in the Late Nineteenth Century', *Journal of Global History*, 5 (2010), 423–46.

Pietsch, Tamson, 'Bodies at Sea: Travelling to Australia in the Age of Sail', *Journal of Global History*, 11 (2016), 209–28.

Polehampton, Henry Stedman, *A Memoir, Letters, and Diary* (London: Richard Bentley, 1858).

Pope, Alexander, *The Works of Alexander Pope, Esq., Volume VI*, ed. by William Warburton (London: J. and P. Knapton, 1751).

The Popular Overland Guide, Hints to Travellers by the Overland Route to India, Australia, and China (London: Ward and Lock, 1861).

Potter, Simon, and Jonathan Saha, 'Global History, Imperial History and Connected Histories of Empire', *Journal of Colonialism and Colonial History*, 16 (2015), https://muse.jhu.edu/article/577738.

Power, William Tyrone, *Sketches in New Zealand: With Pen and Pencil* (London: Longman, Brown, Green, and Longmans, 1849).

Power, William Tyrone, *Recollections of a Three Years' Residence in China; including Peregrinations in Spain, Morocco, Egypt, India, Australia; and New Zealand* (London: Richard Bentley, 1853).

Pratt, Mary Louise, *Imperial Eyes: Travel Writing and Transculturation* (London: Routledge, 1992).

Rainey, Thomas, *Ocean Steam Navigation and the Ocean Post* (New York: D. Appleton & Company, 1858).

Rediker, Marcus, *Between the Devil and the Deep Blue Sea: Merchant Seamen, Pirates, and the Anglo-American Maritime World, 1700–1750* (Cambridge: Cambridge University Press, 1987).

Rendell, Jane, *The Pursuit of Pleasure: Gender, Space and Architecture in Regency London* (London: Athlone Press, 2002).

Richardson, David Lester, *The Anglo-Indian Passage, Homeward and Outward; Or, A Card for the Overland Traveller from Southampton to Bombay, Madras, and Calcutta: With Letters Descriptive of the Homeward Passage and Notices of Gibraltar [etc.]* (London: Madden and Malcolm, 1845).

Richter, Amy G., *Home on the Rails: Women, the Railroad, and the Rise of Public Domesticity* (Chapel Hill: University of North Carolina Press, 2005).

Roberson, Susan, *Antebellum American Women Writers and the Road: American Mobilities.* (New York: Routledge, 2012) .

Romer, Isabella Frances, *A Pilgrimage to the Temples and Tombs of Egypt, Nubia, and Palestine, in 1845–6, Volume 1* (London: R. Bentley, 1846).

Rosa, Hartmut, *Social Acceleration: A New Theory of Modernity* (New York: Columbia University Press, 2013).

Russell, William Howard, *My Diary in India, in the Year 1858–9* (London: Routledge, 1860).

Rybczynski, Witold, *Home: A Short History of an Idea* (New York: Viking, 1986).

Said, Edward W., *Orientalism* (London: Penguin, 2003).

Sala, George Augustus, 'The Streets of the World: Their Ins and Outs, their Lights and Shadows, their Houses and their Inhabitants', *The Welcome Guest* (London: Houlston and Wright, 1861).

Schivelbusch, Wolfgang, *The Railway Journey: The Industrialization of Time and Space in the 19th Century* (Berkeley: University of California Press, 1986).

Seabright, Sarah, *Steaming East: The Forging of Steamship and Rail Links Between Europe and Asia* (London: Bodley Head, 1991).

Sekula, Allan, *Fish Story* (Düsseldorf: Richter Verlag, 1995).

Shanley, Mary Lyndon, *Feminism, Marriage, and the Law in Victorian England* (Princeton: Princeton University Press, 1993).

Sheller, Mimi, and John Urry, 'The New Mobilities Paradigm', *Environment and Planning A*, 38 (2006), 207–26.

Simmel, Georg, 'The Metropolis and Mental Life' (1903), *Georg Simmel on Individuality and Social Forms*, trans. and ed. by D. Levine (Chicago: University of Chicago Press, 2011).

Simms, Frederick Walter, *England to Calcutta by the Overland Route in 1845: From a Manuscript Left by F.W. Simms*, ed. by Frederick Simms (London: Harrison and Sons, 1878).

Smith, Albert, *To China and Back: Being a Diary Kept, Out and Home* (London: Chapman & Hall for the author, 1859).

Smith, Crosbie, *Coal, Steam and Ships: Engineering, Enterprise and Empire on the Nineteenth-Century Seas* (Cambridge: Cambridge University Press, 2018).

Spalding, J. Willett, *The Japan Expedition: Japan and Around the World; an Account of Three Visits to the Japanese Empire, with Sketches of Madeira, St. Helena, Cape of Good Hope, Mauritius, Ceylon, Singapore, China, and Loo-Choo* (New York: Redfield, 1855) .

Speid, Mrs John B., *Our Last Years in India* (London: Smith, Elder & Co., 1862).

Stead, William T., *Gladstone: A Character Sketch 1809–1898* (London: 'Review of Reviews' Office, 1898).

Steinberg, Philip, *The Social Construction of the Ocean* (Cambridge: Cambridge University Press, 2001).

Stocqueler, Joachim, *The Hand-Book of India, a Guide to the Stranger and the Traveller, and a Companion to the Resident* (London: Wm. H. Allen & Co., 1844).

Stocqueler, Joachim, *The Route of the Overland Mail to India, from Southampton to Calcutta* (London: Gallery of Illustration, 1850).

'Supply – Civil Service Estimates' (1 August 1867), *Hansard's Parliamentary Debates, Third Series, Vol. 189* (London: Hansard, 1867).

Taussig, Michael, 'The Beach (A Fantasy)', *Critical Inquiry*, 26 (2000), 249–77.

Taylor, Bayard, *A Visit to India, China, and Japan: In the Year 1853* (New York: G.P. Putnam & Co., 1855).

Taylor, Miles (ed.), *The Victorian Empire and Britain's Maritime Worlds, 1837–1901: The Sea and Global History* (New York: Palgrave Macmillan, 2013).

Taylor, Tom, *The Overland Route: A Comedy in Three Acts* (New York: Robert M. De Witt, 1866).

Thackeray, William Makepeace, *Notes of a Journey from Cornhill to Grand Cairo by Way of Lisbon, Athens, Constantinople and Jerusalem: Performed in the Steamers of the Peninsular and Oriental Company* (London: Chapman & Hall, 1846).

Thomas, Martin, and Andrew Thompson, 'Empire and Globalisation: From "High Imperialism" to Decolonisation', *The International History Review*, 36 (2014), 142–70.

Thompson, E.P., 'Time, Work-Discipline, and Industrial Capitalism', *Past & Present*, 38 (1967), 56–97.

Thomson, Mrs. Charles, *Twelve Years in Canterbury, New Zealand: With Visits to the Other Provinces, and Reminiscences of the Route Home Through Australia, etc. (From a Lady's Journal)* (London: S. Low, Son and Marston, 1867).

Tillotson, John, *The Overland Route to India: Historical, Descriptive and Legendary* (London: J.E. Lloyd, 1859).

Timbs, John (ed.), *The Year-Book of Facts in Science and Art: Exhibiting the Most Important Discoveries and Improvements of the Past Year* (London: David Bogue, 1855).

Tomlinson, John, *The Culture of Speed: The Coming of Immediacy* (London: Sage, 2007).

Train, George Francis, *An American Merchant in Europe, Asia and Australia: A Series of Letters from Java, Singapore, China, Bengal, Egypt, and the Holy Land, etc.* (New York: G.P. Putnam & Co., 1857).

Trollope, Anthony, *An Autobiography, Volume 1* (New York: Harper & Brothers, 1883)

Tytler, Harriet, *An Englishwoman in India: The Memoirs of Harriet Tytler, 1828–1858* (Oxford: Oxford University Press, 1986).

van der Chijs, Jacobus, *Mijne reis naar Java in 1869 en terugkeer over Engelsch-Indié, Palestina enz. in 1870* (Utrecht: C. Van Der Post Jr, 1874).

van Heerdt, Jacob, *Mijne Reis met de Landmail van Batavia over Singapore, Ceilon, Aden en Suiz tot Alexandrië in Egypte* (The Hague: K. Führi, 1851).

Vernon, James, *Distant Strangers: How Britain Became Modern* (Berkeley: University of California Press, 2014).

Virilio, Paul, *Negative Horizon: An Essay in Dromoscopy*, trans. by Michael Degener (London: Bloomsbury Publishing, 2006).

Virilio, Paul, *The Original Accident*, trans. by Julie Rose (Cambridge: Polity, 2007)

Votolato, Gregory, *Ship* (London: Reaktion, 2011).

Walker, William, *Tom Cringle's Letters on Practical Subjects, Suggested by Experiences in Bombay, Originally Published in the Bombay Daily Newspapers as Letters to the Editors* (Bombay: Education Society's Press, 1863).

Walton, John (ed.), *Histories of Tourism: Representation, Identity and Conflict* (Clevedon, UK: Channel View Publications, 2005).

Warburton, Eliot, *The Crescent and the Cross; Or, Romance and Realities of Eastern Travel, Volumes 1–2* (London: Henry Colburn. 1844).

Warf, Barney, *Time–Space Compression: Historical Geographies* (Oxford: Routledge, 2008)

Warner, Maria, *Phantasmagoria: Spirit Visions, Metaphors, and Media Into the Twenty-first Century* (Oxford: Oxford University Press, 2006).

Waters, George, *Indian Gleanings and Thoughts of the Past* (Chatham: G.H. Windeyer, 1864).

Weber, Max, *The Protestant Ethic and the Spirit of Capitalism* (London: Allen & Unwin, 1976).

Westgarth, William, *Victoria and the Australian Gold Mines in 1857: With Notes on the Overland Route from Australia via Suez* (London: Smith, Elder & Co., 1857).

Wilson, Kathleen (ed.), *A New Imperial History: Culture, Identity and Modernity in Britain and the Empire, 1660–1840* (Cambridge: Cambridge University Press, 2004).

Wohlfarth, Irving, 'Et Cetera? The Historian as Chiffonnier', in *Walter Benjamin and the Arcades Project*, ed. by Beatrice Hanssen (London: Continuum, 2006).

Newspapers and periodicals

All the Year Round
Annual Register
Asiatic Journal and Monthly Register for British and Foreign India China and Australasia (1843–45, *Asiatic Journal and Monthly Miscellany*)
Blackwood's Magazine
Chambers Edinburgh Journal
Civil Engineer and Architect's Journal
Edinburgh Magazine and Literary Miscellany
Edinburgh New Philosophical Journal
Fraser's Magazine for Town and Country
Hampshire Advertiser and Salisbury Guardian
Herapath's Railway Journal
Hobart Town Daily Courier
Household Words
Illustrated London News
Indian Medical Gazette
Kidd's Own Journal; for Inter-Communications on Natural History, Popular Science, and Things in General
Law Times
Leisure Hour
Literary World: A Journal of Popular Information and Entertainment
London Daily News
London Journal
London Saturday Journal
Macphail's Edinburgh Ecclesiastical Journal and Literary Review
Malta Times
Manchester Weekly Times
Mechanics' Magazine
Morning Post
National Magazine
Parlour Magazine of the Literature of all Nations
Punch, or the London Charivari
Shetland Journal
Singapore Free Press and Mercantile Advertiser
Southern Literary Messenger: Devoted to Every Department of Literature and the Fine Arts
The Times
Titan: A Monthly Magazine

Index